MARC SUMMERS'

DECLARE WAR ON YOURSELF

How to Get Your Act And Life Together to Become the Best Version of Yourself

"If we did all of the things we were capable of doing, we would astound ourselves." – Thomas Edison

GETTING YOUR ACT TOGETHER IS WAR

Only 3% of us have our act together because we're not willing to go to war with ourselves to improve and become the person we're capable of being. The person we're meant to be. The person left behind once the nonsense is destroyed. We're not willing to go to battle and fight for the mentality, behavior, habits, and life we want. We're not willing endure the pain, separation, and loneliness of the path to getting better – the path very few take. We're not willing to attack our limiting thoughts, beliefs, emotions, behavior, and habits and destroy them. We're not willing to engage, conquer, and dominate the enemy – ourselves.

Declaring war on yourself is anything but fun. It's hell. It sucks. It's painful. It's unforgiving. You're in a foreign land, the enemy doesn't want you there, and you quickly discover there's no place for hesitation, feelings, complaining, excuses, or a lack of effort. Every minute of every day you're faced with making the right decisions, choosing the right path, and taking the right course of action or you will lose the war and the part of you you're trying to destroy, the enemy, wins.

The enemy does whatever it takes to keep the high ground. To keep you immature, childish, and irresponsible – but you will not retreat. You will, not only, hold your ground, but you will push forward and hit the enemy with everything you have until you overwhelm it, break it, and destroy it.

There will be casualties and injuries. You will lose some battles. Your ego, pride, and confidence will get bruised and banged up. You will have days where your head is up your ass and you make horrible decisions. But it's ok. It doesn't mean you lost the war. It just means you're learning.

The war with yourself will always be at your doorstep, staring you in the face, taunting you, and daring you to become weak and scared. You have a rendezvous with death – the death of your former self.

YOU ARE YOUR OWN WORST ENEMY

We blame why we're not where we want to be in life, thinking the things we should be thinking, doing the things we should be doing, and living the life we should be living on situations, circumstances, and everyone around us - but in reality, our life is 100% the product of our decisions.

98% of everything "happening" in your life IS within your control and the other 2% of everything that is "inevitable", you still have the power to decide how it affects you and how you respond to it. You still have the power to prevent it from breaking you, getting you off track, and distracting you from what you should be doing.

The enemy isn't your parents, your spouse, your kids, your boss, your friends, or your co-workers – the enemy is YOU.

The enemy is the person inside that wants to be comfortable and lazy. The enemy is the person inside that wants to avoid pain. The enemy is the person inside that wants to take the easy route. The enemy is the person inside that wants constant attention, approval, and admiration. The enemy is the person inside that wants to continue making bad choices because they "feel" good. The enemy is the person inside who doesn't want to separate themselves from the people, places, and things that are negative, destructive, and counterproductive.

YOU ARE DECIDING to hold yourself back. YOU created the life you have right now. YOU are the only one to blame for what you're feeling and experiencing. YOU are to blame for how everyone is treating you.

You don't have the power to control the people, situations, and circumstances around you. You only have the power to control yourself. Getting your act together means you're going to war with yourself and destroying the thoughts, emotions, behaviors, and habits that are holding you back and keeping you from being the person you want to be.

MY PERSONAL LETTER TO YOU

Getting your act together is very lonely because very few are willing to endure and do what it takes to become the person they want to be and have the life they want. It's an uphill battle - you're not going to see too many friends along the way. You're going to spend more time with yourself than anyone else. Through it all, you have to trust that, deep down, you're doing what's right and you're going to win. You have to assure yourself that when it gets hard, you're going to keep fighting and keep pushing to win the war within and conquer yourself.

Most people try getting their act together and fail. Some will support you along the way and be happy for you – but most won't care. They might even like you less because your fight reminds them of what they aren't doing and fighting for. What separates you from everyone who has tried the path you're on and failed is you're not going to quit and you're going to keep taking the punishment and getting back up until you get it right.

Having your act together, naturally and effortlessly, causes you to stand head and shoulders above the 99% of those who don't make it the utmost priority to have their mind and life in the right place.

Most of us go our entire lives following the masses, listening to voices of mediocrity and failure, living fake and empty "Social Media Lives", and focusing on everything except what truly matters. We create the appearance of wealth, health, happiness, and love and at the end of the day, we're broke, never truly happy, and we never have the inner-peace we believe is found in buying "stuff" we can't afford and getting "likes" from people we don't like, don't know, and don't care about.

When you work on conquering YOURSELF instead of working on conquering people and things that are a complete waste of time, you will find a real sense of peace, love, and happiness.

Nothing is more painful than being out-of-control of your mind, emotions, and habits and nothing gives you more inner-peace and happiness than having your mind, emotions, habits, behavior, and life on the right track and in order.

Starting right now, make changing your life and having your act together your highest-priority. Make it your biggest goal. Make it more important than what everyone around you is focused on.

Getting your act together helps you get ahead and create the life most people want but are unwilling to work for.

As an Aircraft Mechanic, making $100,000+ a year, I daydreamed about working for myself, actually getting paid for my efforts, making what I felt I was worth, not having to answer to anyone, and living life on my terms – even if it meant being broke for a while.

I'd tell myself, "I'll get there one day" - but I'd never do anything about it!

Then, when I decided I was no longer content with mediocrity and realized I could be spending my valuable time doing something much better, important, and productive, that's when my life changed.

Right now, as you read this, I am where I used to only imagine being. I am now the person I used to dream of being. I am now living the life I used to dream of living. I have my act together more than ever before – and it only took a decision. A decision to move in my own direction and NEVER look back, never stop, and never give up. A decision to be tough, focused, and stubborn. A decision to, as Grant Cardone says, pay the price today so I can pay any price tomorrow.

Right now, it's time to toughen up and make that same decision. Promise yourself you're going to knock off the bullshit, get your act together, stop wasting time, and live the life you know you're capable of living. For me, it all started with a promise to myself, and you're no different.

CONTENTS

INTRO: TOO MANY OF US DON'T HAVE IT TOGETHER

WHEN I LEARNED I DIDN'T "HAVE MY SHIT TOGETHER"

The thought of not having my act together never really crossed my mind until the day, about 8 years ago, my co-worker, Martha, told me, "Gah, Marc! Get your f*cking shit together, dude!"

She wasn't joking, either.

She had a look of disgust and the way she said it communicated how much she simply couldn't comprehend how I was neglecting to do something so simple.

Her brutally honest facial expression mixed with her reaction slapped me in the face, woke me up, and made me realize just how much I actually didn't have my act and my "shit" together.

Even though I was pissed about it and thought the way she reacted was overly dramatic and completely unnecessary, I just couldn't get over the fact that part of me knew she was absolutely right.

It all came about because I had asked for a cigarette AND a lighter – two things I could easily afford and didn't have, simply, because I was lazy.

Sometimes you have to hit people with a sledgehammer to wake them up and have their strict attention. She woke me up, had my attention, and it didn't feel good.

It was just a lighter, no big deal, but it made me realize I had a lot of work to do on myself because not having a lighter in my pocket and bumming cigarettes was only a very small "sign" that I didn't have it together and it meant my complacency was spilling into all areas of my life.

It's not the big things that communicate how much you do or don't have your act together – it's the small things.

WHAT HAVING YOUR ACT TOGETHER MEANS

The same way not having your act together is the product of poor decision making, having your act together is the product of predictable and consistent good decision-making skills. It's, according to the dictionary, organizing yourself, your life, and your affairs so you are able to achieve what you want and deal with things effectively.

- You have your thoughts, emotions, behavior, habits, and life handled, organized, and squared away. None of it is unpredictable or out-of-control. None of it is difficult to deal with.

- You're at or exceeding the level of competence that would, typically, be expected from someone your age and/or in your situation.

- You're not trapped in the middle of destructive situations and cycles that set you back physically, emotionally, or financially.

- You're not burdening anyone with anything you can, and should, be handling on your own.

- You're not in a position of being helpless and others aren't going out of their way to get and keep you on track.

- Others look to you as the example, admire what you're doing and how you're doing it, and aspire to get their act together like you.

Having your act together doesn't mean you don't have problems like everyone else, it means you're better at handling them and preventing them from reoccurring in your life instead of whining, bitching, complaining, and doing nothing.

It means you have a cleaner, sharper, more professional, and more organized way of responding to and solving problems than most.

SOCIETY'S DEFINITION OF HAVING IT TOGETHER

We're so focused on external "signs" of having it together that we completely overlook what's actually important - having it together internally!

When we see anyone who has it together in every way, we're only seeing the outside and trying to mimic what we're seeing. We're failing to understand the outside appearance of having it together is an automatic byproduct of having it together internally. It starts on the inside and works its way out – not the other way around. Having your act together externally only follows when you ACTUALLY have your act together internally. Looking like you have your act together doesn't magically cause you to actually have your act together.

The ability to buy the latest, largest, and coolest flat-screen TV to impress people doesn't mean you have your act together. The ability to buy material things to give yourself the appearance of having it together doesn't mean you have your act together. The ability to buy the latest phone, car, biggest truck, or the newest house that you really can't afford doesn't mean you have your act together. Going to a college you can't afford, taking out loans, going into debt, memorizing information you can learn free on the internet, getting a degree no longer worth the paper it's printed on, framing it, hanging it on your wall to impress people, and getting a job that barely affords you to live paycheck to paycheck doesn't mean you have your act together. That's actually becoming a dumb idea. Creating the illusion of having your act together on Facebook, Instagram, or Snapchat doesn't mean you actually have your act together.

We want to "look" like we have our act together, but we don't want to invest the time, energy, and effort it takes to actually get it together.

WE LIKE TO THINK WE HAVE IT TOGETHER

So, because of our addiction to believing external appearances tell the truth, thinking and falsely believing we have it completely together has become so deeply ingrained and automatic that even the thought of stopping and questioning our thoughts, emotions, actions, behavior, and life never occurs to us.

We think finishing high school, going to college, having a job, a few bucks in our pocket, food in the fridge, a roof over our head, a car to get us from point A to point B, and an iPad for the kids to play on means we have our act together and we've made it! That there are no further levels of personal development to strive for! We believe we've reached the pinnacle of being an adult and living a successful life but what we don't realize is that it doesn't take a lot of brains and effort to get a job, put money in your pocket, pay bills, buy food, get a car, and keep our children alive and entertained. Those are the basics! By default, that's what you're SUPPOSED to be doing! You can be a complete mess of a person with a very low IQ and still be able to pull off the bare minimums. You don't get a medal for the basics. You don't get a trophy for meeting the basic requirements. It doesn't mean you have your act together.

We set the bar and our standards so low that we automatically label those who have a better life and their act together more than we do as "lucky". 99% of the time, it's not luck at all! They try harder, work harder, and never quit. They're more determined, make better decisions, take more action, and are more consistent with what they have to do to get what they want, be who they want, and live the life they want. They push harder, complain less, and endure more "pain" and discipline than everyone else with the same time and opportunity is willing to. When it comes to having it together, they simply want it more than everyone else.

SIGNS YOU DON'T HAVE YOUR ACT TOGETHER

- You don't feel personally responsible and accountable for your life and results

- You're not actively working towards long-term goals and results

- You always have the same problems and "bad stuff" happening

- You're emotionally out-of-control, everything is a "big problem", and you experience constant emotional highs and lows

- You're regularly involved in drama, gossip, and immature situations

- You always need "help" because you refuse to make an effort

- You always have an excuse for your problems and shortcomings

- You talk about what you're going to do but it never gets done

- You lose interest and motivation when anything gets boring or hard

- You're addicted to time-wasting activities like TV and social media

- You're always broke, in debt, and you never save

- You're extremely sloppy, disorganized, and always losing things

- You don't keep your word, you get up late, and you're never on time

- You waste time on dysfunctional friendships and relationships

- You're more worried about having fun and avoiding boredom than the consequences of not working and bettering yourself

- You're not concerned with doing things the right way

- You're not concerned with taking care of yourself, being healthy, and making good food choices

ONLY 3% OF US ACTUALLY HAVE OUR ACT TOGETHER

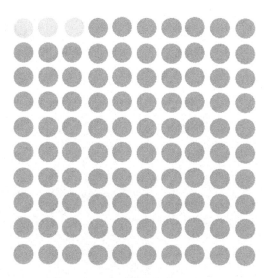

For every 100 people, only 3 are actually on the right track, thinking the right thoughts, feeling the right emotions, taking the right actions, developing the right habits, and getting the life they want.

A lot of us are pretty close, but we're not quite there yet. We just need that extra boost, motivation, education, and whatever it takes to eliminate the habits, distractions, and nonsense getting in our way.

Only 3% of us are actually willing to do whatever it takes to have our act together as much as possible. We're willing to put in the time, energy, and effort. We're willing to endure the pain. We're willing to endure the boring times. We're willing to take risks. The rest of us are wasting time, unfocused, following the crowd, worried about what others think, hesitant, making excuses, avoiding pain, and letting our emotions run the show. We're making fun a priority and putting the activities and habits that push us closer to being the person we want on the back burner.

LIFE IS TOO SHORT NOT TO HAVE YOUR ACT TOGETHER

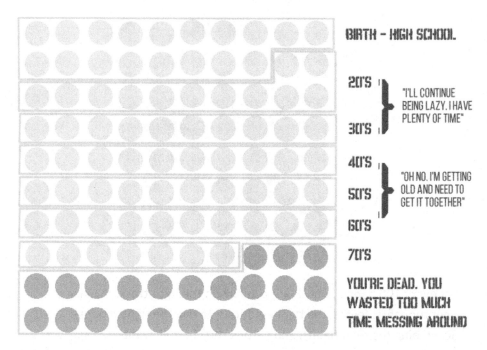

The diagram above provides a visual representation of how short life actually is and how little time you have to get your act together.

From birth through high school, a quarter of your life, is spent growing up, learning, and figuring out the basics. In your 20's and 30's, you're having fun, enjoying some money, and not feeling anything will take a turn for the worst anytime soon. In your 40's and 50's, you're feeling the pain of your decisions from your 20's and 30's and scrambling to figure things out. In your 60's and 70's, regret sets in, the pain and consequences of your bad decisions become more permanent, and you wish you had done things differently.

Right now is the time to act and do what's necessary before it's too late.

NOT HAVING YOUR ACT TOGETHER IS A CONSCIOUS DECISION

No person, place, situation, or circumstance is causing you to not have your act together. You're making that conscious decision yourself.

Every little choice you make every second of every minute of every day is pushing you towards having your act together or away from it.

- No one is forcing you to go out, "have fun", drink, and stay up later than you should knowing you have to work the next morning

- No one is forcing you to stay up until midnight taking selfies, playing games, and scrolling through the newsfeed on social media so you can compare your life to everyone else's fake "social media life"

- No one is forcing you to hit the snooze button and get up late

- No one is forcing you to show up late to work

- No one is forcing you to eat fast food or at restaurants instead of saving money, buying groceries, and making your own food

- No one is forcing you to drive a car or live in a house you can't afford

- No one is forcing you to be broke instead of saving for something better

- No one is forcing you to stay at a job you hate and to keep making the same amount of money you do

You're choosing to be unhappy, feel like other people are "luckier" than you, feel like you need to "get it together", to be lazy, to stay in your comfort zone, and to not do anything about it!

YOU ARE CHOOSING to be where you're at right now in your life and only you have the power to change it.

PART 1: THIS IS WHY WE DON'T HAVE OUR ACT TOGETHER

WE'RE NOT ASKING FOR HELP

Seeking help, training, and guidance doesn't make you stupid, incompetent, less valuable, or uncool. It makes you smart and educated - but it requires maturity, honesty, and security. Not asking questions because you "know everything" communicates you're immature, dishonest, and insecure. Not a place you want to find yourself in.

Let's be clear – graduating high school and going to college doesn't make you "educated". It doesn't mean you never have to ask for help. It doesn't mean you know more than everyone around you. It doesn't make you better. Lose the "I'm educated and better" mindset.

A real "education" is asking questions, collecting useful information, and regularly applying it towards reaching goals and improving your life. A real "education" is gaining specific knowledge to better yourself and others, creating something bigger than yourself, and then contributing to the world using what you're learning. A real "education" is acquiring valuable knowledge that, when passed on to others, will change their thoughts, emotions, behaviors, habits, and lives.

Jim Rohn said, "Formal education will make you a living; self-education will make you a fortune." **Here's what he actually meant –** "Formal education *(school and college, the stopping point for most people because they think they know everything and they've actually achieved something in life)* will make you a living *(you will learn just enough and be just smart enough to get a job working for someone you hate and at a job you hate. A job that will tell you when to wake up, when to take a break, when to eat, when to go home, when you can see your family, when you can spend extra time with them, how much money they think you're worth, and how little of a raise they'll give you over the course of a year or two);* self-education *(being smart enough to ask questions, not thinking you know it all, and seeking to always get better)* will make you a fortune *(you will see, learn, and understand a different way of doing things. A way that only 1% see, learn and understand. A way that will give you the life you want, the job you want,* *the money you want, and everything else. A way that will make you free, happy, and fulfilled)."*

So far, 100% of the credit for anything I've done, goals I've reached, and the person I've become goes to asking questions, seeking help, and not being too proud to say, "I don't know what I'm doing and I can use some guidance, training, and help." I KNOW I will never come close to knowing everything and I ask more questions than a 4-year-old because there's so much to learn and such a short period of time to learn it.

Knowledge and asking for help maintains accuracy in your thinking, emotions, behavior, and habits. It helps keep everything in focus. It helps you stay grounded, updated, and in touch with reality.

Asking for help is now easier than ever before because, before the internet, you'd have to ask around to find someone familiar with a certain topic or you'd have to go to the library and read the available books to try and find an answer. Now, you simply search it. I Google EVERYTHING and it doesn't matter how small or stupid the question is - if I am curious or need to know something specific, I'm 99% sure some other person has, since the invention of the internet, asked the question before, a somewhat intelligent and common-sensed person gave a useful reply, and there's a searchable record of the information exchange sitting somewhere on the internet.

The only thing that makes you an idiot is not asking questions. Never assume to know it all. More knowledge is available on the internet than ever before and it's growing, multiplying, and compounding day in and day out. No matter how small it is, seek guidance. See what others have to say and compare it to your own experience and judgment.

WE'RE SLOPPY IN OUR THINKING, BEHAVIOR, AND HABITS

Tai Lopez says, "The average millionaire has made 10,000 good decisions. That's called 'meticulous'. The rest of us are f*cking sloppy."

He's right. Having your act together requires absolute meticulousness.

Meticulous – "showing great attention to detail; very careful and precise." Another definition is "taking or showing extreme care about minute details; precise; thorough."

Being meticulous is "paying attention", to "detail". Not just any attention, but "great" and "extreme" attention. You "care" and you give a damn about what you're doing. You operate with "precision". It's harder to be sloppy when you're "meticulous-minded".

Not having your act together is the sum of sloppy decisions – the decision to be not go to bed on time, to get up late, to avoid folding clothes and washing dishes, to not be on a schedule to get done what needs to be done and when it needs to be done, to thoughtlessly spend money, and everything else we do that's extremely sloppy.

When we don't have our act together, we're careless, sloppy, and lacking attention to detail – we're not meticulous.

If you're sloppy and lacking attention to detail in the little areas of your thoughts, emotions, actions, behavior, habits, decisions, and your life, there's a 99% chance you're the same way when it comes to the big things that matter the most.

Choose RIGHT NOW to start being meticulous in every area of your life. Choose to pay better attention to detail, to give a damn, and to start being precise in your thinking, behavior, and habits. Choose precision. Choose to pay attention to the things most are overlooking.

WE'RE AVOIDING PERSONAL RESPONSIBILITY

Most of us refuse to look inwards and admit we don't have our act together. We refuse to say, "I don't have my act together, I can make improvements, it's my fault I'm having these problems, and my choices have led me to this point in my life."

It's so easy to do - but our emotions, ego, and our inner-child won't let us. It's not in your ego's best interest.

We like to think "Everyone around me needs improvement, but I'm not going to admit I've made a lot of bad choices because that would embarrass me and make me look stupid. That would make me look less smart. I have a reputation to live up to."

Most of us say, "I know tons of people who don't have their shit together!" but only very few of us will say "I can't talk about anyone because I know I don't have my act together as much as I'd like."

And since we're so good at avoiding responsibility for our lives and problems, when things get really bad and something BIG needs to change, we seek external solutions like stimulants, depressants, Psychiatrists, Psychologists, and even religion. We completely overlook the idea that maybe our problems are stemming from our thoughts, emotions, actions, behavior, habits, and decisions and we might have to do some WORK on ourselves, figure it out, and try to fix it, ourselves!

But, we're lazy and we want someone else to fix our problems.

I never discuss religion but I'm going to touch on it for a second because I have, what I think, is a good point – many of us, not all of us, only go to church and get extremely religious when things are really bad and not going our way. When things are great, we aren't really serious about religion, church, and God. But when things are bad, we run to church looking for a "quick fix" to the problems WE created and that WE should be responsible for.

We shouldn't be abusing religion and using it a "quick fix" to the problems we created and should be handling ourselves.

It's kind of shitty to communicate, "I created these problems in my life but I'm not going to make the effort to fix them! That would be crazy! So, I want you to fix them all for me so I can continue being lazy and unaware and I don't have to change, think, or realize that I might be a big part of the problem."

If your kids kept getting into trouble, took no personal responsibility for their actions or life, and they ONLY gave you attention when they had problems and needed you to fix those problems FOR THEM so they didn't have to make any kind of effort, would you just say, "No problem at all! I'll fix all of your problems, pay your bills, bail you out of jail, and you don't have to worry about being a responsible adult and making good choices. You're such a perfect kid."?

If you're clinically sane, your answer is probably, "Hell no! That's crazy! I would make them accountable and expect them to take full responsibility and fix their problems themselves!"

There's a big difference between understanding your ability to fix the problems you created yourself and irresponsibly choosing to do nothing about your problems except ask someone else to fix them for you.

Take responsibility for your decisions, actions, results, and your life.

Stop crying on social media and sharing posts about how "hard" life is, stop finding people and things to blame, and stop finding reasons why you're less "lucky" than everyone else. If your life isn't what you want it to be right now, you are the cause of it. Take the blame and fix it yourself.

OUR INNER-CHILD IS RUNNING THE SHOW

There's a part of your mind that doesn't care about you, your feelings, your thoughts, your future, or your well-being. It wants what it wants right now and it'll throw tantrums, cry, beg, complain, stomp around, and do whatever it has to until you give it what it wants.

It's the child in your mind. It's the part of you that never wants to grow up, be responsible, and do the hard things to get your act together. It's the part of you saying you don't have to get out of bed, it's ok not to exercise, it's ok to call into work today and be lazy, it's ok to act dramatic, childish, and emotional, and it's ok to give up when anything is boring or hard.

Your inner-child is a tyrant and wants to be in control of everything you think, feel, say, and do throughout the day and it doesn't care about improvement, moving forward, and reaching goals.

We go through puberty and grow up physically, but most of us never force our inner-child to grow up as well. We continue to let it run around, act spoiled, wreak havoc, and do whatever it wants.

One of the most important parts of getting your act together is getting the childish part of your mind under control. Eben Pagan says, in his program On Being a Man, "The boy must die". I say, "The childish part of your mind must die." It has to go. It needs to be disciplined. It needs to be controlled. It needs to be educated. It needs to grow up and start being more responsible. It needs to get with the program. When it's fighting for power, wanting to take over, and wanting its way, tell it to, "Sit the f*ck down and be quiet". It has to know you're the adult, you're in charge, you're running the show, and it has no part in influencing your thinking, feelings, behavior, and habits. It has to know you're the boss and you're not playing around anymore. Give it boundaries.

SELF-CONTROL AND SELF-DISCIPLINE ISN'T A PRIORITY

Self-discipline and self-control keep our inner-child in check.

We don't have the power to control 99% of everything around us - we only have the power to control ourselves, what's happening within us, and how we're interacting with and responding to the world. That 1% we do control, we are out-of-control of 95% of it. We have the power to control our thoughts, feelings, emotions, reactions, what time we get up and go to sleep, our work habits, or social habits, our eating habits, our spending habits, how we treat others, and how we spend our time. We have power over ALL of it – but we're choosing to be controlled instead of controlling ourselves. We're allowing ourselves to act overly-dramatic and emotional, to get up late and go to sleep late, to show up to work late, to not stay sharp and focused, to produce less than we're capable of, to get involved in gossip and pettiness, to eat food we shouldn't be eating in excess amounts, to spend more money than we earn on things we don't need, and to be horribly irresponsible with our time.

WE ARE ALLOWING IT!

We're failing to discipline ourselves to manage our thoughts and emotions, to go to sleep and get out bed early, to show up on time, to work hard, to produce, to rise above and avoid petty people and situations, to eat healthier and exercise, to save money, and to use our time in a wise and effective manner.

We're failing to tell ourselves "no", our inner-child is in charge, and self-control and self-discipline is at the bottom of our priority list.

Self-control and self-discipline has to come first. It has to become more important than anything else in your life. It has to be life or death.

OUR EGO IS TOO IMPORTANT

The biggest reason we're not accepting personal responsibility, our inner-child is running rampant, and we're lacking in self-control and self-discipline is because we're too weak to accept any devastating blows to our fragile ego.

We're afraid our over-inflated sense of "self", our ego, will crumble and we'll lose our identity, the thing that makes us "who we are", because we're overly-concerned with having an "identity" and sense of self.

We have this wonderful image of ourselves in our mind, an image we created of who we THINK we are, and it will all fall to pieces if we admit we're not actually THAT great and we've been erroring in our ways. It means we'll have to pick up the pieces and start from scratch and, for most of us, that's just too scary and too much work. We don't have the desire, willpower, and motivation to do such a thing. It's too far out of our comfort zone and it'll make us look vulnerable and weak.

Our ego says, "You're already cool and an awesome person, you already have a reputation, and let's not mess that up. Let's keep pretending we are who everyone thinks we are and who we present ourselves to be to the world on social media."

Your ego is destroying your life, your potential, and the possibilities of having the life you really want. Your ego is that scared little bitch inside of you that is overly concerned with what everyone thinks and whether or not they're impressed by your hobbies, personality, and life.

Stop making your ego so important. Stop worshipping yourself. Stop designing your life and actions around your ego and self-image. If you don't get rid of it, you will live the rest of your life waking up and thinking, "Why do I keep having these same problems in my life and why won't anything ever go my way?"

WE'RE ALL TALK AND NO ACTION

The ego says it's cool to talk about all of the amazing things we want to do with our life and be the person we want to become but it also warns against actually putting ourselves out there and risking the embarrassment and failure that possibly comes with "change" and doing something different.

Henry Ford, a man of action, said it best, "You can't build a reputation on what you're going to do." Most of us are all talk, but no action.

Talk is cheaper and words are more worthless than they've ever been. Social media now gives us the opportunity to "talk" and run our mouth as much as we want, about whatever we want, and whenever we want and we always have an audience! We get the attention our ego craves and wants more of!

You can get on social media, tag yourself at the gym, talk about "it's time for a change in my life", talk about how "hard" you've been working on yourself, get a bunch of "likes" and "comments", and THINK you're actually doing something positive. You're actually tricking yourself into thinking you're making some kind of progress! Talking about what you're doing or going to do isn't the same as taking action and the time you're using to talk about it could be spent actually doing the thing you're talking about doing!

Right now, as I write this, no one knows I'm writing this book. No one in my family, none of my friends, etc. No one. You know why? Because it's better to talk about what you've DONE than what you're going to do. What you've "done" holds more weight. It's more powerful. It's money in the bank.

Do it first, and then, if you still are desperate for attention, share your progress. Discussing progress is better than discussing only plans!

WE PREFER SHORT-TERM

Getting your act together never happens overnight - and that's the problem. We live in a society where we can have everything we want overnight. We can have it all right when we want it. We've become too accustomed to short-term gratification and never having to wait for anything. Although it's a major convenience in a lot of areas of our lives, it has very real and negative effects on our thinking, actions, behaviors, habits, decisions, and life. It makes us impatient. It gives us anxiety. Waiting used to be a sign of strength but now, it's only an inconvenience.

We're spoiled, lazier, unmotivated, and lacking patience. Our mind is weak and no longer able to handle the minor discomfort and inconvenience of the self-control and self-discipline necessary to create a smoother and higher-quality life. We're unable to wait for what we want.

As a result, we're not making an effort and we're refusing to put in the time and work necessary to get our act together and get out of our comfort zone to become better versions of ourselves.

We spend more time playing on our cell phones and watching TV than we should and our mind is constantly being primed and programmed with advertisements selling you "easier, quicker, no waiting, no effort required" solutions to every one of our problems. Businesses are using our laziness, weak-mindedness, lack of motivation, and short-term gratification thinking to sell us products and we don't even realize it! They know how lazy we've become and they're using our weaknesses to take money out of our pockets!

It's now wide-spread belief we can actually make short-term efforts in anything we want and achieve long-term results. If you want long-term results, make long-term efforts. That's the only way to do it. You have to be willing to do what needs to be done for as long as necessary.

OUR ATTENTION SPAN IS GETTING SHORTER

It's important to learn how to focus for longer and longer periods of time in order to see things through to completion. We have more incomplete projects than ever before. If something takes too long, we're giving up and moving onto something that doesn't take as long so we're not "bored" and unentertained.

The dream of every lazy kid today is to be a YouTube star because it's fast and easy. They press a button on their phone, say whatever they think will get attention, and then hit another button to upload it. YouTube, practically, does all the rest. No work, no waiting, no patience involved.

Fast and easy is now more appealing than ever before because we currently have shorter attention spans than goldfish – according to a study done by Microsoft. The attention span of a goldfish: 9 seconds. Ours: 8. This is the effect our short-term gratification and digitized lifestyle is having on our brain. Our minds are getting used to lightning speeds and faster and faster results and as a result, if something takes longer than 8 seconds, we lose focus and quit caring. If a web page takes 4 to 5 seconds to load, it's considered, by experts, incredibly slow.

Because our attention span is diminishing, we're giving up on getting our act together. We get bored, we give up. It's not "fun", we give up. It's not "cool", we give up. It takes "forever", we give up. We have to do certain things over and over again, we give up.

Lightning fast phones and computers are, literally, rewiring our brain to only wait a certain period of time before cutting off one operation and moving into another that gives it what it wants. We get bored and give up faster and more often than ever before!

At the rate we're going, it won't be long before the first words of all babies will be, "I'm bored".

WE'RE AFRAID OF TAKING RISKS

Les Brown says, "Imagine being on your deathbed and standing around your bed, the dreams given to you by life, the ideas you that you never acted on, the talents, the gifts, the abilities that you never used, and there they are standing around your bed looking at you with large angry eyes saying, "We came to you, and only YOU could've given us life, and now we must die with you forever!" And the question is, if you died this very moment, what will die with you? What dreams? What ideas? What talent? What greatness that you showed up to bring? Don't allow the fear of failure and the attractiveness of playing it safe in life to draw you in. You can't get out of life alive. You've got to die to leave here."

A lot of us have good ideas and great goals but, for some reason, we fail to take action and see them through. It feels "risky" to put the blinders on, focus on ourselves, focus on goals, and to say "nothing else matters" until we get to where we want to be. We allow emotions, fear, and our ego to get in the way and stop us from doing great things and becoming the great person we want to be.

Nelson Mandela said, "There is no passion to be found playing small and settling for a life that is less than the one you are capable of living." Denzel Washington said, "I found that nothing in life is worthwhile unless you take risks." These are highly-respected, successful men, and, what most would call, "great" men. To say the least, they have achieved a lot.

We'd rather play it safe, stay in our comfort zone, and not experience anything "hard" or difficult. We're afraid to risk losing friends, experiencing uncomfortable emotions, others having negative opinions about us, or looking boring and uncool. We afraid to risk "not having fun" like everyone else. We trade having our act together for the temporary convenience of having fun, entertainment, and feeling comfortable.

WE ONLY DO EASY, FUN, AND PAINLESS

We're struggling to get our act together because we're choosing to be complacent, weak, and lazy and we only want to do what's easy, fun, and painless.

It's easier, more fun, and less painful to:

- Avoid personal responsibility

- Avoid self-control and self-discipline

- Stay in our comfort zone

- Keep everything the same rather than change for the better

- Stay up late instead of going to bed on time

- Hit the snooze button rather than get up and deal with being tired

- Buy fast food than to spend time buying groceries and cooking

- Have constant entertainment so we don't have to read or think

- Complain, find blame, and take the victim route with problems

We dream of the day we'll have our act together, but we're unwilling to do what's necessary to make it happen. We avoid the work involved. We avoid the discomfort. We avoid the pain. We're unwilling to live life differently because we're too worried about blending in with the crowd. We don't want to be the oddball. We don't want to be the person always working and never having fun. We don't want to be "uncool".

Instead of living life the hard way so our future will be easier, we're choosing making every minute of every day as easy as possible. Then, when the easy and painless choices catch up to us and start making life difficult, we complain, seek pity, and say things like, "life is so hard" and "life is a bitch".

If you're harder on yourself than life can possibly be on you, you will find life is pretty simple and not as hard as everyone makes it out to be. Stop taking the easy route – it's crowded, slow, and you're surrounded by whiners and complainers. The hard route is like driving on a highway with no traffic and no speed limit – if you stay on it, you'll get to where you're going faster than you can imagine.

Do what average people say "no" to. Become comfortable with pain. Become friends with pain. Pain teaches, toughens you up, and makes you stronger. Experience and a relationship with pain helps you keep going when most give up and quit. Instead of avoiding pain altogether, like most of us do, use it and learn from it. Avoiding pain today guarantees you're going to, by default, endure a different, and much worse, pain tomorrow.

Endure the pain of controlling your spending habits so you don't have to endure the pain of being broke.

Endure the pain of getting up early, exercising, and working towards goals so you don't have to endure the pain of being lazy, fat, and unsuccessful.

Endure the pain of telling yourself "no" so you don't have to endure the pain of getting older and wishing you had made better choices.

Endure the pain today so you can avoid, even worse, pain in the future.

No one fully enjoys the hard road, but it's the right one to be on.

WE DON'T HAVE ENOUGH GOALS

If you want life to go your way, you need to over-plan, over-prepare, and forget what anyone says about it. Have more goals and hit more targets than everyone else. Have goals in between goals, goals on top of goals, so many goals you're not sure how you're going to reach them all and so many targets you're not sure if you can hit them all in one lifetime.

We have things we want, things we'd like to experience, and we want to be as comfortable as possible, but we aren't willing to create as many goals and targets as necessary to make sure everything we want to happen actually happens. We aren't willing to spend more time and energy on our goals than everyone else.

We're waking up each day, wasting time, wandering through life aimlessly, and upset others are "luckier" and having a better life than us. There's no luck to it. It's about goals. It's about eating the big elephant one bite at a time. It's about figuring out the actionable steps involved in getting what we want, turning those steps into attainable goals, and then working each day to cross as many goals off of the list as we can.

If you're bored and can't figure out what's stopping you from having your act together, look at your goals.

Are they flowing off of the page? Are there so many you feel overwhelmed? Do they take up page after page after page? If not, start filling your list up with things you'd like to accomplish, see, do, create, contribute, etc. Start thinking about what you want, what you can accomplish, and what you can achieve and get to work.

With a lot of goals, the time-wasting activities naturally disappear and you're forced to focus on what's important. You're forced to spend your time more wisely. You're forced to knock off the nonsense.

WE'RE OK WITH MEDIOCRITY AND LOSING

"You were, literally, born phenomenal!" – Eric Thomas

You weren't born to be mediocre. You weren't born to be OK with losing.

The average healthy adult male releases anywhere between 40 million and 1.2 billion sperm cells in a single ejaculation and out of all of those sperm cells, YOU MADE IT! You're the only one that fertilized the egg! You made it through the "warfare" and the complex series of environments it takes to reach the egg so you can have life. You beat out millions of other "people" for the privilege of being alive and having consciousness and now you're throwing it away by accepting a life of mediocrity and losing! The process it took for you to be here right and reading this book meant that you had to fight and win!

Even as a tiny sperm cell, you were "programmed" to fight and win. Why are you not fighting to win now? You beat millions of others when you didn't even have consciousness! Now, with your ability to think and strategize, what could you possibly do in your life? You're not battling millions of other people – you're only battling yourself!

For most, life is not a competition – but it doesn't mean you have to lose, come in last, and live a mediocre life. It doesn't mean you have to keep getting knocked down, defeated, and stepped on. Live up to your full capabilities and potential. Stop wasting your powerful abilities doing weak and mediocre things!

Being OK with losing has infiltrated every single area of your mind and everything about you and your life is a product of it! Every single part of your mind should be overly-obsessed with fighting, winning, improving, moving forward, and not accepting average and mediocrity. You should be obsessed with getting what you want and not settling for mediocrity! When this is your mindset, your life reflects it.

WE GIVE UP WHEN OUR EGO GIVES UP

Many of us do ambitious things because it makes us look good to family, friends, and on social media but as soon as it gets boring, tough, and our ego tells us it isn't fun anymore, that's when we throw in the towel and give up. That's when we find something new, different, and exciting to do and the cycle of doing something "fun" and "cool" but never sticking with it, long-term, begins. If it feels good and it paints us in a light that makes us look better or more ambitious to those around us, we'll do it, but as soon as we start feeling the pain, emotional discomfort, and the boringness involved in reaching that goal, that's when the ego calls the fight and decides it's too hard and not worth the pain.

We let our ego run our life for us and dictate what we should and shouldn't be doing. We're not giving ourselves what we actually want – we're giving the ego what it wants.

Your ego isn't your friend. Your ego doesn't have your best interests in mind. Your ego is a terrible influence and only wants to put itself first. It wants the money, comfort, and the great life but it's too good to risk anything to get it. It wants the attention and admiration but doesn't want to spend the countless hours behind closed doors working, studying, sharpening the sword, learning, and becoming better.

From now on, take ego completely out of the equation. It's no longer a tool you need. It doesn't help or contribute in any way when you're getting your act together, getting the life you actually want, and becoming the person you want to be. It actually does everything it can to stop you from improving because the ego's two best friends are your emotions and inner-child. When the ego is in distress, they come running to help out. If you know what you're doing and it will dramatically improve your life, ignore anything trying to stop you or hold you back.

WE ONLY "TRY" WHEN WE HAVE SUPPORT

We start something new, work really hard towards it, but then give up when we notice no one around us really cares about what we're doing. We give up when we notice no one is "liking" or "commenting" on our posts about it. We give up when no one is patting us on the back or lifting us up on their shoulders to celebrate our hard work. We give up when we notice no one is really interested in hearing about it.

Getting your act together requires independence and freedom from the thoughts and opinions of others.

99% of the time, no one truly cares and they're so absorbed with themselves that they don't have the time or desire to look at what you're doing, form an opinion on it, and then go out of their way to communicate to you what they think about it.

When it comes to your goals, stop needing everyone's support. They're YOUR goals, not theirs – and that's why they don't care. Stop looking for people to support you in YOUR dreams. Stop expecting others to stop what they're doing and pay attention to what you're doing. Your goals and dreams are none of their business and you shouldn't expect anyone to make it their business.

Stop getting on GoFundMe and begging people to give you money and support you. If it's YOUR goal, YOUR dream, and YOUR life, find a way to get the money yourself and be your own support system.

Here's the truth - things are going to get hard and some days, you're going to look at your situation and it's going to be a hard pill to swallow. You will be in tears. You will question yourself. You will be in a lot of pain. But the only person that'll be patting you on the back and telling you "It'll be ok" will be YOU. No one will be there when you're in pain and in tears. No one will be there to make it easier. It's not their fight, it's yours.

WE ONLY "TRY" WHEN IT'S A NEW YEAR

We should be making the effort to become better 24/7/365 - not only when everyone is making "New Year's Resolutions".

New Year's Resolutions are jokes – jokes that aren't funny – and 92% of them fail because we aren't serious about it.

It's pitiful that we're doing it just to follow traditions, be trendy, and feel like we're actually making progress.

Those who are winning, living the life we all want, and have their act together are shaking their heads at every single person who talks about and posts about "New Year's Resolutions".

Those who only "try" once a year are the ones spending their entire lives "hoping" and "wishing" to get their act together – but never will.

New Year's Resolutions are for lazy people who aren't willing to get up every single day and do what's necessary to change their life.

You should be making a New Day's Resolution every night you go to sleep and every morning you wake up. Throughout the day, you should be making New Hour's resolutions to keep yourself on track, keep your habits in order, and keep moving forward in the right direction.

You don't have to wait to improve. You don't have to wait until a certain date to improve. You can start anytime you want. You can start right now.

Most of us say, "I know I have to stop doing this or start doing that, but I'm going to be lazy and start or stop doing it on this particular date. That way it isn't hard, I'm not feeling stressed, and it's not a burden. I don't want there to be any actual work involved."

This attitude is the reason we're broke, in debt, and full of problems.

WE'RE CREATING AVOIDABLE PROBLEMS

Unexpected and unavoidable things do happen and come up from time to time, but of all the problems we have right now, 95% are avoidable. 95% of the problems we have, we create on our own because we fail to control ourselves and think before we make decisions.

Those who have their act together have the habit of stopping and asking themselves, "If I make this decision, is it going to be a problem? Is it going to come back and bite me in the ass? Is it going to put me in a bad position?" They go into every situation with a contingency plan. They look at all the possible outcomes and what could go wrong and base their decisions on what would produce the best result.

The rest of us are failing to have contingency plans. We're failing to look ahead and figure out the possible negative consequences of our actions and decisions. We're not making an effort to avoid things going downhill. We're all putting ourselves through the pointless cycle of creating problems, getting upset about those problems, and then getting, even more, upset about having to fix them when it was all completely avoidable in the first place!

Being broke is avoidable if we're disciplined and smart enough to put ourselves on a budget. Being unhealthy is avoidable if we're disciplined enough to not smoke or do drugs and to prioritize the healthiest foods over the tastiest. Being in dysfunctional relationships is avoidable if you take the red flags seriously and are smart enough to distance yourself from certain people and situations.

Making our problems bigger is also avoidable but we're letting them grow out-of-control. When you're in a hole, stop digging. Instead of letting problems persist and grow by focusing too much on them, place your energy and focus on the solution and fixing the problem.

WE'RE NOT LEARNING FROM MISTAKES

Be smart enough to learn from your mistakes.

Mistakes are the driving force behind success and the main ingredient in learning and becoming better. The wisest and most successful people aren't the ones who are the luckiest – they're the ones who have made the most mistakes. Mistakes are the best friends you will ever have because they aren't focused on sparing your feelings - they're focused on helping you and teaching you what you need to know in order to drive forward in the right direction.

When someone spares your feelings, you don't learn because it doesn't jolt you. It doesn't make an impact. It's easily forgettable. When they, deliberately, overlook your feelings and tell you, point blank, what you need to hear, you may get your ego and feelings hurt, but you'll never forget the lesson. You'll never forget the jolt you got from the truth.

When a mistake slaps you in the face and it hurts really bad, instead turning it into a negative event, see it as a positive opportunity. Tell yourself, "This is good. I'm going to learn something valuable and unforgettable from this pain."

We're allowing mistakes to make us feel like a failure and we're lowering our personal value. We wrap mistakes up in "I'm an idiot and I'm not good enough." Instead of learning from the pain and welcoming it, we push it away and find things to numb it or kill it – like avoidance, complaining, blaming, drugs, drinking, denial, etc.

We're not asking ourselves, "What sequence of events or thinking led me to make this mistake? What minor errors, when added up, led up to this mistake? What am I not seeing? What's the lesson to be learned here? What did I do wrong that I'll make sure not to do again? Where did I lose my focus? Where was I not paying attention?"

WE FOCUS ON WHAT DOESN'T MATTER

Over the past few years, if you would have placed your focus on only one or two really important things, where would you be now?

We focus on "fun", pleasure, getting everything we want NOW, avoiding pain, and remaining entertained. It's all we care about. Our potential, desire, and need for becoming better and having a better life is going down the drain because we're too comfortable. Rather than focusing on working to improve our current situation and future, we're focused on things that don't improve the quality of our life and push us closer towards our goals. We're spending, on average, 4 years of our lives looking down at our phones, on social media, watching TV, and being entertained by what doesn't matter – and it's a very safe bet to say the number of years we spend doing these things will only increase as time goes on. Some of us are even spending up to 7, or more, years of our lives playing video games!

We're focused on maintaining our social media reputation, going out, going on vacations, getting home to relax, do nothing, and be lazy, watching the game, going to parties, going to barbeques, going to the mall to spend money, going to see the latest movie, getting the latest video game, etc.

We're so focused on chasing our next Dopamine release that we're failing to plan, prepare, and take action for a better future.

80% of everything you're focused on throughout the day will never matter in the long run. You're only focused on temporary conveniences so you can have fun and avoid boredom, stress, and work.

Start asking yourself throughout the day, "Is what I'm focusing on right moving me closer to my goals?" and, "Is what I'm focusing on right now going to help me become a better version of myself?"

WE CONSCIOUSLY IGNORE LITTLE THINGS

U.S. Navy SEALs have a fierce reputation for being the world's most elite, high-caliber, and high-impact individuals – organized into teams of highly-trained men who have their act together beyond comprehension. One of their secrets – meticulousness and attention to detail. No detail is too small for them to get right. That's what makes them the best.

The little details you're paying attention to are adding up to a bigger picture, like having your act together, and when your life is a mess, it's because you're overlooking and missing the smaller details that matter.

In school, if you fail regular assignments but get a perfect score on important tests, you still fail. The little grades are just as important because they make up most of your grade.

Going to bed and getting up late, not flossing your teeth, not picking up after yourself, playing on your phone, not staying focused, choosing fun over work, spending money on little things you don't need, and choosing to get upset and worried instead of remaining calm are little things adding up. Within a year's time, it adds up to very big problems.

When you become meticulous and pay attention to the little details, you notice big changes.

Tony Robbins says he was getting frustrated one day when he was playing golf because the ball kept going in the water and his instructor told him he was only a little bit off. So, after paying attention to tiny details in his stance, he was back on target and putting the ball where he wanted it. Something as small as shifting his body a millimeter was creating a 30-foot to 50-foot difference in where the ball landed.

The little things you're consciously overlooking and ignoring are making a huge difference in your life, behavior, and results.

WE'RE NOT CONTROLLING EMOTIONS

The world's most successful and elite people who have their act together in every way all something in common – they keep their emotions under control. They don't allow emotions to slow them down and get in the way of what they're doing. When an unnecessary emotion comes up, they kill it and drive forward. They push through it. They don't freak out and spend time on it.

The same cannot be said for those of us who don't have it together.

Emotions are running our lives and 99% of the emotions we experience on a daily basis are a complete waste of time.

We're addicted to our emotions and they're keeping us from remaining calm, driving forward, and focusing on what's truly important.

We believe experiencing emotional highs and lows is completely normal and if we're experiencing a lack of emotion, we're bored. That's why we're interested in the latest gossip and "beef" between people. That's why we're interested in crazy situations on the news. That's why we watch dramatic TV shows. That's why we're addicted to social media and listening to people rant, rave, and complain about how they're offended, what they don't agree with, and how life is hard. We crave the emotional rush because we're overly-addicted to emotions.

We're unnecessarily feeling emotions over little events and then feeding into them so they grow out-of-control. We're allowing unnecessary emotions to thrive and they're stopping us from keeping the right mindset and taking action.

Baby emotions become big events and these "big events" stop us cold in our tracks. Little drama between us and family, friends, and co-workers cause us to call into work, stay in bed all day, and lose productivity.

WE'RE COMPLAINING AND NOT CHANGING

Instead of creating and being the change we want to see in our lives, we just complain and hope someone else will fix it for us.

A lot of us bitch, whine, and complain all day long at our jobs and when we have an opportunity to raise our hand and speak up in a meeting, we stay silent. When we have an opportunity to pull the boss to the side and give some feedback about what's bugging us, we choose to walk the other way so we don't look like we're kissing ass. We cry and cry about how things need to change but we never speak up, offer solutions, or do anything about it. We keep going to the same job day in and day out and we complain instead of finding a new job or making our job more tolerable.

The same goes for our personal lives. We bitch about how our kids act but we don't change our parenting habits. We complain about how we look and feel, but we don't change our eating habits. We complain about being broke and not making enough money at work, but we don't change our spending habits, job, or our work ethic. We complain about our spouse but we don't seek counseling or to get away from them. We complain about our home life but we choose to keep living there.

If you're complaining about something you can fix, then fix it and be quiet. If you're complaining about something you can't fix, then offer solutions to those who can fix it or get away from it entirely.

If there's something you don't like about yourself, change it. If there's something you don't like about your occupation, change it. If you don't like your income, change it. If you don't like the results you're getting, work on changing yourself first because that may be 90% of the problem. Instead of complaining, you have the power to make things better.

WE'RE CONSTANTLY REACTING

Having your act together means you and your life are the product of your conscious decisions and actions.

For those of us who don't have our act together, we're failing to consciously make wiser decisions and to take action. We're reactive instead of proactive. We're reactive instead of responsive. We're unconsciously reacting to everything happening within us and to us and, over time, we become the product of our reactive decisions and actions.

We're broke because we're constantly reacting to emotional excitement, short-term gratification, and the inability to wait. We're not taking time to stop, think, and be proactive about what our money could and should be used for. We're overweight and unhealthy because we're reacting to being hungry and instead of being proactive, demonstrating some mental toughness, and waiting to eat something healthier, we're doing what's easier – using the drive-thru of fast food restaurants. We're complaining, angry, and worried because we're failing to take time and think about the current situation and how much control we, realistically, have over it.

90% - 95% of what you're thinking, feeling, saying, and doing is an unconscious reaction - and it's why you're feeling like you don't have control - because you don't, your reactions do. Reactions are running your life and you're not giving any thought to what you're going to do next. You're just unconsciously doing it.

You will feel and have more control when you choose to start being proactive and responding to everything happening within, to, and around you instead of reacting. Responding is taking time to stop, think, and make a wise decision before you take action and move forward.

Stop reacting. Unconscious reactions lead to decisions and actions that pull you the opposite way of where you're trying to go.

WE'RE TOO BUSY WATCHING OTHERS

It's easy to watch TV, get on a gossip website, or open a magazine and see athletes, musicians, celebrities, and CEO's living lives we think we'll never have. We follow them, look up their Wikipedia pages, read about them, watch their videos, buy their products, and become addicted to what they'll say and do next. It's easy to get on social media and spend hours looking into the lives of other people - how they're living, what they're doing, what they're thinking, how much more fun their life seems, and how much "better" they seem to be. It's easy to form the opinion they have more friends and people love them way more than people love us and they're more successful and "happier" than we are.

And here's what most of us don't see and understand - it's all just a mirage. It's not real. The people you're watching who appear to have these flawless lives are painting a picture of what they WANT you to see – not what's 100% accurate and true about themselves.

Athletes, musicians, celebrities, and CEO's are normal people and they all hire public relations personnel and "image consultants" to help them have and maintain a favorable APPEARANCE to the public eye.

You're wasting your time watching others and comparing your life to theirs. You're not missing out on as much as you think you are and you're not as unfortunate as you seem to be.

As Grant Cardone says, you should be on the field and not in the stands. People should be reading YOUR books instead of you collecting all of theirs. People should be watching your videos and subscribing to your channel instead of you watching their videos and following them.

Use the hours you're spending watching other people on TV and on social media to invest in yourself. To invest in accomplishing the goals and hitting the targets that make you who you want to be.

WE'RE TOO BUSY FOLLOWING THE MASSES

If 99% of the world's money is in 1% of the population's hands, is it possible the 1% with 99% of the money knows or is doing something different and/or better? Is it really a coincidence only 3% of us actually have our act together?

It's not a massive conspiracy. It's not a conglomerate of rich families controlling the world. It's simply human behavior and mass psychology – the larger the group, the lower the IQ.

"The masses" don't produce. They don't have lists of goals. They don't get results. They only want entertainment and pleasure. They flock to mediocrity. They don't resonate with the idea that time is passing by and they're doing NOTHING with it. They have their hands out and want to play now and avoid work as much as they can.

Is it a coincidence the world's elite consciously avoid the habits of the masses like social media, TV and the news, gossip and drama websites and shows, destructive music, destructive people, playing games on phones, and constantly going out to drink with friends? Is it a coincidence most of the world's elite don't have "entertainment" and "fun" at the top of their lists?

The 1% who are choosing to do things differently are getting 99% of the results.

Separate yourself from the masses. Whatever you notice society is doing in droves, avoid it. There's ALWAYS something wrong with it. Sit back, watch, and, with enough time, you'll usually see it producing very negative and destructive results.

Avoid getting sucked into the "fads" and "trends". Avoid getting sucked into the things "everyone is doing". It will only move you backwards.

WE'RE TOO BUSY SEEKING ATTENTION

Attention is the new drug and it helps us maintain our fake and over-inflated sense of self. It's cheap, feels good, and the high only lasts a short while. The more of it we get, the unhappier we are, and the more we need to experience that high again. We go to great lengths and do ridiculous things to get attention, "likes", and comments. We go to bed feeling drained even though we haven't done anything physically exhausting. If the attention gets taken away, we get angry, upset, and display classic addiction behavior and reactions.

When we need to give OURSELVES attention, our brain sends a signal to our dopamine receptors but they're so fried, used up, and worn out from selfies, twitter, social media, and external attention that they're worthless and can't respond to such a normal command. They only respond to people on a little phone screen giving us fake approval.

This is our new "normal".

Social media gives us the power to seek as much attention as we want. Anytime we need a dose of attention, we pull our $1000+ computer out of our pocket, snap a selfie or type something clever, and we get our "hit" so we don't have withdrawals. What makes it, even more, messed up is we "post" about how others need to get their act together and yet the only reason we're "posting" in the first place is for attention!

A 2015 study revealed that men and women spend 5 HOURS + a week taking selfies and young adults are expected to take up to 25,000 selfies in their lifetime.

This is why we don't have our act together.

Seeking attention wastes time, moves you mentally and emotionally backwards, and the more you get, the more of a problem it becomes.

WE'RE FILLING OUR MINDS WITH GARBAGE

We're piling our minds with garbage on top of garbage and, as a result, everything we're thinking, feeling, saying, and doing is complete garbage.

If we don't put value in, we don't get value out. If we put garbage in, we get garbage out. If we put stupid in, we get stupid out. If we put ignorance in, we get ignorance out.

It's really THAT simple – just like if you eat garbage food every day, your body and health reflect garbage eating habits and choices.

You're a product of your environment – everything happening around you is entering your mind through your eyes and ears. It's automatic and you can't prevent it. Your mind automatically absorbs all incoming information and as it finds a home, it primes and programs your mind. Your thinking, emotions, words, actions, and habits automatically and directly reflect what you're allowing to enter your mind.

Yes, I said allowing. You have a choice. No one is forcing you to watch, read, and listen to negative and destructive garbage in books, on the radio, TV, or social media. No one is forcing you to spend time with people who take value instead of give value.

You're choosing what goes into your mind.

- You don't have to watch negative programming on television

- You don't have to listen to negative podcasts and music

- You don't have to watch the news feed on social media

- You don't have to hang out with people who are a waste of your time

The difference between those who are successful and have their act and life together and those who are unsuccessful and can't get their act and life together is what they choose to program their mind with.

WE'RE REFUSING TO BE THE EXAMPLE

Having your act together more than everyone else doesn't make you a square or uncool. It automatically causes you to stand out as the person others look up to and as a leader. It makes you the person whose life is easier and more rewarding. It makes you more intimidating and more likely to be treated the way you expect. It makes you the person people ask about and are intrigued with.

Being the example, not only for ourselves but for those around us, has its rewards but also comes with an interesting position - less fun and more responsibility. Eyes are on you, you're required to think longer and harder about what you're doing, and you're under the microscope and under more scrutiny. You have to watch your step more carefully and it requires more self-awareness.

Because we're becoming lazier, less responsible, less disciplined, and we only want what's fast and easy, we're avoiding the position of being the example. We don't want the difficulty of filling those shoes.

If getting your act together is your ultimate goal, you're going to, by default, wind up being the example. It's impossible to have your act together and not be the example - not wanting to be the example is a clear indicator of not having your act together yet.

Set the example for those around you. Show everyone exactly what they should be doing to get on, what they consider, is the right track. Don't cut yourself slack. Give them a show. Show them what's possible. Show them exactly how much you have it together. Be on time, be dependable, keep yourself together, make good decisions, take action, and be consistent.

Be the example for how you want others to conduct themselves around you by how you treat them. Be the person others look up to and want to, eventually, become.

THE TALENT VS. SKILL MYTH

A lot of us believe we don't have our act together or have the life we want because we're not "talented" and we weren't born with a set of special "gifts" that no one else has.

"Skill" isn't something you're born with or you're not.

Some people may have more appropriate body structure, height, and muscle response times for certain activities, but they've gone from being good at what they do to "great" by beating on their craft day in and day out, being obsessed with what they do, and spending more hours practicing than any of us would be willing to. They've turned something they were kind of good at, a talent, into a sharpened skill.

Anyone can become talented, they just have to pour time and effort into what they want to become better at.

Many of the most "talented" people in the world were horrible when they began and they gained "talent" and skill through constant dedication to getting better at it.

If you just beat on your craft day in and day out, you will develop skill and talent. If you think everyone around you is "better" at something than you are, you can EASILY pass them up if you put in more time and effort than they are to getting better at it. You can surpass their level of "skill" by just practicing and working on it day in and day out. If someone seems "talented" but they don't work on improving it as much as you do, you'll become better than them.

Will Smith says, "The separation of talent and skill is one of the greatest misunderstood concepts for people who are trying to excel, who have dreams, who want to do things. Talent you have naturally. Skill is only developed by hours and hours and hours of beating on your craft."

SKILL LEVEL – WORK ETHIC

MASTERY/OBSESSION/GREATNESS ↑

HARD WORK AND PRACTICE ↑

NATURAL ABILITY/TALENT ↑

NO SKILL

PART 2: THE REALITY OF HAVING YOUR ACT TOGETHER

EVERY DAY IS A BATTLE

Every day you wake up, the battle will be at your doorstep and you will, in a lot of cases, fight the same battle every single day for weeks and months. You will be faced with difficult decisions from the second you open your eyes until you lay your head on your pillow to go to sleep.

In every situation, battles will take place in your mind and you will be forced to draw a line in the sand and pick a side – the side where you continue being sloppy, lazy, and having a screwed-up life or the side where you make progress, improve, and move in the right direction.

Those who can't handle the daily battles never get their act together and live the rest of their lives hoping, wishing, and saying, "I should have."

You don't have to win 100% of the battles, but you have to, at least, try. You have to make an effort. If you make an effort and still lose the battle, the lesson still remains. You still learned something new about yourself. You learned something new that doesn't work. You added a new item to your list of what not to do.

You have to charge the enemy and stop hiding in the trenches. You can't think, "I'll fight this battle tomorrow." You're in the middle of it every single day and you have to stand up and fight with everything you have to win each battle.

Here's the thing – the enemy will keep getting up and coming back day in and day out until it either wins or tires out and gives up. The more battles you win, the weaker the enemy becomes and the more you'll learn about the enemy's tactics, tricks, and hiding places.

When you win one battle and defeat the enemy, you will move onto a new battle. You will, undoubtedly, fight daily battles for the rest of your life – so hunker down, get comfortable, and reload.

IT MEANS REPROGRAMMING YOUR MIND

Getting your act together means removing years of garbage from your mind. Ever seen the show "Hoarders" where people keep collecting junk until they, literally, can't navigate through their home? They have to climb over things and it's a fire hazard and a very unsanitary and unhealthy situation. We do the same in our minds. We collect junk from daily consumption of garbage music, garbage programming on TV, and garbage social media. Our minds are so filled with garbage that there's no room to think, rationalize, and fit anything else in. We're mental hoarders and the collected junk influences our thoughts, emotions, behaviors, and habits and causes us not to have our act together.

What classifies it as "garbage"? Anyone and anything that doesn't have a positive influence, teach, add value, and move you in the right direction. Anyone and anything that doesn't help you have and keep your act together. Anyone and anything that is pointless, doesn't make a difference, and is a complete waste of time.

Having your act together means changing yourself and reprogramming your mind by removing the garbage and replacing it with value, quality, and substance. Replacing it with what pushes you in the right direction.

Once you reprogram your mind, a major shift happens in your thoughts, emotions, behaviors, and habits. A major shift happens in the results you're getting. More favorable things "happen" to you and around you. Change your consumption habits, who you spend time with, and monitor what you're putting into your mind. Once the garbage is out, it has to stay out. There's no reason or room for it anywhere in your life.

Change starts with YOU. If you don't change, your life doesn't change. Getting your act together means letting go of everything you think you know and being open to becoming an entirely different person.

IT MEANS MAKING THE RIGHT DECISIONS

Every second of every day, you're presented with the opportunity to make decisions and every one of those decisions, no matter how big or small, will positively or negatively impact your life and situation. The small decisions aren't felt right away. Sometimes it takes weeks, months, and even years to feel them. But rest assured – those small decisions are adding up. You're layering one tiny bad decision on top of another and they're growing into a monster you can't tame.

Warren Buffet says, "Chains of habit are too light to be felt until they are too heavy to be broken."

It's not only the big decisions that matter, like having a job, paying bills, taking care of your family – it's also all of the tiny, and seemingly insignificant, decisions in between. The things that are easily overlooked.

No matter how small the decision, IT MATTERS. It has to be right. The devil is in the details and the details accumulate to big problems if they're missed.

Getting out of bed on time is a good decision, but you also have to decide to turn around and make your bed, pick up your clothes, etc. Making your bed is a good decision, but you also have to decide to do it the right way and not just throw it together. Brushing your teeth is a good decision, but you also have to decide to do it right. You have to make the decision to floss as well. Skipping flossing for years can lead to gum disease, gingivitis, and horrible breath. Each day, the decision to skip flossing seems very small and insignificant, but it adds up to big health problems in the future.

Having your act together means making the right decision every single time you're presented with the opportunity. Even though it's a pain in the ass, the more you do it, the easier it becomes.

WE ARE WHAT WE REPEATEDLY DO

"We are what we repeatedly do. Excellence, then, is not an act, but a habit."
– Aristotle

"You are a product of your decisions and not your circumstances." – Steven Covey

We are deeply habitual and we rarely make our own choices. We like to think we do but, on average, 95% of what we do is completely automatic, unconscious, and requires NO THOUGHT and the other 5% is consciously selected.

Through our daily conscious thoughts, emotions, behaviors, and habits, we prime and program this automatic part of our brain. We have a seat at the table and we get a vote.

You can start to positively influence this 95% of automatic behavior by using the 5% you do have control over to consciously make good decisions and have good habits. Over time, the 5% of these conscious and controlled decisions seep into the unconscious part of your mind and influence, prime, and program your automatic behavior.

You've chosen to be a product of your everyday thoughts, feelings, behaviors, and habits. You've chosen to think, feel, and do the things that are making up your current position in life.

Every day, no matter what you're doing, you're commanding your brain to automate your thinking, feelings, and actions. 24/7, you are commanding your brain to make your decisions automatic and unconscious. The more you think, feel, or do something, the more you command your brain to "become" it – whatever "it" may be.

Start choosing to program your mind with better thoughts, feelings, behavior, and habits. Develop more awareness about the process.

YOU CAN ACCOMPLISH ANYTHING

"Crazy", "huge", and "impossible" are words used by those who don't accomplish anything. Those who accomplish a lot, and in a short period of time, see anything and everything as doable, reachable, and possible.

Accomplishing is easily simplified if you just break down the big goals into smaller goals. As small as you want them to be. Instead of thinking about how long it will take, break each year into each month, each month into each week, each week into each day, each day into each hour, each hour into each minute, and each minute into each second. Make it manageable. Instead of zooming out and thinking/looking at/focusing on the big picture and letting it scare you, only focus on accomplishing one tiny goal at a time. Break everything down into manageable pieces.

My thought process is, "For the next 45 minutes, I'm placing my focus and energy only on hitting this one target and accomplishing this one goal." I only focus on those 45 minutes. I'm not concerned with the next 5 hours, the rest of the day, the rest of the week, the rest of the month, the rest of the year, or the rest of my life. I worry about tomorrow when tomorrow comes. I only worry about each goal/target as I approach it.

BUD/S has a 70% - 80% drop out rate but the Navy SEALs who make it take it one evolution, run, swim, minute, and even step at time.

With this mindset, ANYTHING can be accomplished. Any giant goal can be broken down into smaller goals and each small goal can be turned into, even smaller, goals. Identify the steps involved, turn them into goals, break each goal down into smaller goals and targets, and then aggressively drive forward with purpose and precision accomplishing each goal, hitting each target, and crossing them off of the list.

"Crazy", "huge", and "impossible" are doable goals. Create the map, create the blueprint, create the to-do list, and get started.

CHANGE ISN'T AS HARD AS YOU THINK

Change is scary because we don't want to leave the safety of our "bubble". We're too used to being in our comfort zones. We're afraid something "bad" might happen if we're not in our place of familiarity. We see change as this huge and painful uphill battle that seems impossible to win – but it's only in our mind.

Change is easy when you start small and change one little thought, feeling, reaction, behavior, and habit at a time – things most don't see as important. Once you get the little things down, move onto bigger and bigger things and by the time you look back, YOU'VE changed. Your life has changed. Your results have changed. Your future has changed. It's only difficult because you're making it that way in your mind. If you believe it's easy, it'll be easy. If you believe it's difficult, it'll be a difficult battle the entire way.

Change starts with a decision. Deciding something about you or your life needs to change. Deciding you're sick of waking up each morning and not being as happy with your results as you want to be. Deciding you're sick of the thoughts and emotions your actions and habits are generating. Deciding you're sick of your life's path. But you have to decide to change, you have to mean it, and you have to stick to it. Draw a line in the sand, step over it, and then build a wall so you can't go back. Cut off people dragging you down – contacts, social media "friends", stop answering your phone and texting them back. Get rid of things that make you unproductive – cable or satellite provider, games from your phone, etc.

When you make the decision to leave your current self behind and move forward into the unknown, you will see change. It won't happen if you don't change your thinking, behaviors, and habits. You can't get different results by doing the same things you've always done.

CHANGE REQUIRES FULL IMMERSION

"If you limit your choices only to what seems possible or reasonable, you disconnect yourself from what you truly want, and all that is left is compromise." – Robert Fritz

When you make the decision to do things differently, doing it only when you feel like it won't work. Doing it only when you're in a good mood won't work. Doing it sometimes won't work. Doing it only when people are looking won't work.

Change requires full immersion. It requires becoming "extreme" in the eyes of society. It requires overdoing it because that's the only thing that gives you the power to pull away from the life-sucking force of your bad habits. Without full immersion, you're easily and continually pulled back into your old habits and your old self.

Changing requires 100% commitment and NOTHING LESS. It requires nothing short of being extreme. Anything worth doing is worth overdoing. You must change your mindset to reflect that belief. It requires taking every ounce of your focus and placing it on your goal of changing yourself, your habits, and your life.

Cut off everything happening inside and around you and fully immerse yourself into the thoughts, activities, and habits that help you change. Put the mission before yourself. Put the path and your purpose before yourself. Put your goal of changing before yourself.

It's perfectly fine if everyone says you're doing too much and spending too much time focusing on getting your act together. You shouldn't be bothered by it. Ignore it. What other people think is none of your business. Since no one else is willing to fully immerse themselves into reaching particular goals, it doesn't mean you have to listen to them.

BIG CHANGES ARE NECESSARY

We want big changes but we're not actually willing to MAKE big changes. We want 100% of our life to change but we only want to make a 20% effort in making it happen. We want things to be different but we don't want to actually do anything different.

If you want your life to change, YOU have to change. Your thoughts, emotions, behaviors, and habits have to change. You have to leave the old you behind and move forward as the new you is being created. You have to be willing to leave everything behind, move forward, and never look back.

EVERYTHING that has contributed to your current state of not having your act together has to go – associations, entertainment, media, etc.

- The people around you are contributing

- The music and lyrics you listen to are contributing

- What you watch on TV is contributing

- What you look at on your phone and on social media is contributing

You can't get your act together and become a different person yet keep the same lifestyle you've always had. You can't get your act together and become a different person and still keep the same people around.

For a shift to happen in your life, a shift has to, first, happen in your mind. For a shift to happen in your mind, a shift has to, first, happen in your environment. You have to consciously make the shift. You have to put time, energy, and effort into it.

Throw out the garbage in your life – even if it means starting from scratch. Clean house, fire everyone and everything keeping you from becoming a better person, and never look back.

YOUR ARE TOUGHER THAN YOU THINK

By default, those who have their act together are mentally tougher than those who don't have their act together.

It's easier to be weak and think we can't "handle" the pressure of getting our act together than it is push through the resistance and pain. Your body gives out before your mind and getting your act together requires more mental exertion than physical. When the mind is willing, everything you want will happen. When the mind is weak, it's because you're deciding to be weak.

Navy SEALs have a 40% rule – if you think you're at your breaking point, you've only reached 40% of your capacity and you can still keep going.

Your mind is more powerful than you can ever imagine.

Lose the weak mindset and thoughts. Quit thinking it's hard. Quit worrying about it being "tough". Quit worrying about hurting yourself mentally and emotionally. Quit worrying about it somehow being unhealthy.

I've heard it all from myself and others – and the truth is, they're all excuses to avoid actually making an effort. The harder you push mentally, the tougher your mind becomes and the easier everything in your life becomes.

Just like, physically, working on your muscles, exercising your mind and willpower causes it to become stronger, healthier, and tougher.

Do the hard things and stop thinking about how much it "hurts".

Embrace the pressure and get used to it. Pressure hardens you. Pressure creates diamonds. When you're not feeling pressure, it's a sign you're not doing enough. It's a sign you're too comfortable. It's a sign you need to push yourself more.

IT'S NOT ABOUT WHAT YOU "WANT"

Those who have their act together never "want" to do what it takes to get their act together – they do it because it NEEDS to be done. In their mind, there's no other choice. It's part of the blueprint. It's a necessary step in the plan. It's what they have to do to keep the "machine" working properly.

We all "want" to be lazy, sleep in late, and to not have to work or make an effort. It's much easier that way. But this isn't about what you want - it's about what HAS to be done. The things you "want" don't create the results. Doing what HAS to be done creates nothing but results.

Switch from thinking about what you "want" to thinking about what "has to" be done. From now on, what "has to" be done is all that matters. Completely forget about what you "want". Get rid of it.

When you get in the habit of consistently doing what has to be done, you automatically get everything you've ever wanted and more. When you get in the habit of doing what has to be done, everything you've ever wanted takes care of itself. When you consistently do what you "want" to do, you always have problems, roadblocks, and a lack of peace and stability in your life and mind.

You're done with what you want. It's not a choice anymore.

Those who don't have their act together may enjoy the short-term pleasures of doing what they want but they, unfortunately, have to lie in the bed they make and live with the long-term consequences of their poor decision making.

Thinking about what you "want" is weak-mindedness. Focusing on what "has to" happen and what you need to do makes your mind stronger, sharper, and more focused.

TWO TYPES OF PEOPLE

What separates those who have their act together from those who don't is their mindset. There's always a defining difference in the way people think and the results they're getting.

There are two types of people:

- Those who see the glass half-full and those who see it half-empty

- Those who see the room is half-lit and those who see it's half-dark

- Those who see the opportunity and those who see the problem

- Those who see the learning opportunities and those who see failure

- Those who see why it CAN be done and those who see why it can't

- Those who see what they want and those who see what's preventing them from getting what they want

- Those who see thorn bushes have roses and those who see rose bushes have thorns

- Those who get the life they want and those who don't

- You're either the hammer or the nail

- You're either the hunter or the prey

- You're either on the offensive or the defensive

- You're either selling or you're being sold

- You're either have the power or you're losing it

- You're either the lender or the borrower

As Grant Cardone says, pick a side and get on it! Decide who you're going to be and stick to it.

ACCEPTABLE OR UNACCEPTABLE – NO EXCEPTIONS

Getting your act together as much as possible is much easier when you dumb everything down to being either acceptable or unacceptable. Not only in the eyes of society, but in your eyes. When you compare it to your experience and everything you've learned about yourself and the results you've gotten so far, is it acceptable or unacceptable?

No exceptions. No "just this time". If it's unacceptable, you don't do it. Period. If it's unacceptable not to do it, then you do it. Period.

It doesn't have to be more complicated than that but we're making it more complicated than that. We're weighing the costs and the benefits and asking others what they would do and what others would think if you did or didn't do it. None of that matters. Is it acceptable or unacceptable?

Don't give yourself wiggle room to be lazy and to make bad decisions. Don't give yourself the opportunity to screw yourself over. Don't give yourself the opportunity to be put in an, even more, compromising position than you're already in.

Draw a line in front of it and decide which side it goes on!

Be as shrewd as necessary to get the life you want. Be stricter on yourself than anyone else will be on you. Be stricter on yourself than life will be on you.

The results you're getting, are they acceptable or unacceptable? The time you're going to sleep and waking up, acceptable or unacceptable? The way you're conducting yourself around others, acceptable or unacceptable? The decisions you're making throughout the day, acceptable or unacceptable?

There are no in-betweens and exceptions.

YOU'RE CHOOSING TO BE AVERAGE

Everyone wants to be above-average but they only want to do average things and make an average effort. Average doesn't help you become the person you want to be. Average doesn't help you create the life you want to live. Average doesn't help you create above-average results.

You're choosing to categorize yourself with everyone else. You're choosing to do the same things and get the same results as everyone else. You're choosing to have the same thoughts and feel the same emotions as everyone else. You're choosing to take part in the time-wasting activities everyone else is taking part in. You're choosing to put in the average amount of time and energy to get better and become the person you want to be. You're average because you're choosing to be average!

Average is a conscious decision. Getting average results is a conscious decision. Having your act together as much as the average person is a conscious decision! Above average isn't an accident. It happens when you decide you're not happy being average. It happens when you make the decision to do what average people won't do. It happens when you decide to put in more than the average amount of time and effort.

Greatness doesn't happen by accident. It comes down to the decisions you're making every minute of the day.

YOU DO HAVE A CHOICE!

To pull away from average and move into the upper-echelon of the elite, the people who have it together, identify what the average person is focusing on and spending time on and then avoid those things. Identify how much work and effort the average person is putting in and do more than they'd ever be willing to do.

Eric Thomas woke me up and changed my life when he said this:

"Innately, innately everything about you is great, everything about you is phenomenal. But the problem is you have consciously chosen to be average.

You are average in school, you are average at your work place, everything you do is average and not because its average but because you made a decision. You made a choice to be average – why? Because the people around you are average, or maybe you grew up in an average environment, or went to an average school, or you work for an average company.

So, you decided… you decided to go against who you are. You decided to go against who you are.

So that's why you go to the basketball game, that's why you spend hours watching your favorite athlete like Michael, and you watch them… you watch them… there's something about this attracted to that greatness because there is something in you that's great. That's why you put those headphones on and you just shut the whole world out and you listen to your favorite artist – you listen to them sing or you listen to them rap and deep down inside you hurt when you listen because it should be you!

You are attracted to greatness because greatness is all in you. But it's easier to watch greatness, it's easier to go see greatness than it is to put in the time, to put in the energy, to discipline yourself, to sacrifice – it's easier!

And so that's why you average, and so you're frustrated because you're not living like you should live. No – you don't have what you should have, you're not being who you should be."

AVERAGE PEOPLE LACK PURPOSE

"A man without a purpose is just spending time."

I can't find exactly who said this but I like to think of it as, "Anyone not on a focused path to make life better for themselves or their family is simply wasting time doing absolutely nothing."

Average people are spending time doing nothing. They're "hanging out", spending hours playing on social media, and when they get home from their job, a job in which they think they're actually doing "something", they're wasting time sitting around, "relaxing", and feeling like they're making an actual effort and difference in their life.

Day in and day out, the countless hours they waste could be contributed towards something much bigger and better. Something that, over the course of time, will change their life.

Average people don't go to sleep thinking about the progress they made on their goals and path throughout the day. Average people don't wake up thinking about goals and targets that need to be reached, met, and hit. Average people aren't on a "path" that's much more important than themselves. They have nothing important to get excited about. Nothing to look forward to each day. Nothing to feel "pulled" towards.

They reluctantly wake up, get dressed for a job they don't want to go to, like and reshare "Monday Sucks" memes on social media, look forward to their days off, and then think about what they can blow their paycheck on to support their emotional addiction to buying things.

Their path is getting the newest TV, video game, smartphone, taking pictures of it, and then sharing everything on social media so they can appear to be on a real path and living a great life. They think their "path" is having a job, paying bills, and filling their life up with "stuff".

AVERAGE PEOPLE "WANT" AND "WISH"

Jim Carrey, in his commencement speech at the 2014 MUM Graduation, said "hope" is a beggar. That hope walks through water and faith leaps over it.

Those who have their act together don't "hope", "want", and "wish", they NEED. They have faith in themselves that whatever needs to be done is going to, inevitably, get done. They have faith that they're not going to let themselves down. The things they want in life HAVE TO happen. There are no choices. There are no other options.

Average people think, "That sure would be nice" and they put little to no effort into it because it's not high enough on their priority list.

When you have your act together, you decide, "This has to happen" and it becomes everything that's important. It automatically shoots to the very top of your priority list.

Turn your wants into needs. Not "I want to do this" but "I need to do this". Turn the things that "should" be happening into things that, no matter what, "have to AND WILL" happen.

Stop with the "It would be nice" mindset. Turn it into a life or death situation and you'll magically create the focus, energy, and drive to get it done.

Eliminate "if" and replace it with "when". Not "if this thing happens", but "when this thing happens".

Average people see it as "luck" and chance. When you wake up every single day focused and determined to do the things that have to happen, you create "luck". "Luck" is the result of doing the right things for the right amount of time. It's forcing yourself to be in the right place at the right time. It's forcing yourself to do what "needs" to be done.

WORDS ARE NOTHING. ACTION IS EVERYTHING

A good plan violently executed beats a great plan executed next week.

Average people talk and "post" but never take action. With their words, they paint the picture they want everyone to see instead of with their actions. Their results don't reflect action. They talk but never "do". Talking is effortless and action requires work. They only want what's easy. They want the appearance of having it together but won't do what's necessary to actually make it happen.

When you have your act together, you're all about taking action and getting things done. Talking isn't important because action gets more done and does the talking for you. Talking and "posting" about being at the gym doesn't make your muscles grow. Talking about saving money doesn't make money appear in your bank account. Talking about getting your act together doesn't change your mindset and results. Let action be your spokesperson. Stop talking and just do it.

Throughout my 12 years as an Aircraft Mechanic, I noticed a common pattern - the mechanics who weren't that good always stood around at the computers TALKING about the big jobs they've done in the past and yet, coincidentally, they were always given small and insignificant jobs because their supervisors didn't trust them with anything bigger. The good mechanics, who were always on the big and important jobs, usually stayed silent and didn't say much about anything. They'd review their job, print their paperwork, get their tools together, and get to work. When the job was completed, they, again, didn't have anything to say about it. The result said enough.

If you want others to take you seriously and be in awe, stop talking and start doing. Move yourself more than you move your mouth.

THERE'S NO ROOM FOR BEING SOFT

If you're soft, life will weed you out, cut you from the team, and you won't get the life you want.

Soft people don't have their act together, they choose to be victims, and they always have a reason and excuse for not having the life they want.

Those who are tough, mentally and emotionally, choose to be the victors and not the victims. They always get what they want. Things happen according to THEIR plans. Things happen on THEIR time.

There's no room for weakness and being soft in your life. You are greater than your circumstances. Make the decision to quit being weak. Make the decision to quit being soft. Make the decision to quit being the victim. Make the decision to get rid of your excuses. Make the decision to take responsibility for everything happening within you and around you.

Become the hammer instead of the nail. See "problems" and challenges as an opportunity to learn and grow instead of an opportunity to curl up into the fetal position and cry about it.

The more you focus on hardening your mind, body, and spirit, the easier everything will become and the less of a negative effect challenges, hardship, and problems will have on you.

The Rock, Dwayne Johnson, says, "Be the person that when your feet touch the floor each morning, the devil says, 'Aww shit, they're up.'"

Become harder than life is so you can turn around and tell the world, "Is that all you got?"

When you choose to stand up and fight the war within your mind, you become battle-hardened, experienced, and more resilient. You develop mental and emotional armor that nothing and no one can penetrate. Find your weak and soft areas, work on them, and become tougher.

IT'S YOUR JOB TO TAKE CARE OF YOURSELF

Having your act together means taking care of yourself and not relying on anyone else to handle what you're supposed to be handling on your own.

If you're a fully-functioning adult - your motor functions are normal, you aren't physically handicapped, and you don't have any psychological disorders preventing you from properly functioning in society, then you're responsible for supporting yourself physically, mentally, emotionally, and financially.

It's not your grandparent's, parent's, or society's job to baby you and provide you transportation, put clothes on your back, food in your mouth, and a roof over your head. You don't deserve free money because you'd rather be lazy and avoid working.

IT'S YOUR JOB to make sure your needs are completely taken care of and when you're interacting with others, you're giving and not taking.

At 17 years old, I had already graduated high school and when my mother kicked me out for continually bringing girls over to her house when she asked me not to, I didn't look for someone else to take care of me. I lived and slept in my car, a car I paid for, showered at the gym, got a better job, saved my money, saved for an apartment deposit, and I paid my own bills. I didn't run around crying to others about my situation. I sucked it up, dealt with it, and got myself out of a situation that I put myself in.

I put all nonsense to the side, put a roof over my own head, put food in my own mouth, and took care of myself so I wasn't a burden to anyone.

You're an adult. Kill the nonsense and laziness. Put the video games down, make money and don't waste it, stop looking to others to babysit your emotions, and start becoming more responsible.

If you can't take care of yourself, you can't take care of others.

LIFE IS EASY OR HARD – IT'S YOUR CHOICE

We live our lives the easy way but then complain that life is always hard and we can't seem to catch a break. The truth is, life is easy if you live it the hard way and hard if you live it the easy way. If you want your life to become smoother and easier, start choosing to make the tougher decisions that most won't make, do the harder things most won't do, and live your life the way most won't live it.

Put goals and progress ahead of fun and entertainment, getting your act together ahead of pleasure, and becoming the person you want to be ahead of what everyone else thinks.

Those who are living the life and having the things you want are living the hard way and making the tough decisions that most won't make. They're getting up at 4 AM, working out, and getting their day started. They're going to bed early while everyone else is watching TV, playing on their phones, or out at the bar having drinks. They're working, making progress, and getting things done while most people are relaxing, taking naps, and out shopping for things they don't need. They're saving money, saying no to the things that aren't good for them, and putting simple pleasures aside while everyone else is spending money, indulging, and consuming. They're putting aside short-term conveniences for long-term gain. They're choosing to suffer and endure so they can become smarter, stronger, faster, and more resilient. They're letting pain push them in the direction they need to go instead of letting comfort and pleasure hold them back.

In every situation, think of the easy thing that most people do and choose not to do it. Choose to take the harder path. Choose to endure the pain that comes with moving in the right direction. For your life to become less problematic and stressful, choose to do the hard things.

YOU HAVE TO BE AT A LEVEL OF F*CK YOU

I saw the movie "The Gambler" twice in the movies because of the scene where John Goodman, Frank, is lending Mark Wahlberg, Jim, $250,000 and he chastises him for not walking away from the table when he was $2.5 million ahead.

Frank says, "You get up 2.5 million dollars any asshole in the world knows what to do. You get a house with a 25-year roof, an indestructible Jap-economy shit box, you put the rest into the system and 3-5% to pay your taxes and that's your base. Get me? That's your fortress of f*cking solitude. That puts you, for the rest of your life, at a level of F*ck You. Somebody wants you to do something, F*ck You. Boss pisses you off, F*ck You. Own your house, have a couple bucks in the bank, don't drink. That's all I have to say to anybody at any social level. A wise man's life is based around F*ck You."

When you have your act together and you're a squared away and high-caliber individual, you are at a level of F*ck You. You have more freedom than everyone else and no one can say anything to you because they have to look at themselves first - and when they do, they're going to realize just how far behind they are.

Get your money, thoughts, emotions, behavior, habits, and life squared away. Get all of it on a level of F*ck You.

If you don't have your act together, you never get to say "F*ck You" to anyone and you can live the rest of your life knowing you had the choice and opportunity and you chose to take the average route. You chose to be lazy and do what's easy. You chose to act like a child, make childish decisions, and to be weak.

What do you want to be able to say to life and to the challenges and problems average people struggle with? "F*ck You..."

PART 3: WHAT ARE YOU FOCUSING ON?

WHY ARE YOU GETTING YOUR ACT TOGETHER?

Yes, you want to become a better version of yourself, but why?

Your "why" gives you the drive, strength, stamina, and advantage you need to make it there.

My "why" for having my act together is it pushes me in the direction of my goals. I get more done, I stay on track, and my thoughts and emotions don't get in the way. My "why" for having my act together is it feels good to be in the state of having it together. To wake up knowing I did a great job and accomplished more than I thought I could the day before and go to sleep knowing I used my time wisely and hit my targets throughout the day. My "why" is running away from feeling guilt. I hate waking up in the morning and going to bed at night feeling like I don't have my act together and guilty that I'm not doing what I know I'm capable of. I'm sure you know that feeling. My "why" is knowing that feeling like I don't have my act together doesn't have to be permanent. I'm 100% capable of always doing better and the negative feelings of laziness and complacency are a conscious choice. My "why" is having my act together sets the example for my child, family, friends, and everyone around me. I'm a positive influence in their life and I'm able to give instead of take.

How is getting your act together going to make you feel better about yourself, improve your life, and contribute to those around you?

What direction will it take you?

What goals will it help you reach?

How is it going to make your life easier?

Where will you end up if you don't get your act together?

WHO IS THE IDEAL YOU?

Keeping up with your ideal self is a constant battle, but it's doable.

Your ideal self isn't the person you want to be because you hate yourself. Your ideal self is the person you know you'll become if you continue making daily improvements to yourself. It's the person you know you're capable of being. It's the person you become when you decide to quit selling yourself short and cheating yourself out of a better life.

Matthew McConaughey said this about his ideal self, "And to my hero - that's who I chase. When I was 15 years old I had a very important person in my life come to me and say, 'Who's your hero?' I said, 'I don't know, I've got to think about that, give me a couple of weeks.' I come back two weeks later, this person comes up and says, 'Who's your hero?' I said, 'I've thought about it - it's me in 10 years!' So, I turned 25 and that same person came to me and said, 'So are you your hero?' I was like, 'Not even close. My hero is me at 35.' Every day, every week, every month, and every year of my life my hero is always 10 years away. I'm never going to be my hero. I'm not going to attain that - I know I'm not. That's just fine with me because it gives me someone to keep on chasing."

Eric Thomas asks, "If you were amazing, what would amazing look like? If you know what amazing is, why haven't you gotten there yet?"

If people saw you and said, "I wish I had it together as much as that person", what would that look like? What thoughts, emotions, behavior, and habits would lead them to make that remark?

What aspects of your thoughts, emotions, behavior, habits, and responses can you improve so you can become the person you know you're cable of being? What limiting thoughts, emotions, behavior, and habits do you need to give up to become your ideal self? What do you have to start doing to reach that goal?

WHO ARE YOU AT THE REACTIVE LEVEL?

Most of us don't have our act together because we're not paying attention to poor reactions to challenges, stress, and lack. We get hungry - we eat fast food. Something doesn't go our way - we get angry and throw a temper tantrum. We get bored - we spend money and find entertainment. Something is difficult - we give up and move on. We feel fatigue - we throw in the towel and lay down.

Your reactions don't lie, can't be faked, reflect where you currently stand physically, mentally, and emotionally, and reveal your strengths and weaknesses. They reveal your thoughts, the effort you put into training your mind, and your daily habits. The more you have your act together, the more your natural and unconscious reactions reflect it.

How are you naturally reacting to challenges? Are you caving in, shutting down, becoming emotional, and making poor decisions? Or are you controlling yourself, choosing to respond instead of reacting, and making logical and wise decisions?

This matters.

Under pressure and stress, you sink to your current level of having your act together. You sink to your current level of your training. There's no time to think, "If I had my act together, how would I respond?" You're either reacting appropriately or inappropriately to the situation. When there's no time to waste and no time to think, your unconscious and automatic reaction needs to be mature, intelligent, and trained. It needs to be deeply ingrained and come from a place of having your act together.

If you are pretending to have your act together, you immediately collapse under pressure. Instead of stress and pressure revealing a diamond, you become rubble.

DO YOU KNOW YOUR LIMITS?

A big reason a lot of men choose to join U.S. Navy SEAL teams and other Special Forces units across the military is because they want to know their limits. They want to know their capabilities. They want to know how far they can push their mind and body until they can't go anymore. They want to find a starting point so they can start building upon it to become stronger, faster, smarter, and tougher - both mentally and physically. They know it'll provide major insight into what they can achieve across all spectrums of life. It's also the same reason a lot of us do extreme competitions, like triathlons and long-distance running.

Do you know your physical limits? When was the last time you physically pushed yourself to the limit? If you haven't done so and you don't have any physical ailments preventing you from doing it, you might want to give it a try. You will learn a lot about yourself. I didn't know I could run 10 miles and still feel like I could run another 10. I didn't know I could do 500 push-ups, 200 pull-ups, and 200 burpees and still have energy to make it through the rest of my day. It was something I had to do to find out for myself and it turned out I could push my body further than I thought it would go. And actually, I still don't know how far I can run and how many push-ups, pull-ups, and burpees I can do before I collapse and need medical attention. I will have to find out one day. All I know is I'm capable of pushing myself further than I think I can and you can too.

Do you know your mental limits? Your mind is tougher than you think and it, essentially, has no limits. You can handle more work, stress, challenges, and battles than you think. You can tolerate more focused activity than you think. Your mind finds a way to make it happen.

Finding your limits is important because when things get tough, it's a reminder you can keep pushing, striving, going, and making progress.

WHAT'S PROGRAMMING YOUR MIND?

Without fail, everything you read, watch, and listen to impacts your mind positively or negatively, it takes value or gives value, or it's a complete waste of time. Every person you interact with impacts your mind positively or negatively, takes value or gives value, or they're wasting your time. There's no in-between and there's no way around it.

The result of what you put in your mind is automatically reflected in every aspect of your attitude, thoughts, emotions, behavior, and habits. Put quality in and you get quality out. Put trash in and you get trash out.

Your mind is a sponge, it absorbs anything it's exposed to, and you can't control the process. What you do control, however, is WHAT you put in your mind so you can better predict what comes out - your own thoughts, emotions, behavior, and habits.

The things you choose to read, watch, listen to, and who you spend time with create "you". They directly impact your level of having your act together. I said "choose" because IT IS a choice.

You don't have to read, watch, and listen to negativity or anything that is a complete waste of time. You don't have to spend time with victim-minded, negative, and lazy people. You can put the negative book and magazine down. You change the channel on the TV. You can choose not to listen to garbage music that gives you a garbage mindset. You can choose to not answer your phone and to walk away from people who are a waste of your time.

What are you ALLOWING to program your mind and what screening process can you implement to have more control of it? How is what you're putting into your mind impacting your thinking, emotions, behavior, habits, and life?

WHAT ARE YOU NOT PREPARED FOR?

When you don't have your act together, you are not prepared. You are not trained. You are not battle-hardened and ready to fight whatever life throws in your direction.

U.S. Navy SEALs, and once again, I talk about them a lot because they're very good at what they do and have their act together beyond comprehension, constantly train to become better and to prepare for anything. In times of war and peace, they focus on becoming better. They focus on finding weaknesses and turning them into strengths. They simulate harsh environments, situations, circumstances, and prepare for dealing with those difficult threats and predicaments. They constantly ask themselves, "What can we train for next and get more prepared for? What are our weak areas? What could catch us off guard? How can we prepare against flanking in this particular situation? What weak areas are we overlooking?" The more they train and prepare, the less shocking and stressful the actual fight is for them. They're better able to keep their heads on straight, their emotions and reactions under control, and to maneuver under pressure and when faced with hostile threats.

Life is full of hostile threats. Life is pressure. Life is difficult. Life wants to destroy you. Life is unforgiving. Life doesn't care about your feelings. Life is war.

To have your act together, recognize there will be daily battles and it's imperative to train and prepare for them. Learn the enemy and its tricks, tactics, and methods of keeping you down and keeping you from becoming the best version of yourself.

What are you not prepared for physically, mentally, emotionally, financially, etc.? Where are your weak areas? Where are you being complacent? What difficulties are you not ready to deal with?

WHAT LEVEL ARE YOU ON RIGHT NOW?

UNCONSCIOUS INCOMPETENT	CONSCIOUS INCOMPETENT
IGNORANCE. UNAWARE OF HOW MUCH YOU DON'T KNOW. UNAWARE OF ERRORS IN YOUR THOUGHTS, EMOTIONS, BEHAVIOR, AND HABITS.	AWAKENING. LEARNING, NOTICING, AND IDENTIFYING PROBLEM AREAS. CONSCIOUS OF POTENTIAL IMPROVEMENT.
CONSCIOUS COMPETENT	UNCONSCIOUS COMPETENT
PRACTICE. WORKING ON NEW AND IMPROVED THOUGHTS, EMOTIONS, BEHAVIOR, AND HABITS. CONSCIOUSLY PAYING ATTENTION TO DETAIL.	MASTERY. SECOND NATURE. YEARS OF CONSCIOUS AND REPETITIVE THOUGHT, EMOTION, BEHAVIOR, AND HABITS.

This is called the Johari Window of Competence and, right now, you are in one of these quadrants. You're either unaware you have things you need to work on (like a fish that doesn't know it's wet), aware that you have problem areas and you're figuring out what to do, consciously and actively working on fixing your problem areas and becoming better, or you've spent years working on yourself and most of it has become second nature. You've mastered it.

LEVELS OF HAVING IT TOGETHER

HAS THE LIFE YOU WANT/
INDEPENDENT/SELF-RELIANT

1% ELITE. NO NONSENSE. STOIC. FOCUSED. DRIVEN. SCHEDULED. FINANCIALLY SET. ALL ACTION. GETS IT DONE. STRAY CALF.

IMPROVING/ GETTING IT
TOGETHER/SEMI-DEPENDENT

2% AWARE. ASKING QUESTIONS. READING. LEARNING. MAKING AN EFFORT. SAVING MONEY. MAKING CHANGES.

FULLY DEPENDENT ON
OTHERS - JOB, SELF-ESTEEM, ETC.

97% UNAWARE. EPICURIAN. AVERAGE. VICTIMS. LAZY. EXCUSE MAKERS. CONSUMERS. IN DEBT. NO ACTION. CONCERNED WITH SHORT-TERM, EGO, PLEASURE, FUN, AND WHAT OTHERS THINK. ADDICTED TO PHONES AND SOCIAL MEDIA. THE HERD. UNABLE TO LOOK UP AND NOTICE LEVELS ABOVE THEM.

97% of us are unaware, dependent, and concerned with fun rather than having our act together. As a result, we're broke and in debt, lazy, making excuses and acting like victims, egotistical, and addicted to time-wasting things like our phones and social media. 2% of us are waking up, seeing how off track the other 97% is, and we're learning, improving, and doing our best to take steps in the right direction. 1% of us are not about nonsense and we're doing what has to be done to have the life we want and deserve. We're focused, driven, taking action, getting our money right, and getting it done every day.

HOW MUCH TIME ARE YOU WASTING?

THE TIME YOU HAVE TO IMPROVE

5,840 DAYS GROWING UP	9,125 DAYS SPENT SLEEPING	10,950 DAYS TO GET IT TOGETHER

AVERAGE LIFE SPAN 25,915 DAYS

Everything you think, feel, and do is either a good use of time or a waste. The people you choose to associate with are either wasting your time or a good use of your time. There is no in-between.

Those who don't have their act together waste 80% of their day being unproductive and counter-productive. They're sleeping in, playing on their phones, abusing social media, watching TV, addicted to listening to music, and just "hanging out" because they're bored.

24 hours a day, sand is falling in the hour glass of your life and it doesn't stop for your feelings and discomforts. As long as the sand is falling, you have to be getting after it, getting things done, and making progress. There's no time to waste being unproductive and counter-productive.

Of the 25,915 days we have to make something happen in life, 5,840 are used growing up into a young adult and 9,125 are spent sleeping. That leaves us with only 10,950 days to get our head on straight, take action, and do things right. Our time is too limited to waste.

Make each second, minute, hour, day, month, and year count.

The 2 - 3 hours you spend hitting the snooze button in the morning could be used to make progress on your goals. The 2 - 3 hours you use staying up

DECLARE WAR ON YOURSELF 1ST EDITION BY MARC SUMMERS | 94

past, what should be, your bedtime could be used getting quality rest instead of watching TV and playing on social media.

How much time are you wasting each morning? How much time are you wasting at night? How much time are you wasting by spending unproductive and counterproductive time with friends, on your phone, and in front of the TV?

If you add up all of the time you're wasting each day and multiply it by 365, you'll find you have enough time to make big improvements in your life in one short year.

WHAT ARE YOUR EXCUSES?

We all have stories for why we're not where we want to be and doing the things we know we should be doing. We all have a thing, a person, or a circumstance to point at and say, "That thing, that person, or that situation held me back and is keeping me from moving forward."

We can all use the "bad childhood", "bad luck", and "life has been unfair" stories and excuses, but at the end of the day, we're using them to dodge full accountability and responsibility and we know it. We're using stories and excuses as tools to avoid having to be absolutely truthful.

The past can't hold us back at this current moment and when we decide to be lazy and complacent, we pull that story out of our pocket and use it to justify our poor decisions and behavior.

Once I decided to quit acting like a child and got rid of my stories and excuses for why I wasn't where I wanted to be, I had no choice but to move forward and make things happen. I had to accept full responsibility for my situations and quit using stories and excuses as crutches.

Your stories and excuses are only holding you back.

What stories about your childhood are you using to justify why you're a victim and why you're not getting your act together? What stories and excuses about your current situation are you using? What stories and excuses do you regularly use for not getting your act together? Quit telling them. Quit using them. Quit repeating them. Let them die.

No matter who you are, how fortunate you are, and how successful you are, shitty things are going to happen to you and you're just going to have to suck it up and roll with it. You can't use them as a wall to hide behind. When something bad happens, say, "Well that sucks but I'm not going to use it as an excuse. I'm not going to let it hold me back."

WHAT'S REALLY IN YOUR WAY?

We have stories and excuses about the things that are, supposedly, in our way, but what about the things that are actually in our way and we're not doing anything about them? What situations, circumstances, and people are ACTUALLY in your way but you're choosing to do nothing about it? Instead of saying, "Excuse me. You're stopping me from reaching my goals. Can you please move?", we're saying, "It's ok that you're in my way. I'll work around you and make my life more difficult." Most of the time, they wouldn't be in the way if you asked them to step aside.

You're in your own way by not deciding to do what you're supposed to be doing. You're in your own way by making excuses and stories instead of sucking it up and moving forward. You're in your own way by not being mentally tough and enduring the pain necessary to get to where you want to be. You're in your own way by allowing situations, circumstances, and people to be in your way. If you're allowing it, then it's your fault and you can't say anyone or anything is stopping you. You're stopping yourself!

When you choose to go to bed and wake up late, you're in your own way. It's not, "Oh I've been stressed at work so I'm not sleeping well." It's, "I didn't go to bed on time so I got crappy sleep and I had trouble waking up." That's the truth and you know it. You're not using stress and work as an excuse. You got in your own way. You stopped yourself from making life easier. You allowed yourself to make poor decisions.

What distractions are you allowing to stay in your way and remain enemies of your success? What addictions are you allowing to get in your way because you're failing to control them? What thoughts, emotions, behaviors, and habits are you allowing to get in your way and keep you from maximum performance?

PART 4: TAKE OUT THE TRASH

ELIMINATE TRASH BELIEFS, MINDSETS, AND HABITS

Trashy thoughts, emotions, behavior, and habits result from exposing your mind to trash. Every thought, emotion, behavior, and habit that doesn't serve you has to go. Everything negative, limiting, and a waste of time has to go. Ask yourself, "Does this belief, mindset, or habit push me towards my goals and getting my act together?" If no, label it as "trash" and throw it out. When it tries coming back up, tell it, "You don't belong here. Get lost."

You can't simultaneously have your act together and retain mental trash. You have to throw it out and replace it with high-quality and valuable thoughts, emotions, behaviors, and habits.

Mental trash is messing up your thoughts and emotions. Trash habits are creating problems and pushing you in the wrong direction. Trash beliefs are keeping you discouraged, unrealistic, and unmotivated. Complaining, thinking you aren't good enough, acting like a victim, making excuses, being too easy on yourself, justifying your shortcomings, etc., means you need to clean up your mindset and replace the trash with positivity.

Clean your mind up. Get rid of the bullshit. Get rid of the nonsense. Lose the limiting beliefs. Lose the mindsets and habits keeping you in your current position. This also includes proactively ensuring you're not exposing your mind to and feeding it trash.

You won't catch all of your trash beliefs, mindsets, and habits in one day. They'll come up one by one from time to time over the next few months and years and, when they do, catch, identify, label, and throw them out as quickly as possible. The more you do it, the easier it becomes.

Once the trash is gone, your mind is cleaner, purer, and more efficient.

POSITIVE HABITS FORCE TRASH HABITS OUT

Whatever you reinforce in your mind wins. What you feed in your mind is what lives and what you starve, dies.

Your mind doesn't recognize words like "don't" and "do". It only recognizes the verb, like "smoke". If you want to stop eating fast food and you tell yourself "don't eat fast food", you're commanding your mind to, "eat fast food". If you say, "I want to eat only healthy food", your mind will hear, "eat healthy food" and it will execute that command and completely bypass "eat fast food".

If you want to eliminate the negative thought, emotion, behavior, and habit, ONLY focus on its positive replacement.

If you keep going to bed late and want to start going to bed earlier so you can get up and get started earlier, only focus on waking up early and getting out of bed. Give your mind the command of "wake up early" instead of "go to bed late". By the time your target bedtime rolls around, you're, naturally, more tired and willing to go to sleep. If you think, "I don't want to stay up" your mind only hears "stay up" and it's executing that command.

If you're quitting smoking and thinking, "don't smoke", you're commanding your mind to "smoke". But if you replace "smoking" with "eating fruit", your mind will focus on executing the "eating fruit" command and not on "smoking".

If you think you're fat, lazy, and need to go to the gym, focus on "go to the gym" and not on "lazy". If you give your mind the command of "lazy", it'll automatically decide you're not going to the gym.

Focus on positive replacements for the trash thoughts, emotions, and habits and don't reinforce the negative in your mind.

MANAGE YOUR EGO

Your ego is holding you back and stopping you from getting your act together. It's keeping you stuck in your place of comfort and mediocrity. It's keeping you from doing things differently and making progress. It's making you inflate your current level of knowledge and giving you the false sense of knowing everything. It's making you think you deserve all of the credit. It's making you think you're better than others. It's giving you a false sense of superiority and the "I'm always right" attitude. It's making you think no one can tell you what to do and how to do it because you already have it figured out.

Your ego is telling you that when problems arise, it's everyone else's fault because they're stupid and you're smart, superior, and educated and there's no way you contributed to it.

Your ego is creating and contributing to a lot of the problems you're currently experiencing because it's a stuck up, maniacal, and self-centered entity living within your mind. It's the part of your brain that's overly-concerned with taking selfies, abusing social media, and constantly saying, "Look at me! Give me attention!" and "I'm better than others!"

It doesn't care about you. It only cares about itself. It's only concerned with looking good, getting attention, and avoiding the opinions of others. It has no interest in helping you get your act together and become a better person. Your ego knows if you get your act together, it's going to get evicted – and that's not what it wants.

Get your ego under control. Treat it as if you're the boss and you have some egotistical employee running around the office and messing everything up. Tell your ego, "Look, I need you to calm the f*ck down. You're messing everything up and I need you to take a back seat, sit down, and shut up."

ELIMINATE THE MENTAL CHATTER

Mental chatter is a major distraction. It's robbing you of energy, peace of mind, the ability to focus, and leaving you drained, tired, and used up. When you know what needs to happen and you know it needs to happen now, mental chatter talks you out of it. It creates doubt, insecurity, and causes you to second guess yourself. It delays and prevents you from taking action.

To reach your goals and get your life on the right track, you need to keep your head on straight. Your mind needs to be clear. You need to be able to hear yourself think. You need the mental space to logically process all incoming information so you know what to do with it and how to apply it.

Mental chatter amplifies anything negative so you don't take action. It holds you back and thinks it's trying to protect you. Mel Robbins says anything you want to do, you have 5 seconds to get started and to take action or your brain is designed to kill it. After 5 seconds, the mental chatter sets in and talks you out of it.

Do your best to operate with a silenced mentality. Kill the mental chatter the second it starts. Stop the self-pity and self-doubt conversations. Stop the inner-negativity. It's a bad habit. Tell the mental chatter, as Jocko Willink puts it, "I'm busy. Come back later when I'm not!"

Stop worrying about what the voices are saying. Stop listening to them. When it needs to happen, silence your mind and just get it done.

Tame your mind. The scared, doubtful, insecure, and disbelieving voices don't get a vote. They have no business in what you do and how you do it. Consciously practice silencing the voices when they're starting to talk too much and create doubt. The more you do it, the easier it becomes until, eventually, it's automatic and your mind is always silent. Kill the thoughts and voices. Kick them out. They're not welcome.

ELIMINATE MICRO EMOTIONS

There are two levels of controlling emotions - 1. Controlling bigger emotions like jealousy, sadness, anger, excitement, etc. 2. Controlling the hundreds, and possibly thousands, of tiny, and almost undetectable, emotions that are always present – what I'm calling Micro Emotions. (Not to be confused with the exterior Micro Emotions of a person's face)

We don't notice micro emotional chatter constantly happening unless we're self-aware and paying attention. Micro emotions show up when we're just "thinking". They're the tiny emotions in between the bigger emotions. They're the small, energetic thoughts in between the bigger thoughts. When you think about past, current, and future events and get anxiety about them, those are micro emotions. When the alarm goes off and you have that whiny feeling of not wanting to get up, those are micro emotions. When it's time to go to the gym and you get the whiny feelings of not wanting to go, those are micro emotions. When you're not feeling 100% and you're, internally, complaining, whining, bitching, and feeling self-pity, those are micro emotions.

We believe they're just thoughts but we're actually attaching tiny emotions and emotional energy to those thoughts and making them into bigger emotions. Those bigger emotions, needlessly created from emotional thoughts, influence decisions. We're thinking too much, attaching micro emotions to our thoughts, and those thoughts become powerful enough to negatively influence our behavior and habits.

The second you detect micro emotions, kill them. Disconnect from them. Get away from them. Don't attach emotion to thoughts. They're keeping you from taking action and reaching goals. If allow them to hang around and start adding up, it becomes a bunch of useless thoughts and emotional chatter. It gets you out of touch with reality. Shut them down.

ELIMINATE THE DISTRACTIONS

Stop allowing things to get in your way. Stop allowing people and things to make your job harder. Do what's necessary to make absolutely sure the path to your goals and getting your act together is clear and free of distraction. Then, keep it that way.

We're spending time on people and things we shouldn't be spending time on. We're paying attention to things we shouldn't be paying attention to. We're spending hours lounging around, entertaining ourselves, and being involved in unproductive and counterproductive activities that rob us of time and set us back.

Whoever and whatever is wasting your time, getting in the way, and being a distraction has to go. You can't afford to be distracted by anyone or anything not contributing or providing value. You can't afford to waste time on anyone or anything getting you off of your path instead of helping you move faster down it.

Stop abusing social media. You don't need attention. You don't need to see what everyone else is wasting time on. Unfollow all people and pages that post distracting, negative, destructive, victim-minded, and loser posts. Better yet, stop reading the social media news feeds. It's a just a big distraction.

Go through your contact list on your phone and delete distractions. People you know you don't want to talk to or spend time with. Anyone setting a horrible and negative example. Anyone not providing value or teaching you. Anyone not making you a better person by speaking to them or spending time with them. Anyone who doesn't' make you feel good.

Disconnect cable and satellite. If there's something you need to see, it's probably on YouTube. Otherwise, most programs are a distraction.

ELIMINATE CHAOS

I'm sure you know someone who always has "crazy" things happening and they label everything as "crazy", "chaotic", and "hectic". You ask how their day or week is going and their response is, "Things are really crazy right now!" Things aren't "crazy". If they are, they're creating it. They're creating the chaos by not controlling their environment.

Nothing about your thoughts, emotions, behavior, habits, routine, and life should be chaotic and if it starts turning in that direction, you should know how to keep your head on straight and deal with it appropriately. You should have preventive measures, controls, and plans in place for when things get chaotic so you don't freak out and get sucked into it. You should have trained, intelligent, and logical responses to chaos loaded up, in place, and ready to unload when it shows up.

Look at your life and find the sources of any chaotic situations you're in. Are you living in a chaotic household where it's always crazy? Separate yourself from that situation and find somewhere peaceful to live. Are you in a crazy and chaotic relationship? Get it under control, seek counseling, or get away from it. Is your job too crazy and chaotic? Find a way to deal with it more effectively or find a different job.

Chaos also stems from complacency. Dishes and laundry pile up, the house becomes a mess, the car starts having problems, your boss gets fed up with you showing up late, etc. It gets overwhelming and chaotic because you're letting it build up instead of handling it.

Eliminate the chaos from your life. It's not logical to deal with it and there's never a good reason for it to exist. It's counterproductive and distracts you from focusing on what's important. Practice **Planned Chaos Elimination** – identify what could go wrong in any situation and strategically design your actions around preventing it.

ELIMINATE WHAT DOESN'T MATTER

Stop placing importance on people, things, activities, thoughts, emotions, and habits that don't matter. Make your list of things that actually matter very small. Reduce it. Downsize. Clean house. Free up physical, mental, and emotional space so you have less to worry about and more room to learn, grow, and become. Prioritize your priorities.

80% of the possessions, activities, thoughts, emotions, behaviors, habits, and things you think are important actually don't matter and aren't useful. They're only keeping you entertained, feeding your ego, and keeping you stuck in your comfort zone. We have too many options. We have too many things happening at once. Our thoughts, emotions, and lives are cluttered with 80% garbage and we're unable to learn and grow because we're refusing to make space for something better.

Past experiences shouldn't influence today's thoughts, emotions, behavior, and habits. Let go of your shitty childhood. Let go of the times people did you wrong. Let go of the times you got rejected. Let go of times you felt embarrassed. Let go of the time you were the high school quarterback or the head cheerleader and the most popular kid in school. It doesn't matter anymore. Good or bad, it's in the past and it's no longer useful. Let go of future worries and expectations. There's little you can do about it right now. You can't predict how future events will play out. You can't predict how people will behave in the future. You can't predict what will or won't go wrong. It doesn't matter right now. All you can do is keep your cool and deal with it when it shows up.

Today's decisions matter. How you choose to think, feel, and behave today matters. Focus on the people, things, activities, thoughts, and emotions that can help you, in this very moment, to get closer to the goals you want, the life you want, and the person you want to be.

PART 5: IMPROVE YOUR RELATIONSHIP WITH YOURSELF

COMMIT TO YOURSELF

Commit to yourself before you commit to other people, things, and situations.

Be loyal to yourself first before being loyal to others.

This doesn't mean being selfish and not thinking about anyone but yourself, it means if you don't have a good relationship with yourself first, and understand yourself as much as possible, then it's harder to do the same with others. If you trust yourself, others will find it easier to trust you. If you're loyal to yourself first, it'll be easier to be loyal to others. If you keep your commitments to yourself, it'll be easier to keep your commitment to others. Solidify your relationship with yourself.

Have an understanding with yourself that you're going to get your act together under your present circumstances and not wait until the right time, it feels right, or you feel like it – you're going to start now.

Put yourself under a binding contract that there's no getting out of:

"Starting right now, on this _____ day of _____ in the year of _____, I, _____, am declaring war on myself to get my act together. No more excuses. No more stories. No more validating my thoughts, emotions, behavior, and habits. No more finding people and things to blame. No more being a victim and thinking life is unfair. No more weakness. Starting now, the nonsense stops. I am taking myself and my life seriously, carrying myself with respect, reaching my goals, and hitting my targets. I'm getting my ego under control and eliminating mental and emotional chatter, distractions, chaos, and everyone and everything not pushing me towards my goals or adding value to my life. I'm aggressively moving through my goals and targets, not looking back, and ignoring anyone and anything wasting my time and getting me off of my path."

ACCEPT WHERE YOU ARE RIGHT NOW

You can't move forward and get your act together if you can't accept where you're currently at physically, mentally, and emotionally. You can't move forward if you fight it and try convincing yourself and others it's just pure coincidence that you don't have your act together. You can't move forward if you keep blaming your results and life on other people and things.

You can only move forward if you, as Jocko Willink and Leif Babin say, "take extreme ownership for everything about yourself, your results, and your life." Accept it on an extreme level – the level most people are afraid to go to when they have to admit their guilt in having a hand in the current state of their life.

Your results are not a coincidence. Your life is not a coincidence. Not having your act together is not a coincidence. It's the result of years and years of choosing to make the same decisions over and over. It's the result of years and years of choosing to have the same thoughts, emotions, behaviors, and habits. It's the result of being too comfortable to change. It's the result of being too much of a wuss to experience a little pain and discomfort so you can learn, grow, and become better.

Accept that YOU have decided every single day for the past few years to be who you are. Accept this is your current reality.

Don't feel too bad about it. Don't feel stupid about it. Don't feel like you're an idiot. Don't feel like others are better than you. Emotionally detach from it, see it for what it is, decide to move forward, and put the immaturity behind you.

Accept you aren't perfect, you have some work to do, corrections to make, and things to learn. Tell yourself, "I put myself in this situation and I'm going to get myself out of it."

BE GRATEFUL FOR EVERYTHING

Our capacity for finding things to complain about is astounding. We are more comfortable than we've ever been, and yet, unhappier and complaining more than ever before.

When you're having a bad day, instead of thinking about what you're "lacking" and the bad experience you're having, be grateful for what you DO have and what you CAN experience. Be grateful you're alive to experience the bad day. Be grateful you get to come "home" to a roof over your head, your family and pets, and something to eat and drink. Be grateful you have a bed to sleep in. Be grateful you're free and not being held against your will. Be grateful you have all of your fingers and toes. Be grateful you have both arms, legs, eyes, and ears. Be grateful you can see, smell, hear, touch, taste, and breathe. Be grateful you're healthy. Be grateful you get another day and another chance.

There's always something to be grateful for. It can ALWAYS be worse. Another situation can always make your current situation look like a walk in the park. There's ALWAYS someone in a worse situation than you.

Louis C.K. jokes about people who aren't grateful, "Everything is amazing right now and nobody's happy. Like, in my lifetime, the changes in the world have been incredible. Flying is the worst because people come back from flights and they tell you a horror story. They're like: 'It was the worst day of my life. First of all, we didn't board for twenty minutes, and then we get on the plane and they made us sit there on the runway.' Oh really, what happened next? Did you fly through the air incredibly, like a bird? Did you partake in the miracle of human flight you non-contributing zero?! You're flying! It's amazing! Everybody on every plane should just constantly be going: 'Oh my God! Wow!' You're flying! You're sitting in a chair, in the sky!"

ADMIT YOUR PROBLEM AREAS

Admitting there's a problem is the first step in having your act together and most of us who are living sloppy and problematic lives don't want to admit anything's wrong or that maybe we're contributing to the problem. We don't want to admit we're wasting time and energy on things and people that don't matter. We don't want to admit we have problem areas in our lives that can be zeroed in on and corrected.

We're too proud. Our ego doesn't let us reveal the truth. It's too afraid of the embarrassment. It's too afraid of the exposure and vulnerability.

If anything affects your thoughts, emotions, behavior, reactions, performance, success, and habits in a negative manner, it's a potential problem area, it requires your attention, and you need to start being honest with yourself about it. It can't be overlooked. It can't wait until later. It requires immediate attention and immediate decisions – fix it or eliminate it and then move forward and forget about it. You don't have time for the same problems to keep popping up in your life, bugging you, and causing distractions and chaos.

Honestly and humbly pinpoint and identify your problem areas. Identify the enemies. Identify what's holding you back and negatively influencing your thoughts, emotions, and behavior, decide what to do about it, and then take action. Identify the distractions and eliminate them. Identify the reasons you're not on track and make the proper adjustments. Identify the sources of your frustration, sadness, anger, and resentment, disconnect from them, and put an end to the nonsense.

Be honest about the relationships that are taking value instead of giving it. Be honest about your time-wasting activities. Be honest about your limiting beliefs and mindsets and how they're holding you back. Be honest about everything you can, potentially, improve.

NO MORE STORIES, LYING, AND EXCUSES

You can't have your act together without moving on from the stories, lying, and excuses - the stories you keep using to justify where you're at and why you do what you do, the lies you repeat to yourself about who you are, and the excuses you use to justify why you're not accepting responsibility, getting it together, and becoming the person you want to be.

It has to go. All of it. You can't simultaneously have your act together and still, hang onto these things. It's either one or the other, but not both.

Since you already know where the stories, lying, and excuses have landed you, the only choice left is to move on from them and let them be part of your past.

You've told the exaggerated stories so many times that you enjoy the validation and pity you receive from them. You've told yourself the lies so many times you actually believe them. You've used the excuses so many times you believe they're actually holding you back and standing in your way.

It's all a bunch of trash - you know it and I know it.

The stories you needlessly repeat to yourself and others don't matter anymore. Quit giving them life. Quit attaching emotions and emotional energy to them. They're not affecting your decisions and abilities in this moment. The lies you keep telling yourself are, simply, a waste of your thoughts and emotions. The excuses you keep using to justify your current position are, simply, you dodging responsibility for your own bad decisions and results.

Anything you're using to pin the blame on, get rid of it. Anything you're using to hide behind, get rid of it.

SELF-RESPECT AND SELF-CONTROL

Having your act together means respecting yourself enough to keep your thoughts, emotions, behavior, habits, and life under control. It means having enough self-respect to stay focused on becoming better every second, every minute, and every hour of every day. It means controlling what you think, say, and do and making sure all of your actions align with and push you towards your goals and targets.

Respect your word to yourself. Respect your self-discipline. Respect your time and energy. Respect your targets and goals. Respect your schedule. Respect your rules. Respect your boundaries. Respect yourself. Respect your life. Respect the amount of time you have to get things done and make them happen.

Respect yourself enough to do what you say you're going to do. Don't tolerate being absent, late, and not keeping commitments. Don't tolerate dishonorable, disrespectful, and disgraceful behavior. Don't tolerate having a victim mindset. Don't tolerate losing because you didn't strategize, prepare, and make an effort. Don't tolerate excuses, stories, and blame for why a goal wasn't reached and a target wasn't hit. Don't tolerate anything that is unproductive, counterproductive, and a waste of time.

Self-control means you're responsible for yourself. You're controlling your thoughts, emotions, behaviors, and habits and not letting them steer you in the wrong direction or get too extreme. You're pulling back when you're doing too much and pushing when you're not doing enough. You're calculating in what you say, what you do, and the timing.

Respect yourself and the world will have more respect for you. Get better at controlling yourself and "bad luck" and unfortunate things will be less likely to happen to you.

REINFORCE BOUNDARIES, ETHICS, VALUES, AND PRINCIPLES

Self-respect and self-control mean having boundaries – you're "bound" and limited, for good reason, to certain thoughts, beliefs, behaviors, and habits and going beyond these borders is unacceptable. These boundaries come from experience and seeing that once you go too far in any direction, it only produces negative results. Your boundaries are comprised of ethics, values, principles, and other strong beliefs about how you should conduct yourself and how others should conduct themselves around you. Beliefs designed to lead you to straight to the outcomes you want.

Your ethics are how tightly you follow what's considered right and wrong by the majority of society. If you're very ethical, your ethical boundary stops you from doing things that are considered ethically wrong. If you're unethical and lacking that ethical boundary, you're ignoring what society considers ethically wrong. It has no influence in your decision-making process. Your values are standards, or boundaries, of behavior and personal judgment that you place value on, find important, and hold in high regard. Anything outside of these boundaries are unacceptable. Your principles are your foundational and fundamental beliefs, reasons, and judgments for thoughts, behaviors, and habits. They're boundaries of meaning. You don't sleep with another man's wife because of your principle boundary and belief that it's just not cool to do such a thing and you wouldn't want someone doing it to you.

What boundaries are you putting in place for yourself and others? What do you consider unacceptable? What is right and wrong? What thoughts, behaviors, and habits are highly valuable? What principles guide your thoughts, emotions, behavior, and habits? Identify and reinforce them.

CHOOSE MATURITY

Immaturity is an easy decision, an easy way out, requires no work, and usually more fun than doing what you should be doing. The problem with immaturity is it produces horrible results and keeps you in the same place you've always been. Maturity, on the other hand, is not as fun, more stressful, and requires honesty, responsibility, and tougher decisions – but leads to better results.

When making a decision, no matter how big or small, you're coming to a fork in the road and having to choose a path – the mature route or immature route, the high road or the low road, the hard thing or the easy thing, what very few do or what everyone does. You can't choose both.

The mature route is uphill and the immature route is downhill. Uphill is harder, requires more effort, and takes longer but it makes you tougher and stronger. In any battle, whoever takes the high ground has the advantage. Downhill is easier and faster but it doesn't challenge you, toughen you up, or make your body stronger. It's also easier to fall forward, roll all the way down, and wind up in a bad situation.

Choose maturity over ego. Prioritize need over want. Get up earlier instead of sleeping in. Go to bed on time instead of staying up late watching TV. Wash and put away dishes instead of letting them pile up. Clean up regularly instead of letting your room or house become a disaster. Pay your debt and bills instead of buying things you don't need. Take the extra 5 minutes to floss your teeth. Take the extra 30-45 minutes to exercise. Buy groceries and eat at home instead of at McDonald's. Avoid gossip and drama instead of being part of it. Take responsibility instead of blaming. Ask for help instead of assuming you know it all. Say "no" to dumb choices instead of indulging.

Choose maturity. It comes first and pushes you in the right direction.

KEEP YOUR WORD

Not keeping your word means you can't be trusted. You're not reliable. You're not dependable. Your value drops. You're no longer needed as much. It does a lot of damage and makes everyone see you in a negative light. It automatically categorizes you as someone who's full of shit.

It's the same when you don't keep your word to yourself and do what you say you're going to do. You need to be able to trust yourself. You need see yourself as incredibly valuable. You should be the most dependable and reliable person you know. If you tell yourself you will quit doing something, respect yourself enough to quit doing it. Don't find excuses and reasons you're failing to keep your word. Suck it up, go through the pain and discomfort, and stop doing it. If you say you'll be somewhere at a certain time, have your act together enough to be there and on time. Have a contingency plan, factor in unforeseen circumstances, add some buffer time, and be there. No excuses.

Keep your word to yourself. You should be extremely disappointed in yourself when you run your mouth and don't follow through. Your word to yourself should be more important than your word to anyone else. If you don't break your word with anyone else, then don't break it with yourself.

Keep your promises to yourself, stick to your plans, and follow through. Take action when you say you're going to take action. Stop doing what you say you're going to stop doing. Get up when you say you're going to get up. Finish what you say you're going to finish. Reach the goals you say you're going to reach. Hit the targets you say you're going to hit. Be the person you say you're going to be. Difficulty, discomfort, opinions, time constraints, etc. should not be distractions.

When you give yourself your word, nothing stands in the way of it.

BE EXTREMELY STRICT

Be extremely strict on yourself. Be hard on yourself. Don't leave anything to chance. Don't fill your life with guess work. Don't be clueless about what you'll face each day. Don't wing it. Don't give yourself wiggle room to mess up or get it wrong.

The stricter you are on yourself, the better. It assures you'll do what needs to be done. It means running an extremely tight ship and keeping everything squared away. Nothing slips through the cracks. Nothing is left to chance. You're paying attention to details most overlook and you're more in control of your thoughts, emotions, behavior, and habits. Being extremely strict is triple-checking everything for accuracy and making absolutely sure you're on the right track.

It's smart and important to implement personal processes and procedures for everything needing to get done. They ensure your time is used wisely and efficiently. Decide what things need to happen, create processes and procedures, triple-check them, rehearse them in your mind, and follow the steps laid out to guarantee it's executed properly. When you notice steps can be improved, implement the changes, move forward, and repeat the process.

If you need to be up at 4 AM, like I do, be extremely strict about it. Mentally rehearse detailed steps for how you'll do it. Be strict about going to bed at the same time every night. No leniency. When the alarm goes off, put your feet on the floor, walk to the bathroom, wash your face off, take a shower, etc., and start your day. Act without hesitation.

If you know the orders are correct and they'll get the desired outcome, then put your emotions away and strictly follow the orders. Don't worry about how long it takes, how hard it is, or how hard you're being on yourself. All that matters is the target, goal, and the outcome.

STOP BEING A BAD INFLUENCE AND A REBEL

The reason we struggle to get our act together is because we're a bad influence on ourselves. We're rebelling against the rules and what we know is right. We're too lenient, too easy, and not holding ourselves accountable. Our inner-child is influencing our decisions.

When you need to be strict on yourself and know exactly what needs to happen to reach each of your goals and hit your targets, the childish part of our mind doesn't like the boundaries and wants to bend and break the rules, rebel, and keep you from moving.

Your inner-child says things like:

- "Go ahead and sleep in. You need it. You're not a robot."

- "You're hungry. Fast food today won't matter. Enjoy yourself."

- "You're tired, skip the gym today. You deserve it."

- "One cigarette won't hurt. You're stressed. Take a load off."

- "Spend that money on whatever you want. Your bills can wait."

You have to take the stairs to be successful. Stop looking for shortcuts and ways to be lazy. Stop being a bad influence. Stop rebelling. Stop bending and breaking the rules. Stop being a bad example. You can't be a bad influence on yourself and a good influence on others.

Stop telling yourself the rules don't matter. Stop trying to go around them. Stop influencing, persuading, and convincing yourself to get off track. Stop listening to your inner-child that wants you to do things you shouldn't. Stop listening when it wants to set you back. Stop listening when it wants to indulge in addictions. Stop listening when it says you're too strict and too hard on yourself. It doesn't know what it's talking about. When it starts talking, make it be quiet.

DON'T THINK YOU'RE BEING TOO STRICT

Even though it's absolutely necessary and the most rewarding, few of us have our act together because, overall, it's not very fun.

A lot of the time, it's boring, uncomfortable, mentally and physically tough, and it seems everyone is having an easier time. It seems you're having the least fun. It seems the excessive and extreme rules and boundaries are taking away your freedom. But this is just the childish part of your mind trying to convince you to give up and quit because it doesn't like constraints, rules, and boundaries. It doesn't want to grow up with you. It wants to be free so it can screw up your life again, lead you back down the wrong path, and undo the hard work you've put into getting your act together.

Instead of being imprisoned by all of the rules and boundaries – you're becoming free. You're no longer being imprisoned by your immaturity, bad decisions, and bad habits. You're breaking the shackles and chains you put on yourself. You're opening the door and walking out of the prison you've chosen to remain in all of your life.

As long as you continue accepting laziness, weakness, softness, and immaturity as part of who you are, the childish part of your mind will keep you imprisoned in a life of mediocrity and failure.

You're not being too hard on yourself. You're not overdoing it. You're not missing out on anything. You're not lacking or losing anything. Don't listen to anyone who tells you otherwise.

The truth is, 99% of the people who say you're "too hard" and strict on yourself don't have their act together. They don't know what it takes. Deep down, they wish they had the strength, endurance, will, and fortitude to do what it takes to get their act together. They quit a long time ago and they're trying to get you to quit too.

MAKE A REAL EFFORT

How much further along would you be right now if, over the last 5 years, you placed every ounce of your focus on what actually matters, you gave it 100% every single day, and did everything you could to push yourself closer to your goals and the life you want? Where will you be 5 years from now if you knock off the nonsense, quit wasting time, and start today?

Will you still be waking up and going to that job you hate? Will you still be broke after paying your bills? Will you still be driving the same car? Will you still be living in the same place barely big enough for you and your family? Will you be more satisfied with your life?

We may be fooling everyone by "posting", saying, and creating the illusion of doing the best we can, but we know when we're actually making a real effort and when we're not. We know if we're giving it 100%.

Starting right now, make a 100% effort from the moment you wake up until the time you go to sleep. Keep yourself focused. Push as hard as you can. Cut yourself no slack. Show no mercy. Don't feel sorry for yourself. If you think you're overdoing it, tell yourself to be quiet and quit acting like a whiny baby. Overdoing it is 100 times better than underdoing it or not doing it at all.

Get up and go. Develop a sense of urgency. Start moving like you're late. Start moving like the bus is leaving without you.

The part of your mind that wants to talk too much, be weak and sensitive, complain, and make excuses, tell it to be quiet. There's no room for weakness. There's no room for sensitivity. There are no outs.

It's not too late. Avoid the regret of knowing you didn't do enough.

TREAT YOURSELF LIKE ROYALTY

If you were the king or queen and had your act totally together, how would you expect to be treated? What standards would you hold yourself and everyone else to? What behavior would you expect? What would you consider acceptable and unacceptable? Would you accept overinflated egos? Would you accept bad habits? Would you accept complaining? Would you accept excuses? Would you accept acting like a victim instead of taking personal responsibility? Would you accept bad influences? Would you accept rebelling? Probably not.

You'd respect your position and expect everyone else to as well. You'd hold everyone accountable, expect appropriate conduct, and wouldn't accept substandard behavior and results.

If that's the case, why are you accepting substandard from yourself? Why are you accepting substandard thinking, emotions, behavior, and habits? Why are you accepting substandard results? Why are you accepting a substandard life? Why aren't you living up to your expectations?

You're the leader and the servant. You make and follow the rules. You give and take the punishment. You set and meet the expectations. Be in charge and obedient. Follow your orders. Respect yourself. Behave the way you expect others to.

Give yourself something to respect. Give yourself something to follow. Give others a reason to treat you the way you want to be treated.

If you want to live like a king or queen, you have to think and behave like it. You have to accept the full responsibility of it.

You are royalty. You are in charge. You are at the top. Put up with whatever is necessary to keep crown and stay sitting on your throne.

PART 6: HAVING YOUR ACT TOGETHER STARTS IN YOUR MIND

YOU MUST CHANGE YOUR MINDSET

Getting your act together is 90% mental. It starts in your mind and everything follows.

Change doesn't occur by:

- Getting more money and buying a nicer car, nicer clothes, a nicer home, nicer furniture, etc.

- Reposting inspirational quotes and photos on social media

- Talking and posting about how you're planning to get your act together

- Listening to inspirational speeches and videos but never taking action

- Getting tattoos of inspirational quotes

Mindset change begins when you tune out the distractions, stare at yourself in the mirror, and realize and accept you're holding yourself back.

It's telling yourself enough is enough, you're not taking any more of your crap, you've caused enough problems, and it's time to knock it off. It's realizing and accepting it's time to make something of yourself, get serious about life, and the fun and games don't come first. It's traveling to the very deep and unconscious parts of your mind and hunting down, dragging out, and killing every ounce of immaturity, bullshit, and nonsense that's keeping you from having your act together.

Mindset change begins when decide to change your thinking, emotions, reactions, and the way you handle and solve problems.

It starts when you look around at everyone else's constant need for attention, poor results, and unhappiness and you decide you're not going to remain in that mediocre state and mindset.

YOUR MIND HAS NO LIMITATIONS

Tim Grover says, "There are so many individuals out there who are so talented in different things and never accomplish anything. The world is filled with talented people and they never accomplish anything. The body has limitations, the mind does not. We focus so much on what goes on from the neck down that we forget it all starts in your mind." Napoleon Hill said, "There are no limitations to the mind except those that we acknowledge."

The only person holding you back is you. When you want to point fingers and blame someone for not getting to where you want to be, do it in front of the mirror. If anyone or anything is actually is getting in your way and stopping you, it's because you're allowing it to happen.

Regardless of whether it seems possible in the present moment, whatever you want and whoever it is you want to be, you have to absolutely believe it's going to happen. You have to be 100% sure about it. You have to see it as clear as day because the clearer you are about it, the more it will light up your path towards it. When Conor McGregor beat Eddie Alvarez and made UFC history by holding two title belts at the same time, he said, "I saw this so clearly. I saw this so clearly. I followed it until it was reality. I'm very confident in my abilities. I back it up with work ethic. I back it up with hours and hours of time and dedication. I never take an hour off this game. I'm very satisfied, very grateful, very happy, but not surprised. I knew it was going to happen."

Someone thinking your "big plans" are crazy and unrealistic doesn't make it true. That's just their opinion. They're not able to see the path that you can see. They can't see it in their mind the way you do. They can't see the hundreds, and even thousands, of tiny little details and steps leading you to what you want. Being able to see it clearly is all that matters.

THE HERD MENTALITY

My oldest brother is very smart, successful, and financially independent and took the time to explain the way he thinks, the way he sees things, and how it's allowed him to have his act together and create a lot of success in his life.

He calls it the "Herd Mentality".

He says, "When ranchers lead herds of cattle to the slaughterhouse, the herd follows a bell steer – the lead cow wearing a loud bell. The stray calf is problematic because he doesn't care about the sound of the bell or who's leading the herd. He breaks away from the herd to follow his own path and this is a problem for the rancher who needs the herd to stick together and a problem for the stray calf who's made into BBQ if caught.

I relate more with the stray calf than the rest of the herd because, when I was young, certain things just didn't make sense to me and I decided to break away from the herd and the herd mentality. When I moved away, it allowed me to gain a higher-ground perspective and see the bell steer leading the 'herd' to a slaughterhouse – as the ranchers planned. Herds are so ignorant, they only focus on the sound of the bell. You can't lead the herd to greener grass when they are part of a huge society, the herd, even when it leads to bad ending because they won't get out of their comfort zone. You'll mostly find that they don't care about the slaughterhouse as long as they're comfortable. They believe they're in the right place and doing the right things because it's what all of the other cattle are doing. This is the 'herd mentality'.

So, all you can do is open your eyes to every path and don't be driven by men for their own gain. Get to safer ground, gain a higher-ground perspective, and just watch the rest of the herd follow the sound of the bell. Once they realize the final destination, it's too late."

We're the "herd". We're the 99% with 1% of the money. We're following the bell steer – celebrities, TV, magazines, internet stars, etc. and we're following the sound of the bell – short-term gratification, phones, games, social media, and the shiny objects in front of us. We're failing to look up and see where we're headed. We follow the sound of the bell and assume we're on the right track because everyone else is following it too.

We're failing to see the slaughterhouse – unreached goals, mediocrity, massive debt, unhappiness, stress, and preventable problems.

The "rancher" is everyone - friends, family, co-workers, etc., trying to keep us is in the "herd" by telling us to be "safe" by not being different. Telling us to stay in the same "safe" box everyone else is in by taking out loans and going to a college we can't afford, getting a general degree we won't use, working at a "safe" job we hate and that barely pays the bills, and settling for a mediocre and unhappy life we can barely afford.

This is how we, the "herd", are living.

Without thought, we're copying everything we see each other doing and getting the same lousy results over and over.

The "herd" is one missed paycheck away from losing everything. They're barely surviving. They're depending on other people to put food on their table and clothes on their back. They're betting their family's survival on another person, the owner of the company they work for, keeping their act together.

They have the same opportunity as stray calves but they're CHOOSING to follow the sound of the bell because it's easier. They're choosing to stay where they're at. They're choosing comfort.

They're refusing change because their friends, family, co-workers, and buddies are doing the same thing.

They're choosing the "herd life". The sound of the bell steer's bell is more important to them than someone telling them they're headed in the wrong direction.

Stop doing what everyone else is doing. They're following the sound of the bell. They're being led to the slaughterhouse. Get away from the "herd".

Get to higher ground and see for yourself what's really happening and where they're headed. You'll notice they're just copying each other.

The Herd Mentality you want to avoid:

- Play it safe, stay in your comfort zone, and don't take risks

- Only do what everyone else is doing so you're "relevant"

- Only work for other people because it's "safer"

- Remain in large groups where you're accepted

- Work on the external instead of the internal

- Keep up with the latest trends, crazes, technology, clothes, and experiences to look relevant, "cool", and successful

- Forget privacy. Create a social media life, take constant selfies, and share your thoughts, experiences, and feelings with everyone online

- Go to college and start your career with tons of debt. Memorizing, mostly useless, information in an overpriced institution instead of learning it free on the internet makes you better than others and is the real and only "education". Take out student loans, get a fancy-titled "degree" you can't afford and won't use, make a "name" for yourself and your family, and get a job living paycheck to paycheck so it'll take you 10 – 25 years to pay off your student debt.

PRIORITIZE HABITS AND ACTIVITIES

How much you have your act together depends on your daily habits and activities and the ones you focus on the most have the biggest impact on reaching goals and becoming better.

Think about and write down everything you do from the time you wake up until you go to sleep. Next to each one, assign it a number of 1 through 10. 1 being the lowest payoff, negative, non-important, a waste of time, you don't learn, grow, or change and 10 being a wise investment of time, big payoff, highly impactful, important to reaching goals and getting your act together, and it makes you better. Example: Watching TV and playing video games =1. Getting enough sleep. = 9.

Draw a triangle on a sheet of paper, divide it into 3 parts by drawing 2 horizontal lines through it, take the top 5 to 7 habits and activities you assigned the highest number to and put them in the very top. Then, take the next 5 to 7 habits and activities with the highest numbers and put them in the middle. Everything left goes at the bottom.

The stuff in the bottom of the triangle is what 99% of us are focused on and why we don't have our act together. This stuff isn't important and wastes our time. The middle section contains secondary habits and activities. These things are ok to do but need to be put on the back burner and done later. The very top of the triangle is where your attention needs to be. Focusing on these habits and activities more than anything else changes your life rapidly and helps you get your act together faster than you can imagine.

This exercise helps you find what's truly important and helpful to you. It helps you become crystal clear, focused, efficient, and productive. Place your focus on everything in the top of the triangle and everything in the middle and very bottom will either disappear or take care of itself.

ACTIVITY PRIORITY PYRAMID

TAKING ACTION. BETTERING YOURSELF. RESONSIBILITY. GIVING. PRODUCING. READING. LEARNING. SELF-EDUCATION. TEACHING/ COACHING/ ADVISING. EXERCISING. GETTING SLEEP. WAKING UP EARLY

MOST HELPFUL 8 - 10

BUILDING SOCIAL LIFE. ATTENDING SOCIAL EVENTS. SHOPPING. VACATIONS. SPENDING TIME W/ FRIENDS. GOING OUT. BUYING THINGS.

SOMETIMES USEFUL 5 - 7

SLEEPING IN. SOCIAL MEDIA. SEEKING ATTENTION. WATCHING TV. VIDEO GAMES. LISTENING TO MUSIC ALL DAY. TAKING SELFIES. DRUGS. ADDICTIONS. GAMBLING. GOSSIP. DRAMA. NEGATIVITY.

WASTE OF TIME 0 - 4

99% OF US

PRIORITIZE THOUGHTS AND EMOTIONS

How petty are your thoughts and emotions? Are they helping you or hurting you? Are they moving you closer to having your act together or farther away?

Figure it out. Do the same exercise you did for your priorities and habits. Draw a triangle and prioritize which thoughts and emotions are worth your time and helping you get closer to who you want to be.

MENTAL PRIORITY PYRAMID

RESPONSIVE. HAPPY. FOCUSED. PATIENT. HUMBLE. DRIVEN. CLEAR. PRODUCTIVE. CALM. COOL. COLLECT. RELAXED. EASY GOING. FORGIVING. SLOW TO ANGER. REASONABLE. UNWORRIED. KIND.

MOST HELPFUL 8 - 10

REFLECTION. RUSHED. DISSAPOINTED. SURPRISED. SHAME. FEAR. ALERT. UNCERTAIN. HESITATION. CAUTION. SUSPICION. SKEPTICISM. PRIDE. VALIDATION. COMPETITIVE.

OUR AUTOMATIC MINDSET

SOMETIMES USEFUL 5 - 7

REACTIVE. EGOTISTICAL. INSECURE. SAD. BOASTFUL. CONTROLLING. NEEDY. DRAMATIC. CHAOTIC. ANXIOUS. WORRIED. ANGRY. BITTER. JEALOUS. COMPLAINING. BLAMING. HOLDING A GRUDGE.

WASTE OF TIME 0 - 4

STOP LOOKING AROUND AT OTHERS

You'll be much happier and satisfied with your situation and life when you stop focusing on everyone around you and start focusing more on yourself.

Pay attention to and focus on yourself – you need all the focus you can get. The better you get to know yourself, the clearer your road map to success and getting your act together is.

Stop focusing on what others are/aren't doing. Stop focusing on how much others have their act together. Stop comparing yourself to others. Stop asking about others because you feel you're in competition with them. Stop looking for clues for how you should be walking, talking, dressing, thinking, feeling, and behaving.

Stay off social media news feeds. They do a lot of psychological damage and give you a false impression of yourself and others. Stop comparing your life to those of your "friends" on social media. Stop thinking about how much fun they're having while you're not having any. Stop thinking about how many social media "friends" they have compared to you. Stop looking at their "likes" and reading the "comments" they post or get. Stop wondering how good/bad your life is compared to everyone else's. It's all a complete waste of time because what you're seeing on social media isn't real. It's not the truth. It's a manipulated representation of their activities, thoughts, emotions, behavior, habits, and life.

In public, don't be the person constantly being nosy and breaking their neck to look at everyone around them. It communicates you don't have an interesting life and you're insecure and bored. It also reinforces the bad habit of not focusing on yourself and the goals in front of you.

You're getting YOUR act together, not everyone else's. What everyone else is doing doesn't affect what you need to be thinking and doing.

GIVE YOURSELF NO ROOM TO FEEL GUILT

When you're not doing what you're supposed to be doing, you're burdened with the constant feeling of guilt. When you go to sleep and wake up, it's there. You feel guilty for wasting time. You feel guilty knowing you could be accomplishing more. You feel like a screw-up and a failure. You feel like a child who needs to grow up already. It's an ugly feeling and no matter what you do to get it to go away, if you're not on the right track, it'll keep coming back.

When you're squared away, on top of everything, have your act together, reaching goals, and hitting targets, the guilt vanishes and you feel the opposite of guilt - pride. You feel a rush of satisfaction, accomplishment, and victory over your day. Isn't this how you want to feel every single day? Then do it. Get rid of the guilt.

Remember, it's 100% certain that if you're not on top of your game every single day, the guilt will return and make you feel stupid. Get familiar with that feeling, if you aren't already, and remind yourself every single day you won't allow yourself to feel that way anymore. That you're not going to be flooded with guilt because you're choosing to take the easy route over the hard route. Because you're choosing to act like a child instead of an adult. Because you're choosing to be lenient instead of strict. Because you're choosing to let your guard down.

You don't have the time or capacity to be feeling guilty because you're making second-class decisions. It's completely avoidable and you're responsible for dodging that bullet every single day.

When you're feeling guilty, you owe yourself an explanation for its presence. You owe yourself an explanation for why you aren't doing what you're supposed to be doing. Become focused, driven, and active and you won't feel guilty from a lack of accomplishment.

GET COMFORTABLE BEING UNCOMFORTABLE

Getting your act together, getting better, and growing is extremely uncomfortable because you're doing things differently from the way you've always done them.

You're shocking and waking your mind and body up. You're seeing things you haven't seen. You're feeling things you haven't felt. You're learning things you don't know. You're experiencing things you've never experienced. Things your mind and body aren't used to. Things the childish part of your mind doesn't like. Things pushing your physical and mental limits. Things forcing you out of your comfort zone. Things forcing you to stretch, adapt, and grow. Things filling your mind with quality and value and forcing the trash out.

You're experiencing the pain and discomfort of a much-needed mental puberty. Get used to it. You're becoming the adult you're supposed to be. Your mind is growing up. You can't avoid the uncomfortable growing pains. They're necessary. That's how you know it's working. You can't appreciate the process unless you develop a relationship with the pain, weirdness, and discomfort.

Once it's learned and experienced, you've adapted to it. It's part of who you are. Your comfort zone absorbs it and expands. It's no longer uncomfortable. It no longer hurts. It's easier. It's second nature. It's unconscious. But you first have to endure the pain. First, you first have to be uncomfortable. First, you have to grit your teeth and deal with it.

When you're feeling extremely comfortable, something is wrong. It means you're not pushing hard enough. You're not learning. You're not experiencing. You're not stretching. You're not growing. If you don't get uncomfortable, you'll become weaker and move backwards.

THE COMFORT ZONE

MOVING FORWARD IN YOUR LIFE INCLUDES CONSTANT MOVEMENT OUTWARD FROM THE CENTER OF YOUR COMFORT ZONE. IF YOU DON'T MOVE OUTWARD, YOU'LL NEVER GROW AND BECOME BETTER.

97% LIVE HERE. THIS IS PLAYING IT SAFE. MEDIOCRITY. AN UNHAPPY AND BORING LIFE.

WHEN YOU FIGHT AND DEFEAT THE ENEMY WITHIN, YOUR COMFORT ZONE EXPANDS. IT'S GOING TO BE UNCOMFORTABLE. GET USED IT. IT'S A GOOD THING.

BECOME FRIENDS WITH SELF-DISCIPLINE

Self-discipline isn't punishment. It's training. It's taking care of yourself. It's parenting yourself. It's mentoring yourself. It's being your own big brother or big sister. It's keeping yourself on the right track. It's showing yourself love and respect. It's improving the quality of your life through boundaries.

Self-discipline is necessary for everything in your life and it's the fundamental mindset, practice, habit, and quality that makes you better. It's an internal force that comes from within. It starts with you. It starts in your mind. It starts with the decision to be disciplined instead of lazy and sloppy. It starts when you're tired of the results you're getting from not being disciplined. It starts when you're ready to knock off the nonsense and move forward.

If discipline is coming from somewhere else like a parent, teacher, counselor, drill sergeant, etc., it's less likely to mean anything to you because it's not coming from within. It's coming from the outside. External discipline doesn't stick. It's not as powerful. It doesn't survive. Anyone helping you become disciplined should, actively, be working their way out of your life and building up your self-discipline. It should reach a point where you no longer need them anymore.

When you decide to get your act together, make an impact, and do what you're meant to be doing, you will develop a healthy, friendly, and respectful relationship with your self-discipline. You will appreciate what it does for you and your life. You will appreciate what it does for your mind. You will appreciate what it does for your friendships and relationships. You will appreciate what it does for your social status. As Jocko Willink says, "Self-discipline will set you free."

Instead of relying on motivation, rely on discipline to get you there.

DO EVERYTHING THE RIGHT WAY

Anything worth doing is worth doing the right way – even when others aren't looking and will never see it. Anything worth your time is worth the extra attention, focus, and effort in making sure it's the best.

Steve Jobs of Apple said his dad taught him to do everything right – even what will never be seen. Most furniture builders use junk materials for the parts you won't see, but his dad made those parts just as beautiful as the rest. He believed in 100% quality and doing EVERYTHING right.

When you develop the mindset of doing everything the right way and to the best of your abilities, no matter how small, it changes your life. You no longer accept second-rate efforts and results from yourself and others. It permeates every area of your life and you become a more solid, squared away, and structured person.

What you do and the way you do it communicates everything happening in your mind and how much you have it together. It communicates your values, lifestyle, and how much effort you put into yourself and goals.

If you do little things the right way, you automatically do big things the right way. If you're putting a new trash bag in your trash can, it can still be done the right way. If you're making your bed, even though you're going to mess it up when you get back in it, it can still be done the right way. If you put your shoes away, you can still take 5 seconds to make sure they're neat, orderly, straight, and the right way.

I keep between 30 and 60 bottles of water in my kitchen cabinet and when I put them in there, the labels face the same direction, they're tightly together, and in perfect order. Even though they're hidden and going to be consumed and thrown in the garbage, it doesn't mean they can't be stored as neatly as possible. It's the principle that counts. Again, nothing is too insignificant to be done to the best of your abilities.

ANYTHING WORTH DOING IS WORTH OVERDOING

In the movie Lone Survivor about Navy SEAL survivor Marcus Luttrell and Operation Red Wings, fellow Navy SEAL Shane Patton says, "Anything worth doing is worth overdoing. Moderation is for cowards." He's right. If you want to get your act together, you have to overdo it. You have to become obsessed.

UFC Champion Conor McGregor says, "There's no talent here, this is hard work. This is an obsession. Talent does not exist. We are all equals as human beings. You could be anyone if you put in the time. You will reach the top, and that's that. I am not talented, I am obsessed." He's saying if you want to reach your goals, become the best, and get it together in any area of your life, you have to become obsessed. You have to overdo it. You have to put in more time and effort than everyone else around you. If it's worth doing it, overdo it. Do it better than anyone else. Become obsessed with it. Learn how to do it right. Make it second nature.

If getting up early is worth your time, do it on your days off too. Do it on the weekends. Do it on the holidays. Do it when everyone else is cutting themselves slack and giving themselves a break. Become obsessed with getting up early so it becomes second nature. So it becomes default behavior. So it becomes a natural reaction.

U.S. Navy SEALs train until what they're learning becomes a natural and complete reaction. In complicated situations, consciously going through the training steps will get them killed. It has to be second nature.

When you're stressed, under pressure, and don't have time to think, you fall to the level of your training. If you overdo everything involved in getting your act together, you'll naturally and automatically do what you've learned without giving it thought.

TRAIN YOUR MIND 24 HOURS A DAY

Your training is never over. Your work is never done. You never reach a point where there's nothing left to learn. You never reach the point where you have it together more than everyone in the whole world.

Everything you think, feel, say, and do throughout your day, see it as learning and training opportunities. Whatever you experience, you learn from. It trains you. Woke up on time today? Good. See it as training for tomorrow. Experienced some micro emotions this morning because you had to make your bed and do it right? Good. Learn from it, see it as training for tomorrow, and it'll be easier. Had a bad day at work and you allowed your emotions to get the best of you? Good. Learn from it and see it as training for the next time you have a bad day. Feeling stupid because you got overly excited and said too much on a date or in a business meeting? Good. Learn from it and see it as training for the next time you're in that situation.

You're either learning from everything happening to you, within you, and around you, or you're wasting it. You're throwing away valuable opportunities to gain knowledge. Constantly be training to become better at something. Constantly train your mind by reading books, watching videos, listening to podcasts, and learning from people who are at and beyond your target self. Take that knowledge and cram it into your mind on a daily basis. Constantly train your body and keep it strong and healthy by exercising and pushing yourself to and past your physical limits. Prevent muscle atrophy. Use them or lose them.

A weak body is a weak mind. A weak mind is a weak person. A weak person gets weak results. Train your body with healthier foods, healthier amounts, and at healthier times. Your body will crave the junk food, but it will get used not having it. It will become trained. It will adapt.

AIM TO INCH CLOSER TO PERFECTION

Not being perfect shouldn't stop you from aiming for it. It shouldn't stop you from inching closer and closer to it.

When you overdo anything that's worth doing and you do it right, your goal should be to reach perfection in that area. To, eventually, do it perfectly. Even though you may never reach the perfection you're looking for, it shouldn't stop you from aiming for it. If you aim for perfection right from the beginning, you'll try harder and get better at it much faster than if you were cutting yourself slack and giving yourself permission to suck at it. Never be ok with being horrible if you know you can improve.

When you do something new, you make large strides in improvement in a short period of time but, eventually, you plateau. A plateau is where most get bored and lazy and quit. This is where you need push hard. This is where you need to work. This is where you inch closer to perfection day by day. This is where the hardly noticeable improvements take place. You get better a little bit a time. When you add up the tiny improvements over a long period of time, the sum is you being closer to perfection than those who aren't pushing and aiming for it.

Don't feel guilty for aiming for perfection. Don't see it as a bad thing. It doesn't make you stuck up. It doesn't make you snobby. Those who have a problem with it are those who settle for mediocrity, live mediocre lives, and never aim for anything big. The closer you get to perfection, the better your life becomes and the more worthless it makes them feel.

Aim to spend more hours focusing, learning, working, and growing than everyone else. Aim to have your act together more than everyone else. Aim to be more focused than everyone else. Aim to be sharper than everyone else. Aim to work harder than everyone else. Aim to get more results than everyone else. Push yourself harder than everyone else.

BECOME COMPETITIVE

Never compete just to see others lose and to boost your ego. That doesn't provide any real benefits to your life and each time you do it, you're expanding your ego and making it harder to control. It's not what winners do. You don't have to prove to others how much better you are than them. This is not the type of "competitive" you should be.

The right type of "competitive" is out doing yourself. Beating yourself. Becoming better. Competing with who you were yesterday, last week, and last year. Making sure that tomorrow's you is better than today's.

At the same time, if you're in business or trying to earn your place in any area of life, you don't want to just lay down and let your competitors trample you. You should be competitive in the sense that you want stay at the front of the pack and not let others make you look bad and put you out of business. This type of competitiveness isn't bad. You're not doing it to boost your ego. It's to keep you alive. It's to survive. It's to maintain and continually improve your standard of living and your place in the world. You don't want to see your competitors lose and go out of business and you don't want to take food out of their mouths, but if you don't defend yourself in a competitive manner, they'll do it to you.

You have to be competitive to get better and keep what you've earned and work hard for. You have to be competitive to see where you stand amongst others, what your weak points are, and where you can improve.

If you aren't disappointed in yourself when you sleep in and wake up late, you're not competitive enough. If you did better last month than you're doing this month, you're not competitive enough. If you're in last place and you're ok with it, you're not competitive enough.

Your competitive spirit will push you to greatness. It will push you to where you want and deserve to be.

BECOME THE REAL DEAL

Grant Cardone says, "Today I'm living the dream other people are just having. You're thumbing through the magazines and looking at TV of how all the big shots are living. That's a waste of freaking time. You're going to the Fontainebleau to tear it up and to see the celebs that walk in, waste of time. You're going to the ball game, I had a guy invite me to see the Dolphin's game this weekend, I said 'Dude I ain't got time for the Dolphin's game, dog. I need to be on the field, not in the stands, you understand? Hey, let them go to the stands, baby. My life is not in the stands. My life is not as a spectator. My life is being a player on the field."

Eric Thomas says, "So that's why you go to the basketball game, that's why you spend hours watching your favorite athlete like Michael, and you watch them... you watch them... there's something about this attracted to that greatness because there is something in you that's great. That's why you put those headphones on and you just shut the whole world out and you listen to your favorite artist – you listen to them sing or you listen to them rap and deep down inside you hurt when you listen because it should be you! You are attracted to greatness because greatness is all in you. But it's easier to watch greatness, it's easier to go see greatness than it is to put in the time, to put in the energy, to discipline yourself, to sacrifice – it's easier! And so that's why you're average, and so you're frustrated because you're not living like you should live. No – you don't have what you should have, you're not being who you should be."

Stop spending time watching and listening to people do things and thinking they're better than you. Aim to become that person. Aim to become the person other people watch and listen to. Quit talking about people who are doing it. Quit worshipping the people who are doing and wishing it was you. Become that person. Become the real deal.

BECOME THE RAZOR'S EDGE

The tip of the spear used to be the highest level you can reach... but not anymore.

It's not good enough anymore just to be the tip of the spear. You may not be the tip of the spear yet, but you will make it there if you keep focusing, pushing, grinding, working, improving, growing, and becoming stronger and sharper. If you keep improving the person you are. If you keep enduring the pain and hardship no one else is willing to endure. If you keep putting in the time and effort no one else is willing to put in.

Even though the tip of the spear is seen as the sharpest and most dangerous part of the spear, it can still be sharpened to a razor's edge.

That's where you want to be.

Don't aim to only become the tip of the spear, aim to become the razor's edge. It's the sharpest and the first to handle business when confronted with a problem.

Aim to be the best person you can be. Aim to be the most top-notch person you can be. Aim to be the sharpest, fastest, and toughest – both mentally and physically. Aim to be the hardest working, the one who takes the most action in the shortest period of time, the wisest, the most knowledgeable, and the most successful. Aim to be the person who has their act, thoughts, emotions, behavior, and habits together the most.

When you're the razor's edge, nothing stands in your way. Nothing stops you. Nothing is tough enough to hold you back. You'll cut through anything standing in your way and trying to stop you, hurt you, and kill your dreams and ambitions.

There is no challenge or problem you can't handle and destroy when you throw yourself and your mind at it.

CHISELED MIND AND HABITS

A chiseled mindset is about getting rid of everything unnecessary. It's being free of all nonsense. It's eliminating the mental fat – everything in your mind not helping you become a high-caliber individual.

Just like becoming physically chiseled requires you burning as much fat as possible, building muscle, and eating healthy, getting and maintaining a chiseled mindset requires getting rid of all mental fat - unnecessary thoughts, emotions, behaviors, and habits, building mental muscle – taking action and getting experience, and feeding your mind healthy food – reading, learning, educating, improving yourself, and only surrounding yourself with knowledge, wisdom, experience, and positivity.

Before a statue is carved into a masterpiece, it's nothing special. It's a huge slab of ugly rock, wood, or whatever it's made out of. Before it becomes a beautiful work of art, it has to be carved and downsized. The useless parts have to be removed and thrown away. Instead of building it from nothing, adding material to it, and molding it the way a clay statue, for example, would be made, the artist eliminates the "fat". He continuously and purposely carves out and removes what he doesn't need layer by layer until the statue bears a resemblance to the final piece of work. The more he "trims the fat" and removes what isn't needed, the more beautiful and striking the statue becomes. Here's the thing, the only way he can take it from being an ugly rock to a beautiful piece of art is by removing and throwing out what isn't needed. The more he keeps, the more it's an ugly, useless rock instead of a valuable piece of art.

In order to be the person you want to be, you have to carve away at yourself and eliminate the thoughts, emotions, behavior, and habits keeping you from becoming a beautiful masterpiece. You can't be a chiseled masterpiece and still keep everything that's unnecessary.

GET YOUR EMOTIONS OUT OF THE PICTURE

When you're getting your act together, remain detached from the process. Get your emotions out of it and to stop "feeling" certain ways about what you're doing. Put your feelings away and just do what needs to be done to get to where you're going. Anyone who acts on emotion can't be trusted and that means you can't trust yourself to do what needs to be done when you're constantly flooded with emotion.

Getting up early, staying focused, working hard, disciplining and controlling yourself, reaching goals, etc. – separate emotions from it. Detach from it. Emotions are not required. They're a distraction and have no place in the process. Consciously remain "emotionally zeroed out".

Society says you need emotions to make things happen and you have to be "passionate, excited, and stoked" about what you're doing. While that sounds lovely, intense emotions use your energy up and cause you to burn out faster. These people start strong, quickly run out of energy and motivation, and give up. For long-term success, save your energy and turn off your emotion. Use your energy to take action.

High emotion isn't the secret behind success and reaching goals. It's putting your emotions away, thinking clearly, and forcing yourself to do what needs to be done regardless of how you feel about it.

Stop attaching emotions. Eliminate "loser" thoughts - "This isn't healthy", "I should sleep more", "I'm going to burn out", "This is hard", etc. Don't feel one way or the other about it. As hardcore as it sounds, have the emotionless attitude of, "I'm going to reach my goals or die trying."

Turn off the emotions. Stop waiting until you "feel" like it. Lose emotions about the past. It's gone. It's done. Don't feel one way or the other about the future. See it as, "I'm busy dealing with today and I'll deal with the future when it gets here. I won't waste my time worrying about it."

CONTROL YOUR ENVIRONMENT

Your ego may say you're 100% unique and original, but you're mostly an exact copy of your environment. You're the product of the people, places, and things you're around the most. Control your environment or it'll control you. If you hang around with those who have their act together and are winning in life, you'll be on the same path as them but if you hang around victim-minded people who don't try to become better, you won't become better either.

Again, your mind is a sponge and it soaks up and programs your mind with all incoming information – even the things you aren't paying attention to. Everything about you reflects your environment. Very little about you is unique. It's all been learned and "programmed".

Program your mind with what will make you better. Simplify your "environmental choices". Ask yourself, "Is this a wise investment of my time? Is it helping my future or current situation? Is it making me smarter? Is it adding value to my life? Am I learning something useful? If no, separate yourself from it. Les Brown says, "It's necessary to get the losers out of your life if you want to live your dream. Those who don't want anything and aren't striving for something better. Birds of a feather flock together. If you run around with losers, you will end up a loser!"

Get away from everyone and everything wasting your time. Weed out your social circle. Those who want to be in your life will prove it and respect your choices. Delete the social media apps. Disconnect your TV.

Run everything through your "environmental filter" and if it doesn't check out or pass the test, separate yourself from it. You're not missing out. It's a waste of time. Most of what you're focused on right now isn't helping you. It needs to go. You might feel a little lonelier and a little more bored, but you'll get used to it, be happier, and more successful.

AVOID NEGATIVITY AT ALL COSTS

Negativity, of course, doesn't benefit you. Many are losing in life and can't get it together because they're negative and failure-minded. They feed off of negativity and allow negative people, places, media, music, and television to penetrate and influence their mind. The most successful people are also the most positive. They didn't decide to become positive after they became successful – they become successful because they were so positive and avoided negative people, places, media, music, and television. They didn't let anything affect their mindset. There's a definite difference between the two. There's a definite a correlation between the success rates of people who feed off of negativity and those who feed off of positivity.

Tom Brady, NFL quarterback of the New England Patriots, is one of the most positive people you'll ever see - even though he's one of the most-hated quarterbacks of all time. Watch any interview – he consciously avoids negativity and automatically chooses to be positive, no matter what. When asked in the post-Super Bowl 51 press conference about his stolen jersey, smiling, his response was, "Those are pretty special ones to keep, you know? But um, what can you do? I'll take the ring and um, that's good enough for me." When talking in interviews and press conferences about Roger Goodell, the NFL Commissioner who tried to make Brady's like miserable during "Deflate Gate", he has a lot of opportunities and reasons to bash Goodell and say negative things about him, but he doesn't. He takes the high road, chooses to be positive, and only says positive things about him.

Find out what's causing you to become negative and get away from it. Eliminate the negative thoughts and emotions. When you have the opportunity to become negative and to say negative things, pause and take a second to take the positive route instead of the negative one.

NO MORE EXCUSES

Retired Navy SEAL commander Jocko Willink said during his TED Talk about a mission that went wrong and he made some mistakes as a leader, "Unlike a team where no one takes ownership of the problems and therefore the problems never get solved, with us, everyone took ownership of their mistakes. Everyone took ownership of the problems. And when a team takes ownership of its problems, the problems get solved. And that is true on the battlefield. It is true in business and it is true in life. So, I say, take ownership, take extreme ownership. Don't make excuses, don't blame any other person or any other thing. Get control of your ego. Don't hide your delicate pride from the truth. Take ownership of everything in your world, the good and the bad. Take ownership of your mistakes, take ownership of your shortfalls, take ownership of your problems and then take ownership of the solutions that will get those problems solved. Take ownership of your mission. Take ownership of your job, of your team, of your future and take ownership of your life and lead. Lead, lead yourself and your team and the people in your life, lead them all to victory."

Excuses are for the weak and those in last place. Excuses are for those who are afraid of admitting their mistakes. Excuses are for those who will never overcome their challenges and shortcomings.

Get over your rationalizations and excuses. Get over the reasons you're not the person you want to be right now. Get over the reasons you're not where you want to be. Get over blaming other people, places, things, situations, and circumstances. Get over trying to wiggle your way out of it. Get over trying to protect your ego and your pride from the truth.

Lose the excuses. Lose the reasons. Lose the rationalizations. Lose the need to be right. Suck it up, deal with it, correct yourself, and move on.

YOU ARE NOT A VICTIM

Owen Cook says, "Those who don't have a larger purpose, when they get in pain, their interpretation is 'I'm a victim. I've been victimized. That thing victimized me. I want to complain!' Every second of this shit out of their mouth is a loss of their life. What are they talking about this for? They don't need to blame anyone for anything. If I get robbed, I say, 'Oh, I guess I shouldn't have put myself in a position to get robbed.' If I get f*cked over, I say, 'Oh, I guess I shouldn't have put myself in a position to get f*cked over.' Sometimes I get screwed over in very unfair ways and I say to myself, 'Oh, a lot of my situation is good and maybe I wouldn't have this situation if these other bad things weren't happening and I'm trying to remove those bad things out of my life. But in the meantime, they're there, and that's part of the life I'm in, so I accept it and I'll work my way out.' Full self-responsibility. And sometimes I truly do get victimized but I don't run around complaining about it. I'm just like, 'Well, sometimes in life, life isn't fair. Sometimes my situation is not totally fair and if I keep working on improving my situation, I'll have less of that in the future. But then again, my kid could get killed in a car accident and all of victim mindset stuff won't mean shit anyways.' Life is going to have an inherent level of pain and unfairness and you try to minimize it as much as you can and the rest you accept. One part of life is improving your execution and situation and another part of it is accepting it's going to be f*cked up either way."

Stop seeing yourself as being a victim. Switch your mindset to, "I was in the wrong place at the wrong time and something happened that I'm not exactly happy with" and leave it at that. Your ego wants to be the victim. Your ego wants justice. Your ego says, "I'm important and this thing made me uncomfortable, angry, and sad and I want someone to pay for it! I want to act weak and helpless!" Stop playing the victim card.

YOU ARE NOT A QUITTER

Quitting is not giving up on what you're doing. Quitting is giving up on yourself. It's allowing your will to die. It's reinforcing, in your mind, you're not fast enough, tough enough, strong enough, smart enough, or good enough to keep going. That you don't have what it takes to get what you want, become the person you want to be, and to have the life you want.

You only lose when you quit. Everything you've worked for and the time, effort, and energy you put into it vanishes when you decide to quit moving forward, pushing, and surviving.

You can crawl, feel sorry for yourself, cry, lick your wounds, call out for your mom, get emotional, and even complain, but you can't quit. In hard times, everything else is acceptable, but quitting is not.

Coming in 2nd, 3rd, 4th, 5th, etc. doesn't make you a loser. It means you finished but you just happened to come in behind someone else. It means you didn't give up and you just have to work on your execution for next time.

Not quitting means you have to, as Gary Vaynerchuk puts it, "crawl through the shit". He says, "Most people aren't willing to eat shit for two years so they can eat Caviar for the rest of their lives." Most people quit because they don't want to have to endure the pain, suffering, lack of comfort, and hard work that it takes to get to where they want to be.

You're not a quitter. You will do what is necessary to get there, to have what you want, to be what you want, and to do what you want.

Grit your teeth, dig in, and endure. Endure the pain, suffering, discomfort, and hard work. Endure the shit. Endure whatever it is you have to go through to reach the finish line.

YOU ARE NOT HELPLESS

Having your act together is making sure you are never helpless. When I learned this, it hit me like a brick wall because I realized I always felt helpless because I was doing it to myself. I was always putting MYSELF in the compromising position of feeling and being helpless. Nothing robs you of your power, confidence, and self-esteem more than feeling helpless and needing something you could provide to yourself if you're smarter and more strategic in your thinking, planning, and execution, but you're not.

Not being helpless is making sure you always have, have access to, and can get what you want and need. It's putting yourself at a level of "f*ck you". It's making sure you're always able to provide yourself and your family everything that is needed. It's making sure you never have to borrow money or anything else and become slave to a lender. It's making sure you are never in a position where you have to give someone or some company power over you because you don't have the power to make it happen yourself.

When you, irresponsibly, spend yourself broke and eliminate your financial options, you put yourself in a helpless position. When you choose to smoke cigarettes, do drugs, and make unhealthy food choices for years and years and have severe health problems, you put yourself in a helpless position. Stop making yourself helpless. Stop engineering situations where you wind up being helpless. Others, who don't have their act together, like to think, pretend, and communicate that they're helpless so they won't have to make an effort. You are not helpless. You have the same opportunities as everyone else. You choose what to do with your 24 hours each day. You choose who and what to surround yourself with. You choose not to help yourself when it's needed. If you are willing and focused, you can avoid ever being helpless.

PUSH THROUGH RESISTANCE

As you move forward and learn, grow, and become, you will feel resistance. It'll come from people, yourself, and life. People will tell you you're working too hard, you're too focused, it's too much, and you need to give yourself a break. To stop being so hard on yourself. The childish part of your mind will create micro emotions, excuses, complaints, and reasons you should slow down, take a break, and not be so hardcore and extreme about it. When you develop new habits, your inner-child resists the change and the growth. It finds the pressure hard to handle. It doesn't like feeling of being uncomfortable.

Life places challenges and obstacles in front of you at the worst times. Multiple bad things will happen at one time and you will feel like giving up. As soon as things look good, life will slap you in the face to keep you from getting too comfortable.

Resistance will always be present and those who never get their act together and become the person they want to be give up and stop moving at the first sign of it. They allow the resistance to become stronger than they are. They allow it to hold them down.

Someone or something will always resist you. You will always resist yourself – and this is good. When you exercise, the resistance of gravity helps you and your muscles become stronger because you're taking what could hurt you and using it to your advantage.

The same happens with your thoughts, emotions, behavior, habits, and mind. When push through the resistance instead of letting it hold you down and stop you, you become stronger. You work those logical, emotional, behavioral, habitual, and mental muscles. You make yourself stronger. You learn lessons and become wiser.

When you feel resistance, think, "Good. Time to become better."

BE PATIENT WITH THE PROCESS

"Overnight successes" don't happen overnight. They spend years behind closed doors ignoring the opinions of others, pushing through resistance and frustration, beating on their craft, and inching closer to perfection. We don't see or think about the thousands of hours they spend behind closed doors doing what most think of as "boring". We only see what they do publicly. We only see their results.

The truth is, they're patient during the process and they don't quit. Nothing is too "painful" to handle because the goal is worth enduring whatever is necessary. They don't act like whiny babies because it's "boring". Even the world's biggest rock stars, the ones who have the most awesome lives, have to lock themselves away in studios for hundreds and even thousands of hours writing songs, getting the chords down, and designing the perfect sound for their songs and albums. It's a very long process and it requires patience but the payoff is huge. It's boring but they're patient enough to go through it. They stick with it.

When getting your act together and reaching goals, you have a lot of boring moments. No one sees the hours and hours you spend working on your self-control and self-discipline. No one sees the time you spend changing your environment and carefully designing it so it's free of negativity and pushes you in the right direction. No one sees the frustration, pain, and resistance you deal with. No one sees the battles taking place in your mind throughout the day. No one sees the war you're fighting to become the ultimate version of yourself.

War with yourself takes patience. You will have long and difficult days. Be patient with the process. Ignore the boring. Ignore the painful. Ignore the discomfort. Stay focused on what needs to be done and be patient. The payoff is 100 times the amount of effort required.

UNDERSTAND THE PATH TO MASTERY

If you're making mistakes, regressing, figuring things out, making progress, and then making mistakes again, you're doing it right.

Getting your act together doesn't mean you don't make mistakes. It means you're making mistakes, learning from them, and using that lesson to push forward. When you make a mistake, don't feel stupid. You found a weak area you can work on, repair, and strengthen.

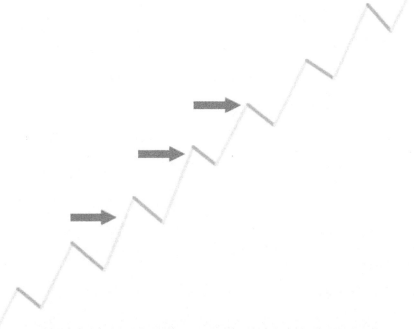

THE PATH TO MASTERY

MASTERING GETTING YOUR ACT TOGETHER MEANS YOU LEARN, MAKE MISTAKES, LEARN FROM THOSE MISTAKES, GET BETTER, MAKE MORE MISTAKES, AND THEN REPEAT THE PROCESS. IT NEVER STOPS. YOU WILL NEVER REACH PERFECTION BUT YOU WILL INCH CLOSER TOWARDS IT.

PART 7: HANDLING PROBLEMS, CONFLICT, NEGATIVITY, AND DRAMA

EVERYONE HAS DARK MOMENTS

The path to getting your act together isn't straight. It's dark and tough. Bad things happen. Life sucks once in a while. You go to bed worried. You wake up anxious and depressed. You get angry because nothing seems to be going your way. You want to give up. You feel like it's pointless to keep going.

Everyone reaching and fighting for something goes through this. They feel the pain and frustration of the dark moments. Life sucks, they're embarrassed, and they're unsure of themselves – but they accept it. They deal with it. They live with it. They welcome it. They adapt to it. They expect it. They know it's part of the process.

Your path will never be perfect. It will never be perfectly flat. It will never be perfectly straight. It will never be a smooth finished surface you can coast on.

Instead of thinking you're a finely-tuned Ferrari that needs perfect conditions to perform, develop the mindset of a 4x4 truck that can handle any nasty environment with ease. It may not go as fast, but nothing stops it from moving forward.

Something will always be in the way. Something will always be trying to stop you and kill your motivation. Something will always seem more "fun" and worth your time. When things are going so well that they seem perfect, something will come up and ruin it. When things are bad, more bad things will happen.

Grant Cardone says, "See, most people think success is a straight line. I'm gonna get out of high school, I'm gonna get a job, and everything's gonna be fine. That's not how it plays out. This is how it plays out – you decide you want something and the line gets all squiggly. That's really what success looks like."

U.S. Navy SEALs are so scary to the enemy because they train in their "green world" more than anything else. They learn how to operate and execute with precision in the dark. You may not see them, but they'll see you and you'll be dead before you even know they're there.

Handle dark moments in the same fashion. When bad things happen, it's night training. It's time to train in the dark. It's time to practice your navigations skills when you can't see 5 feet in front of you. In the dark moments, put on your night vision, push forward, and keep moving. Get used to operating and executing in the dark.

97% of us don't have it together because we don't learn to navigate, operate, and execute in the dark. Instead of moving forward with caution and using our hands to feel where we're going, we give up because we can't see anything and fear stops us. The lights go out, we experience hardship, and we give up. We quit working as hard. We quit making an effort.

The 3% of us who do succeed get down on our hands and knees and crawl through the dark. We walk slowly and feel our way through the dark. We walk face first into things if we have to. The dark doesn't stop us. Fear of not seeing doesn't stop us. When problems pile up and the lights go out, we think, "Good. Time to train. Time to get stronger. Time to learn how to move faster in the dark."

You will never avoid problems, stress, and obstacles. You will never avoid the dark. All you can do is learn how to move with purpose, precision, and focus through it. There's no reason to let it stop you and keep you from placing one foot in front of the other.

When it gets dark and everyone else around you is letting it stop them, keep moving. Get down and crawl. Stick your hands out and feel around. By the time you can see light again, you will be miles ahead of everyone else and miles closer to your goals.

YOUR EMOTIONS MAKE THINGS WORSE

"Problems" aren't as bad as we "think" and "feel" they are. They're more imaginary than real. We take simple problems, add emotion to them, and allow them to grow out of control. Hamlet says, "There is nothing either good or bad, but thinking makes it so. To me, it is a prison."

Do you develop emotion when you see a rock? Do you see it as a problem? Does a rock make you angry and upset? Does it make you extremely happy? I hope not. It's just a rock. It just "is" what it is. It's not good. It's not bad. It's a very neutral thing. It's neutral because we, naturally, don't make analytical and emotional investments in it.

Your perceived problems are no different than a dumb rock. That person, event, and thing you see as a "problem" isn't good and it isn't bad. It just "is what it is". It's neutral. It's nothing and you're turning it into something bigger and worse through your thinking, emotions, and perception of it. Assigning and labeling it as "good" and "bad" doesn't make it true. It doesn't make it fact. It's just your perception of what you think, feel, see, and believe when you look at that person, event, or thing.

Very few things you label as "big problems" are actually real problems. Most of them are, literally, nothing. They're as unimportant as a rock. Traffic jams are not "problems" but you allow them to make you angry and unhappy because you create the "problem" using your thoughts, emotions, and perceptions. People aren't actually THAT stupid, you aren't actually that much of a smarter driver, and your day isn't as bad as you think it is. Things are only "problems" because we're making them into problems. We create the illusions of a "problem". If it actually is a problem, we're making it worse than it actually is.

What everyone sees as a problem, see it as nothing. See it as a rock and, logically, not emotionally, figure out how to handle and solve it.

DETACH AND REMOVE EMOTION

When something arises that can easily be perceived as a problem, detach yourself, your ego, and your emotion from it and handle it. Emotion makes it bigger, worse, and causes you to lose motivation in handling it.

The more emotion you develop during a traffic jam, the angrier you'll get about it and the bigger of a problem you'll think it is. But if you remove all emotion, you'll realize you didn't cause the traffic jam, there's nothing you can do about it, and being angry doesn't help. The reality is that when a lot of vehicles are in a small area, they're entering and exiting the roadway, and they're all going different speeds, there will be, with 100% certainty, a multiplied chain reaction and pattern of slowing down and speeding up. There will be people on their phones, people not paying attention, traffic accidents, large objects in the road that fell off of a truck, etc. So many things can go wrong and the chances of a traffic jam are extremely high. Once you take all of this into consideration, getting upset is completely pointless, ridiculous, and a waste of your time.

When you detach from the situation and remove all emotion, you'll see what's happening more clearly and it won't seem so frustrating and difficult. Don't allow thoughts and petty emotions to make people, situations, and things worse than they actually are.

When you have to clean your bathroom, instead of feeling, "Dammit. I don't want to do this! It's hard and nasty!", just detach from it and think, "This has to be done and thinking about it won't make it happen." Remove emotion, get to work, and before you know it, you're done, your bathroom is clean, and it wasn't as hard as you anticipated.

When faced with anything, even remotely, challenging, remove emotion, detach from it, and deal it. Quit seeing it as and making it a big deal. Quit being dramatic about it. Don't feel one way or the other about it.

NEVER GO PAST DISAPPOINTED

I learned something else interesting from my brother when I was talking to him and seeking his thoughts, opinion, and advice on a situation that was making me "frustrated", "irritated", and "angry".

He cut me off and said, "Well, Marc, that's where I think you're making a mistake. You're letting this thing make you upset. You don't have to allow anything to make you feel any kind of way. The reason you're feeling this way is because you're allowing it and you're wasting your time, energy, and happiness. You're giving away your joy. The reason I'm not upset, frustrated, or angry about this situation is because I never go past disappointed. I never let anything make me unhappy. I'm disappointed in what's happening but that's as far as I will go with it. I don't get angry, frustrated, and upset, I get disappointed. I choose to stop myself at "disappointed" and I hope this situation gets figured out. I'm not allowing anyone or anything to rob me of my happiness. Going past disappointed is creating negative energy and I have no time or space in my life for any kind of nonsense. So, I think you need to re-evaluate your thinking process on this one, back track a little bit, and just stop yourself at disappointed. Get rid of the anger and frustration part. It's not helping or solving any problems. When you come to the fork in the road where you can be disappointed or angry and frustrated, choose to only be disappointed and let everyone else go down the other path. Anything more is a waste of time."

He's right. When you allow ANYTHING to make you angry, frustrated, upset, depressed, etc., you're giving it your personal power. You're giving it your happiness. You're allowing it to rob you of peace and joy. The next time something bad happens or someone lets you down, be disappointed but stop at that. Never allow yourself to become emotional and out-of-control with frustration, anger, and rage.

STOP AND LET IT SETTLE

In dating, I teach men when they feel things are going south, the attraction is fading, and they don't know the right move is, the best thing to do is to just stop, take a step back, let it settle, let the emotions settle, and then let her take the next step. I teach this because when most men see things going in the wrong direction and they feel they're losing their power and her, they freak out, overrespond, and overcorrect. They overdo trying to fix it. They buy flowers, text and call more often, and they smother her with questions and attention. I've noticed, from experience, that the best thing to do in this situation is to not do anything drastic. It's best to completely stop, calm down, put the emotions away, don't bombard her with questions, take a step back, and just watch to see what she does.

This approach, pretty much, works well with all conflict, drama, and problems. When things are going wrong in your life and you're noticing problems coming up, instead of freaking out and doing drastic things in an effort to fix them, just stop, calm yourself down, put your emotions away, and open your eyes. Look to see what's really going on. Look to see if you're making the conflict, drama, and problems worse with your thinking, emotions, and perspectives. Look to see if you're making all of it bigger and more complicated than it really is.

When the smoke clears and you're not so amped up on feelings and emotion, it's easier to decipher what actually happened and whether you should just walk away from it or fix it. If you're going to fix it, the solution is clearer and less complicated than originally anticipated.

Overall, "don't jump to conclusions" means to stop, lose the emotion, think, observe, and respond instead of react. 90% of the time, when we react emotionally instead of logically and we don't stop to think about what we're doing, we look back, feel stupid, and realize we could've handled the situation in a more appropriate manner.

PULL YOURSELF TO THE SIDE

In order to detach, remove emotion, never go past disappointed, and let things settle, I consciously stop, pull myself to the side, and have a talk with myself. I have a meeting in my mind before I let anything escalate. This is when my logic is strongest and my emotion hasn't taken over. I consciously walk myself through the situation as if the logical, more level-headed, and adult part of my brain is talking to the highly-emotional and childish part of my brain and telling it, "Now before you jump to conclusions and freak out, let's put the emotions away, slow down, calm down, and look at this from a logical perspective. It's VERY possible you're making this bigger and worse than what it actually is." I let the logical side of my mind ask the emotional side questions so the emotional side has the opportunity find the right answer.

When you're emotionally bent out of shape, detach from it, talk to yourself, ask yourself questions, and figure it out. You know yourself the best and what's happening in your mind.

I had something distasteful happen and I just couldn't get over how shitty it made me feel. No matter what I did, I couldn't calm my mind and emotions down so I could get over it. Nothing worked. Not even a 6-mile run through the cold rain. Later that night, as I was lying in bed, I had a meeting in my mind. I let the experienced, adult, level-headed, and straight-thinking part of my mind ask questions to the emotional and childish part of my mind. I asked, "Was this your fault?" and the childish side answered, "No". I asked, "Is there anything you can do about this?" "No." "Is being upset going to change anything?" "No." "Is it possible you're making this bigger and worse than what it really is?" "I am doing that." Then I told myself, "Now that we have a clearer picture on what's going on, it's time to let it go." This meeting lasted for 5 – 10 minutes and once it was done, I felt 99% better and it was no longer a big deal.

REDUCE IT TO ITS LOGICAL EQUIVALENT

So, to help myself get over what I thought was a "problem", I simply reduced it into its real and logical form. I stripped it of all thoughts, emotion, and nonsense that could have been making it worse. Once it was down to its logical equivalent, I could see how much of a problem it actually wasn't because I was no longer blowing it out of proportion and making it seem bigger than what it actually was.

The logical part of my mind told the emotional part, "Look, dude, calm the f*ck down. You're being too dramatic and making things worse." It also said, "Ok, Mr. Emotional wussy man, I'm going to ask you a series of questions that will help you to calm down and I want you think really hard about the answer. I need you to be completely honest."

I turned it into the adult talking to the child. The detached person talking to the attached.

Once the logical and emotional parts of my brain were done discussing it and figuring it out, I felt better, saw my own behavior more clearly, and understood the situation better. I figured out that I was upset for no reason, the other person, realistically, didn't do anything wrong, and I was only feeling victimized because I was letting my inner-child have too much input in the discussion. I wasn't controlling my emotions. I was acting like a victim. I was acting like a crybaby about it. I was acting like a big wussy. Once I realized this was happening, I took full personal responsibility for the situation, calmed myself down, and got over it.

Instead of making a huge deal and getting bent out of shape about the things you don't understand, sit down and figure it out. Detach your mind from it and have a discussion with the part of yourself that's refusing to detach. Take the big emotional mountain and strip it down and reduce it so it becomes a molehill.

USE A "DRAMA BOOK"

What I also did, something I've done a lot, is I used what I call a "drama book". I call it a "drama book" because instead of posting, talking about, and sharing negative feelings and problems with the world, something that reflects poorly upon you and makes you look weak, I get the negativity and "drama" out by writing, by hand, in a "drama book". All of your drama and petty, weak, and victim-minded thoughts go in it. It doesn't judge you. It doesn't talk about your business when you're not around. It's 100% personal and private. It's the same as journaling, except you only dump your negativity and drama into it so you're not dumping it on other people and putting your business online.

The important thing is getting the nonsense, weakness, and "poor me" thoughts out of your system. There's a magical process that takes place when you take a pen or a pencil and actually write out on paper what's in your mind. It creates a "release" you don't get from talking about it or typing it out.

It's very weak, childish, and socially and emotionally irresponsible to dump all of your problems, negativity, and drama onto another person so you can "feel better". If you need to vent because you just can't take it anymore, go to the store, buy spiral notebook that's only used for your "drama book" purposes, write in it every time you're having negative and dramatic feelings, and then put it away where no one will read it.

There's no specific time you have to use it and there's nothing you have to, specifically, say in it. When you're overwhelmed by negativity, drama, self-doubt, weakness, and being a victim and it's stopping you from focusing, moving forward, and reaching goals, your "drama book" is a tool to help you relieve the pressure. To get the negativity out. To get the nonsense out of your system. It does wonders for your peace of mind.

IGNORE CRITICISM

Regardless of what you're doing, someone will find a reason to criticize you and talk trash. It's a part of life. You can't have your act together and still care about what others think.

If you know you're on the right path and doing what you're supposed to, then ignore the opinions and criticism. It's usually coming from people who think they have it together but don't. It's usually coming from people who have no room to talk and criticize.

When you clean up your environment and choose to separate yourself from negative and failure-minded people, you will be criticized and told you think you're better than others. You will be called "stuck up". You will get told you forgot where you came from. You will hear you've "changed".

When you become busy working towards a better you, a better life, and better goals, you will get told you're not making enough time to have fun. That you're working too much. That you're working too hard. That you need to cut yourself some slack and give yourself a break. That you're being too hard on yourself.

When you decide to become an entrepreneur, make your own hours, and become your own boss, you will be told it's not safe. That it's not stable. That you need to find a "real" job. That what you're doing isn't smart. That you're only working for yourself because you think you're too good to have a normal job like everyone else.

You will hear it all. There will always be an opinion lurking around the corner and it will come from a person who's inexperienced, unmotivated, and all talk and no action.

Don't let petty words and criticism influence your habits and decisions.

THE AUTOMATIC FORK IN THE ROAD

When you're on your path and drama, conflict, and problems arise, imagine coming to a fork in the road and having the option of taking the path of negativity and drama or the path of avoiding it altogether.

Most people choose to engage and get involved and it causes a lot of negativity and unhappiness. It causes a lot of preventable problems.

You have a choice every single time. You can choose to go down the path of peace of mind rather than the path of drama. You can choose to separate yourself from petty nonsense, drama, and conflict.

Many engage in negativity because they're bored, in the wrong environment, and they don't have goals to keep them busy and moving forward. They don't have anything to remain focused on.

When talking about negativity, my brother, the same one I've talked about twice in this book, says, "Negativity, to me, is like radio static. On the older radios, you had to keep turning a knob until you found a clear station you wanted to listen to. In between the clear stations, there's a bunch of radio static that isn't pleasant to listen to. When I hear something negative or someone's talking about something that I don't care to hear about, it sounds like that ugly radio static. I don't listen to it. I just turn the knob until I hear something that's worth listening to."

When I'm talking to someone and they start getting shitty with me, I tell them we will continue this conversation another time when they can calm down and learn how to talk to me correctly. If someone is arguing on the phone in my home, I ask them to step outside. If people get into a fight and it has nothing to do with me, I separate myself from it until they hash it out. 100% of the time, I consciously choose to take drama and conflict-free route. It preserves my peace of mind and keeps me happy.

PART 8: MANAGING YOUR ENERGY

ENERGY IS IMPORTANT

Many of us aren't paying attention to the thoughts, emotions, habits, people, and things that are robbing us of energy and we're wasting it instead of using it wisely. Those accomplishing a lot more than you, seem inhuman, and have tons of energy only focus on what gives them energy instead of what takes it away. They know smoking makes them feel tired, anxious, and worthless, so they avoid it. They know drinking a lot does the same, so they avoid it. They know unhealthy food takes energy instead of creating it and so they make healthier food choices. They know not having a sleep schedule destroys energy so they make sure to go to bed and wake up at the same time. They know negative, destructive, and unhealthy environments rob them of energy, so they choose the people and things they give their attention to very carefully.

Over the last 10 years, add up all of the days you mismanaged your energy and decided to go to bed too late and wake up too late. Add up the extra hours you spent sleeping in instead of getting up early and doing something productive. What could you have accomplished if you managed your time and energy more wisely? If you went to the gym all of those days instead of sleeping, what would you look like now? How much healthier would you be? If you used those days and hours to work on a new business for yourself, how far along would you be? Would you still be working a job? What would your financial situation look like? How would it be different?

We are Oscillatory and move to and from like a pendulum. We expend energy and renew it. If we expend too much energy without renewing, we burn out. If we rest too much without spending energy, we lose strength, momentum, and stamina. We become weak and lazy and don't grow. When we exercise, we break the muscle down and allow it to recover. Necessary for muscle growth. You need the right balance.

STAY RELAXED

We're wasting energy by constantly being on edge and unable to stay relaxed. We're always worried. We're always stressed. We're always anxious. We're always upset. We're always angry. We're in a constant state of negativity. This burns through your energy reservoirs and leaves you feeling all used up and worthless.

When you do this day in and day out for years, you look back and wonder why you haven't moved forward, accomplished anything, and become better. It's because you didn't have the energy and your free time was spent renewing and recovering from your destructive and negative mental and emotional cycle.

Staying in a constant state of mental, emotional, and physical relaxation reserves your energy. Do your best to remain in a constant state of being "chill" and "cool" about everything and not let your thoughts, emotions, reactions, and responses reach any extremes. Remain balanced and keep everything mellow, calm, and peaceful.

In every category, the highest performing people in the world are always calm, still, relaxed, and not bouncing off of the walls. They're not going from one extreme to the other. They're not experiencing intense and extreme emotions. They're, naturally, reserving their energy by remaining calm.

Plus, when you're always relaxed, you're a more likable and approachable person. You're more trustworthy. You're the one people seek out when they need something important done because they know you're not going to freak out and mess it up.

Regularly practice relaxing and eliminating extreme emotions when they come up.

TURN YOUR BRAIN OFF AND FOCUS

Constant mental and emotional chatter robs you of energy. You're drained of the fuel you need to push forward and get things done. No matter what you're doing, practice shutting your brain off. Shut down the thoughts and emotions and get it done. Forget what happened yesterday. Forget what you're doing that day. Forget what's happening tomorrow, next week, and next year. None of it matters in the moment. All that matters is focusing on what needs to happen right then and there and making sure it gets done right and on time. Eben Pagan says 100 watts in a light bulb will light up a room but if you take those same 100 watts and point them all in one direction, it becomes a powerful laser that cuts through steel and shines for miles.

When your mind and emotions are running, you're as weak and ineffective as a light bulb. It's good enough to light up a room, but you won't cut through the hard stuff and you won't go the distance. But when you turn your mind off and place all of your focus in one direction and on one thing, you will get things done better, faster, and with less energy. Not only will you get things done, you will get more things done because you will be able to move from one thing to the next with no thought and emotion interrupting and distracting you. Eliminate the thoughts, emotions, people, and things preventing you from focusing for longer periods of time. Turn off your phone. Put it on silent. Log out of your social media accounts. Work in a quiet room. Go somewhere where people in your environment won't be a distraction.

The most important and powerful skill you can possess is to keep your attention focused on one thing and in one direction. You need the ability to think about one single thing for a very long time without internal and external distractions and interruptions. This means you can focus for hours each day and repeat it daily for months and years at a time.

WE NEED STRESS

Most of us see all stress as bad. In reality, stress teaches. It points out weaknesses. It helps you grow. It helps you find your limits. It helps you become better. It keeps you humble.

Resistance and finding your limit create stress. While running, you're not stressed when you start. It takes time until you feel the pain. The further you go, the more and more stress you feel in your muscles, joints, body, and mind. The more it sucks. The harder it gets. The more it hurts. The weaker you feel yourself getting. Stress from running isn't doing damage and it doesn't stop a lot of us from ever running again. If we run all of the time, it doesn't hurt that bad, it makes us stronger, and we enjoy it more.

The first time you went to a gym was probably really stressful and, within a short period of time, you were in pain and your body said you were ready to go home. Again, that stress makes you stronger. If you work out 5 days a week, you probably find the stress fun and therapeutic.

We expand our mind, body, capabilities, energy, comfort zone, and ourselves through stress. We grow by pushing until we're stressed. When the stress sets in, we push a little more and then we rest and recover. Once we've recovered, we do it again. Without stress, we wouldn't push our limits. We wouldn't reach. We wouldn't strive. We wouldn't try harder. We wouldn't fight for what we deserve. We wouldn't learn. We wouldn't grow. We wouldn't become better. We wouldn't get stronger.

When you feel stress, it's a sign you're coming to the end of your comfort zone, arriving at a weak area, and you need to push past it and use it to learn, grow, and become stronger.

Next time you're stressed, instead of running away and letting it victimize you, think, "Good. I'm reaching a limit. I'm reaching the edge of my comfort zone. This is an opportunity to learn, grow, and become better."

INCREASING YOUR ENERGY RESERVOIR

It's important to keep your energy levels up so you have the energy to get things done and be productive. It's equally important to learn how to increase your energy throughout the day and throughout time. This doesn't mean temporary energy sources like cocaine, energy drinks, coffee, and caffeine. This means eating, drinking, and doing things that naturally give you energy instead of taking it. It means your lifestyle.

The most obvious way is getting enough sleep and resting your body.

It takes a lot of energy to process unhealthy foods like pizza, cake, fast food, alcohol, soda, etc. They make you feel tired and worthless.

Greatist.com says it's good to drink water and green tea and to eat chia seeds, bananas, quinoa, oatmeal, almonds, beans, and to avoid junk food, white bread, candy, and anything that's hard for your body to process. Personally, I eat lots of vegetables, salads, and fish. When I eat McDonald's and drink soda, I want to sleep all day, I'm unfocused, and don't get anything done. When I eat light and healthy foods, I have more energy, I'm more focused, and I get more done.

Exercise increases energy. Physically working out, running, jump roping, and anything that creates good stress on your mind and body increases your stamina and energy. You can go longer and longer periods of time without losing focus or energy. The more you do it, the more your mind and body adapts to the stress and provides more energy.

When doing anything that requires a lot of focus and placing stress on yourself, when you want to take a break, push yourself to go just a little bit longer. Push yourself to go just a little bit further. Push yourself to make it a little bit harder. Over time, you massively increase your "energy reservoir" because your mind and body adapt to it. When the pain is setting in and you want to stop, do just a few more reps than usual.

DISCONNECTING AND RENEWING

"Every now and then go away, have a little relaxation, for when you come back to your work your judgment will be surer. Go some distance away because then the work appears smaller and more of it can be taken in at a glance and a lack of harmony and proportion is more readily seen." – Leonardo Da Vinci

As you expend energy and focus on goals, avoid getting sick of what you're doing, burning out, and giving up by taking breaks, disconnecting, and getting away for a moment. It's good for productivity and sanity.

We get so involved in our lives, work, and goals that we get stuck in them and we can't see them for what they really are. We can't see their true form. We get emotionally wrapped up and blinded to what the right moves and decisions are. Leonardo da Vinci said to take breaks, completely disconnect, and get it out of your mind. To focus on something else and give your mind and body a break. When you come back, you see it clearer and it's more manageable. You see what you didn't see before. You understand it in a way you didn't before.

In the book, The Power of Full Engagement by Jim Loehr and Tony Schwartz, Jim, a performance psychologist, spent hundreds of hours figuring out the differences between the greatest tennis players and those who weren't. To his surprise, there weren't any that met the eye. But when he paid closer attention, he noticed differences so small you miss them if you're not looking for them. "In the sixteen to twenty seconds BETWEEN points, the best tennis players were able to lower their heart rates by as much as twenty beats per minute." Completely disconnecting and resting for as little as twenty seconds helps you recover and do better. Instead of wearing yourself out and burning out, take the time to disconnect, renew, and come back to it.

QUALITY OF RECOVERY

If you don't get your rest and recovery cycle down, everything else in your life suffers. If you're always tired, you're not as effective, in the best mood, motivated, and productive.

Quality of sleep matters. If you drink yourself to sleep, your body spends energy eliminating toxins and you wake up feeling tired and worn out. If you leave the TV on while you sleep, your brain still receives, processes, and programs itself with whatever is on. This uses up energy – energy you're trying to restore and renew. It's like trying to charge your phone while using all of your apps. It goes against the purpose. Your phone charges fastest when it's off or you aren't using it.

We consider weekends to be recovery time from a long week of "work" but then we go out and destroy our energy by gorging ourselves with junk food, drinking alcohol, doing drugs, and partying and when Monday rolls around, we feel worse than we did at the end of Friday's workday!

Doesn't sound very smart.

When we're stressed out, we sit down, watch TV, and "relax" by watching things that are dramatic, negative, and overly emotionally stimulating

It's important your "recovery" and renewal consist of chilling out, calming down, grounding yourself, and disconnecting from everything negative, extreme, and intense. Disconnecting from everything overstimulating to give our mind and body a break.

Remember, junk food, alcohol, drugs, etc. cause a very negative type of stress and do not assist in recovery. Exercising, training, and anything else good for the mind and body causes positive stress and helps disconnect the mind and does wonders for recovery.

PART 9: GETTING IT TOGETHER PHYSICALLY

HYGIENE AND HEALTH

We have every option available to be very clean, hygienic, and responsible but some of us aren't capitalizing on those opportunities. We're not giving strict attention to the details of our hygiene and health.

When someone misses the details, you notice. If they haven't brushed their teeth, you avoid talking to them, if possible. If they haven't flossed in a while, you smell the rotting food that's been in their mouth for days and weeks. If they're wearing clothes that came out of the dirty laundry, you know it. If YOU notice it and choose not to be direct about it, other people notice when you do it and are choosing not to say anything as well.

Bad hygiene is embarrassing, hard to forget, and burns horrible opinions about you into people's minds. They talk about it and remember when you don't have your hygiene squared away. I love Matthew McConaughey. He's one of the nicest and likable guys you'll ever meet, a skilled actor, and I'm not personally bashing him, but people, magazines, and websites talk about his questionable hygiene A LOT. So much that it leads you to believe he probably has some problem areas.

I can't stress enough how important it is to have good hygiene because it affects your health as well. Not just everyday hygiene like brushing, flossing, and wearing deodorant, but going for regular check-ups with doctors and specialists. Dentist checkups and cleanings get what a toothbrush, floss, and Listerine miss. They do preventative maintenance, take x-rays, and help you avoid big problems. The difference between going to the dentist and not going can mean keeping your teeth or them rotting and falling out.

Here's hygienic details you should be paying attention to:

Oral Hygiene: Brush your teeth when you wake up and go to sleep. Failing to do so means you have food rotting in your mouth all day and night. Floss to get the rotting food from in between your teeth. It only takes 5 minutes to start rotting once it's in your mouth. This negatively affects your health. Last, rinse with an Antiseptic mouthwash to get the rotting microscopic food particles out and to kill the leftover bacteria and germs. Dentists recommend going in for checkups and cleanings every 6 months.

Skin and Hair Hygiene: Wash ALL of your skin thoroughly, not just your armpits and crotch area. That's called a "Whore Bath". Wash your face, back of your neck, back, inside of your belly button, your ass, arms, legs, and the bottom of your feet. Scrub. Don't just put soap on and think you're clean. I know telling you this is completely ridiculous, but many people still bathe like 4-year-olds! If the inside of the collars of your button-down shirts are dirty and brown, you're not washing good enough. Use white towels to dry off. If they start losing their brightness after one or two times, work on your shower skills. Wash all hair thoroughly because hair and the skin under it holds odors.

Clothing: Once dirty clothes are in the hamper, don't take them back out and wear them! Cologne and perfume don't mask that unique and unpleasant smell. Once you wear jeans once or twice, wash them. You may not smell them, but a gust of wind ensures everyone else does. And please, don't put the same underwear back on after taking a shower.

OPERATE ON CALM

We covered this already but we'll talk about it again. When you have your act together, you're not bouncing off of the walls, fidgeting, and displaying a lot of nervous ticks. You're, physically, calm, still, and composed. You're not all over the place. You're not overly energetic and anxious. Your energy doesn't make others feel uneasy and nervous. You walk, talk, and move in a confident, calm, and composed manner. Your gestures don't freak people out. You're not feeling insecure and unsure. You're not suffering from severe mental and emotional chatter.

Make it your highest priority to operate on calm. When the mind is calm, the body is calm. When the body is calm, the mind is calm.

When you're emotionally all over the place, you're physically all over the place. Your heart-rate is elevated, you're in fight or flight mode, and you appear very paranoid and sketchy. It's hard to relax, sit still, and even your eye contact and speech reflects your sketchy mindset.

When you're not physically calm, you're less likable and approachable. You're less likely to make friends. You're less likely to be trusted. You're less likely to be picked for teams and projects. You're less likely to be seen as dependable. You're less likely to be seen as the person who keeps it together under stressful circumstances. You have less opportunities. Those who are calm, relaxed, and don't seem to care as much have better luck than those who care too much. It's not a coincidence. Caring too much kills your physical and mental composure.

Your physical composure communicates everything about you and everything happening in your mind. When you're unable to relax and chill out, pay attention to what's happening in your mind and get it under control. Tame your mind and the body will follow. Tame your body, and the mind will follow.

EXERCISE

Exercise calms the mind and body. It helps you keep it together by getting rid of excess energy and releasing chemicals and hormones into your system that positively affect your mind and body.

Excess amounts of unused energy, if not spent in a healthy way like exercising, turn into thoughts, emotions, behaviors, and habits that aren't so healthy and effective.

Ever noticed how a good workout or run makes you calm, cool, collected, and composed and your mind isn't going crazy? The excess energy is being used for something positive - to work on your body and muscles. It didn't remain in your body long enough to turn into anxiety, negative emotion, and counter-productive thoughts.

When you don't use your energy for something positive and productive, it turns into something negative.

So, to operate on a level of cool, calm, composed, and confident, make sure your energy is getting spent and not finding negative outlets and not becoming negative thoughts, emotions, actions, and habits. When you feel anxious, worried, self-conscious, and anything negative, exercise. Spend that energy. Do something physical. Get the energy out of your system so it doesn't create more negativity. Do push-ups, sit-ups, pull-ups, burpees, run, hit a punching bag, jump rope, or go to the gym. Even yoga helps. Physically get rid of that excess energy. That's why prisoners get more angry and violent when they can't lift weights and exercise.

Fully-engage and use up your energy so you're able to fully disengage, disconnect, and relax. Depleting your energy means you'll get better-quality rest, recovery, and renewal. Our energy must work in a perfect balance like day and night, summer and winter, fire and water, etc.

LOSE THE STIMULANTS AND DEPRESSANTS

We're an over-stimulated and over-depressed society. In 2013, Mayo Clinic found 70% of Americans take prescription drugs. 50% take more than one prescription drug, and 20% take more than 5 prescription drugs. 83% of adults drink coffee just to have enough energy to get their day started or to keep it going. 20% of people use some sort of tobacco product. 56% of people drink alcohol regularly. 10% regularly use illegal drugs.

Yes, some prescriptions are absolutely necessary for treatment, but the majority of cases are preventable just by taking care of yourself. People take drugs for cholesterol, antacid, hypertension, diabetes, stress, sleep, etc. If we, collectively and as a society, had our act together more, took preventative measures, and took better care of ourselves, these numbers would be a lot lower. If you get on a strict sleep schedule where you actually get 7 – 9 hours of sleep a night, you wouldn't need so much coffee, energy drinks, and sleeping pills just to function properly. If you learn to manage yourself, stress, and emotions better and quit freaking out every time something comes up, you won't need to depend on medication, alcohol, and tobacco to "calm your nerves" and more medication to counteract the effects of regular drinking and smoking. If you watch what you eat, and I don't mean "watch what you eat" by watching it go into your mouth, you will be physically healthier and won't need medication to handle the problems your body is having from being irresponsibly obese. Even if you're not obese, you won't need medication to counteract the effects of junk food on your body and health.

Most of us don't know what it's like to be completely sober because we need stimulants to simulate natural energy, depressants to counteract the overuse of stimulants, and medication to dampen the negative mental and emotional effects we experience as a result.

GET ENOUGH SLEEP

The Centers for Disease Control and Prevention states 33% of us aren't getting enough sleep and, over time, it's leading to problems. Chronic sleep loss increases the chances of heart disease, heart failure, heart attacks, high blood pressure, stroke, diabetes, organ failure, etc.

Getting enough sleep is extremely important and a very wise investment in learning, becoming smarter, remaining calmer, functioning properly, staying on track, being happier, and having your act together. A lack of sleep affects your thoughts, emotions, behavior, habits, and results and when you're tired, you're more negative, emotional, irritable, and irrational. You make decisions and exhibit behavior you normally wouldn't if you weren't tired. In other words, you're dumber.

In 2011, Duke University conducted a study to learn how being tired affects decisions and risk-taking and noticed the participants who didn't get enough sleep were making more emotional decisions than logical and calculating risks using emotion rather than logic. At the end of the study, the well-rested participants outperformed the tired ones, took smarter risks, and made wiser decisions.

When you're tired, you don't retain as much information – meaning you don't learn as well. While you're sleeping, your mind is completing the process of programming and storing all of the information you received during the day.

Catching up on the TV shows is not a valid excuse for not getting enough sleep. Checking your social media news feed is not a valid excuse. Going out to drink and hang out with friends is not a valid excuse. Drinking coffee 2 hours before you're supposed to go to sleep is not a valid excuse. Mismanaging your time and schedule is not a valid excuse.

Getting enough sleep doesn't make you weak, lame, and uncool.

FOOD AFFECTS YOU PHYSICALLY

There's a very real and direct connection between having your act together and your eating habits – meaning what you eat, when you eat it, how much of it you eat, and how often you eat it.

Out-of-control eating habits reflect weak-mindedness and, of course, self-control issues. When most of us get the slightest bit hungry, instead of having self-control, holding out, and dealing with being uncomfortable, we're weak and allowing emotions to get the best of us. We let our inner-child run the show and we go to the nearest fast food place and eat the tastiest and unhealthiest thing we can find. Then, we take pictures of our food, post it on social media, and take pride eating unhealthy amounts of unhealthy food. It's messed up.

Eating habits affect your mood, emotions, behavior, habits, mind, and body. Food affects the way you feel. Food affects the way you look. Food, clearly, affects your health. Years of poor food decisions lead to obesity, tooth decay, high blood pressure, high cholesterol, heart problems, diabetes, Osteoporosis, types of cancers, depression, and eating disorders.

Pay strict attention to what you're putting into your body. Control your eating habits and decisions. Your food choices reflect your patience, wisdom, and mental strength. The way you eat is the way you live. If you make sloppy food decisions, you're making sloppy decisions in most areas of your life. If you make wise food decisions and don't eat emotionally, chances are your decision-making process is the same in all areas of your life. They're all connected.

Be strict. Tell yourself "no". Treat your body right. Stop eating emotionally. Stop letting taste override health. Stop eating out of boredom. You only have one body and you need to take care of it.

PART 10: GETTING IT TOGETHER EMOTIONALLY

EMOTIONAL CHESS

The top predictor of success is emotional intelligence and control - not athletic ability, money, confidence, looks, height, race, family name, friends, and even, education. It's the ability to get your emotions out of the way so you can do your job, move forward, and stay on track.

Recognize when your emotions are getting in the way and hindering your ability to think, focus, and perform. Instead of feeling committed to remaining emotionally-transparent, start thinking, reflecting, and strategizing the way a chess or poker champion would. Revealing your emotions makes it easier for others to lose respect for you, take advantage of you, and destroy you. It gives them the unfair advantage. They own you. They corner you. The playing field is uneven.

It's immature and lazy not to control your emotions. It's irresponsible. It's weak. It makes you look like a jackass and a crazy person. You can't trust emotionally-weak and out-of-control people. You can't depend on them. It's hard to respect them. It's hard to like them. They devalue themselves.

When you start thinking revealing your emotions is a good idea, remember it's a waste of your time and it will, more than likely, backfire. Think to yourself, "If I don't keep it together and calm down, will this set me back? Will I look weak? Will I lose my peers respect? Will I lose trust?"

This is very real and important. Forget the, "I don't give a damn what people think!" attitude that you lazily use across the board. Others losing respect for you because you're emotionally-weak and them laughing at you because you're a horrible dancer are two very different things.

You're surrounded by sharks waiting to taste blood. Waiting for weakness and vulnerability. Waiting for their next target. Waiting to screw you over. Waiting to take advantage of you. To avoid putting yourself in compromising positions, control your emotions.

STOP SHARING EMOTIONS

The need to constantly share your feelings and emotions is pathetic and puts you in a position of looking and feeling helpless. As you've learned, you are never helpless. Don't create that appearance. Don't look weak and pathetic to anyone.

Expressing your feelings to the world doesn't improve your situation or position. It does nothing to move you forward. It doesn't give you power. It only takes power away from you, sets you back, and reveals your weaknesses. You're pulling your own feet right out from underneath you.

As Jocko Willink says, "You don't have to be transparent all the time. You have to win the game."

It doesn't matter if others think you're a jerk or not transparent enough. What matters is keeping power to yourself and not giving anyone the opportunity to see right through you and take advantage of you.

When you're sharing your feelings, acting like a victim, and complaining about what isn't fair, the person listening may actually care about you and be a good listener, but unconsciously, they're lowering your value in their mind. They're lowering you on their list of importance. They're unconsciously losing respect for you. They're unconsciously feeling they have more power over you because, more and more, they're able to see right through you. You're losing cool points. The big image they have of you becomes smaller and smaller.

When you keep your feelings to yourself, the opposite happens. I've heard it called "expectation". In their mind, they fill in the blanks with positive things, even if they aren't true. Then what they're imagining about you grows bigger and bigger and they gain more and more respect and admiration for you. The less others know about you, the better off you are. Let them create their own story about you in their mind.

DON'T GET SUCKED IN

You've already learned that no matter who you are, what your background is, what your life is like, or how good of a person you are, bad things happen and there's not much you can do about most of it. You can only control how attached you allow yourself to become to the situations and occurrences. You can only control whether you get sucked into them or not.

The problem with most of us is we allow bad things to suck us in and shake us up. We get emotionally triggered. We get emotionally invested. We allow the bad things to affect our peace of mind and happiness. We allow them to rob us of personal power.

It takes awareness not to get sucked in and become emotionally invested. It takes practice. It takes knowing whether or not you can persuade the situation or circumstance.

If not, have enough awareness to know when you should just let it be. Work around it. Don't bring it home with you. Don't take it to bed. Don't carry it around during the day. Push it out of your mind and forget about it because whether you think about it or not, it doesn't change it. It doesn't make it better and it doesn't make it worse.

If you do have some control, still, remain detached and reverse engineer it. Figure out which actions led up to the problem. If it wasn't your doing, figure out the solution. Once you've figured out the solution, break the solution down into actionable goals and steps and give yourself a deadline to get it done. Leave emotions out of it. They don't help. They only get in the way. Once the problem is solved, move on from it and forget it happened. Don't keep memories lying around that trigger emotions and cause you to act like a victim. Once it's done, it's done. There's no need to get sucked back into it after the fact.

ZERO BASED THINKING

Zero-based thinking works like hindsight.

Based on experience, you help your decision-making process by thinking back to particular events, situations, circumstances, and decisions, looking at the outcome, removing all of the emotions clouding your judgment at the time, and figuring out how you could have handled yourself and/or the situation better. Once you've figured it out, you're storing that information away in your mind and pulling it back out when you're in that situation, or something similar to it, again.

We naturally do this semi-unconsciously, but it helps you to better control your emotions in the present and future if you start consciously practicing it on a regular basis.

During the particular event, situation, circumstance, and decision-making process, you were more emotional about it, naturally, because it was new. It was the unknown. It was darkness. It pushed you out of your comfort zone and forced you to feel vulnerable. You'd never been in the middle of it before and weren't exactly sure how to deal with it. It seemed a lot bigger and scarier than it actually was.

But once you return to it, or something similar to it, and you know what to expect, it's easier to leave emotion out of it since you've spent time returning to it, mentally training for it, rehearsing, and planning what you would do if, ever, in that situation again.

Again, in your mind, you're returning to the event, stripping it of all emotion, looking at it logically and for what it really is, being truthful with yourself about what really happened, and training yourself for possible future occurrences. You're undoing the life-changing event your emotions made it into and revealing the truth about it. You're preparing, empowering, and arming yourself for the future.

EMOTIONALLY ZERO OUT

Emotionally zeroing out doesn't mean being a robot. It doesn't mean you're a cold-hearted asshole. It just means you're intelligent enough to know and understand how feelings aren't very useful or helpful in many situations. That you get better results when you ignore emotion.

It's stripping yourself of emotion not pertaining to or helping your current situation. Consciously choosing not to "feel" one way or the other about it. Emotional favoritism, ties, biases, and prejudices don't hinder you.

When something happens that you don't like, zero your emotions out and deal with it. When it's dealt with, zero your emotions out and move on from it. Remaining emotionally neutral makes it much easier.

Forget how you feel. It doesn't matter. Leave the feelings to the emotionally-weak. It clouds your judgment, slows down your thinking process, and leads to misguided decisions.

EMOTIONAL ZERO SCALE

EMOTIONALLY ZEROED OUT IS STAYING IN THE MIDDLE. NOT BEING TOO HAPPY AND CHEESY AND NOT BEING TOO DEPRESSED AND ANNOYING. FORCE YOURSELF TO STAY CENTERED.

NEGATIVE EXTREME

DEPRESSED, COMPLAINING, VICTIM

ZEROED OUT

CALM. COOL. COLLECT. CONTENT. MELLOW. WHATEVER MINDSET.

POSITIVE EXTREME

TOO EXCITED. TOO HAPPY. HIGH-STRUNG

EMOTIONAL SEVERITY

A big contributor to having your act together is not turning baby emotions into monster emotions. On a level of 1 through 10, 1 being nothing and 10 being extreme, losing a loved one registers a 10. It's understandable. Everyone has their own grieving process but it could be said that some of us take longer than necessary and expected to get over a death because we're lacking the maturity and responsibility to pick ourselves up, accept it's a very sad part of life, and move forward. On the same scale, a 1 is getting upset because someone offended you, you dropped your piece of pizza on the floor, or you had to sit in traffic. You can't change it and it's a waste of time, energy, and emotions.

Expressing your emotions on a baby level makes you weak, unstable, immature, and childish. It's not that big of a deal. Get over it. You're too old to be complaining because you're emotionally sensitive.

EMOTIONAL SEVERITY

SITTING IN TRAFFIC	BEING OFFENDED	HAVING A COLD	PAYING BILLS	POLITICS	CAR ACCIDENT (NON INJURY)	DRAMA / CONFLICT	KIDS NOT LISTENING	LOSING YOUR JOB	LOSING YOUR HOME / MONEY	BUSINESS GOING UNDER	CAR ACCIDENT (WITH INJURY)	LOSING A PET	DISEASE / SERIOUS ILLNESS	DIVORCE / SEPERATION	LOSING A LOVED ONE

1	5	10
NOT A BIG DEAL	DISAPPOINTED	VERY UPSET

PART 11: GETTING YOUR HOME ACT TOGETHER

YOUR HOME REFLECTS YOUR MIND

There's a direct correlation between your mind and your home. The way you think and carry yourself flows into every part and aspect of your life. Your attention to detail is reflected in everything you own and do. Your home makes it instantly noticeable how much you respect yourself, how much you have your act together, and how much attention you give to detail. Your home reflects your thoughts, emotions, habits, and self-discipline. It's impossible to fake.

If your home is sloppy, trashy, unorganized, unsanitary, and details are overlooked, it's easy to guess you're sloppy, trashy, unorganized, unsanitary, and overlooking details in every other area of your life. If things break and you let them sit instead of fixing them, it's easy to guess you're ignoring and choosing not address other problems in your life. If your home is calm, neat, organized, squared away, clean, and the details are handled, it communicates you're a calm, neat, organized, squared away, clean, and detail-oriented person. It communicates you respect yourself and you stay on top of everything. If you're constantly losing and misplacing things and you don't know everything's exact location at all times, it communicates your mental weakness, incompetence, and absent-mindedness.

If you understand this correlation, you can very accurately guess, in most cases, what someone's home looks like and how much attention they give it just by looking at the how they conduct themselves.

Look at your home right now. Look at every single detail. What you're seeing is a direct reflection of your mind. You're looking at the product of how much you have your act together.

It doesn't matter how much you talk about how you have your act together, your home says different. Your home tells the truth.

IT SHOULD FEEL SAFE, SECURE, AND HAPPY

Your home is your domain. Your territory. Your place to drop your guard and relax. Your place of peace. You place of solitude. Your place away from the world. You place of safety, security, and happiness. Not just for you, but for everyone in your family.

Your home environment shouldn't be hostile and negative. It shouldn't be chaotic. It shouldn't be unpredictable. It shouldn't be wild and "crazy". It shouldn't be frustrating. It shouldn't cause anxiety. It shouldn't be somewhere you avoid. It's no place for disrespect, hostility, chaos, and negativity. Nothing about your home should make you feel trapped, cornered, hostile, and unhappy.

It should be purposely designed as a place of happiness. A place free of negativity. The one place you feel you belong.

If your home isn't everything you want in a home, something needs to be done. Something needs to change. Whoever or whatever is causing the lack of peace needs to go. If it's a home you're sharing with family or roommates, find somewhere else to go or find a way to manage your money better so you can afford your own place. If it's your place, ask them to quit killing the peaceful vibe or go. Your happiness comes first and the quality of your living environment is more important than being afraid of hurting someone's feelings.

A calm, quiet, and peaceful efficiency apartment that isn't very special is ten times better than living in a large, luxury, and multi-bedroom home with a pool and a crazy, chaotic, and negative environment.

Unpredictability, chaos, and negativity have no place in your home. You shouldn't have to live with or around anything or anyone robbing you of your happiness and peace of mind. Design your home environment to your specific wants and needs.

RESPECT YOUR HOME

Respect your home 100% of the time and expect all roommates, family, and children to as well. If it's not YOUR home, you should still respect it, regardless of what everyone else is doing. It's the mature thing to do. It should be automatic. It should be the standard no matter where you are.

Your home is an extension of yourself. If you don't allow family, friends, and guests to disrespect you as a person, you shouldn't allow them to disrespect your home.

Expect guests to conduct themselves in a respectful manner towards you, your home, and everyone in it. Expect them to respect the boundaries and rules. Expect them to respect your other guests. Expect them to respect your furniture and pets. If you're picky about furniture, like I am, expect them to know it's not cool to put their feet on couches and furniture without asking. If someone makes a mess, expect them to respect your home enough to clean it up. If they're arguing in person or on the phone, expect them to respect your home enough to step outside.

Not respecting your home and expecting everyone else to as well ruins the environment. It ruins the peace you've designed your home to have. It ruins the point of having your own domain with your own rules. It ruins the positive energy. It ruins the safe space provided for yourself, your family, guests, and even, pets.

It's not ok to disrespect your home just because it's yours. Follow the same rules as everyone else. Be the example. How you treat yourself is how you treat your home. If you don't care about and respect yourself enough to take good care of yourself physically, mentally, and hygienically, it's easy to assume you don't respect your home either. If you don't care about your personal appearance, it's safe to assume you don't care about your home's appearance.

EACH PLACE SERVES A SPECIFIC PURPOSE

Designating specific areas in your home for specific purposes keeps your home structured, clean, calm, and free of confusion. The more cluttered, chaotic, miscellaneous, and weird your home is, the more cluttered, chaotic, and weird things are in your mind.

The basics of how rooms and things in your home should work:

- Logically, eating and drinking anywhere in the home, except for the kitchen, dining room, and dining table, is unacceptable. Food and liquids don't belong on the couch, in bed, or in the bathroom. It's just sloppy and weird.

- The living room is to "live". It's for entertainment. It's where you hang out. It's where you spend time. It's not for eating on furniture.

- Couches, loveseats, recliners, etc. are for your butt, not your feet. They're not dining areas.

- The dining room and dining room table is not a storage room or storage rack for papers and boxes.

- The bedroom is for sleeping and sex. It's not an entertainment room where you sit in bed all day and watch TV and play video games. Hanging out in your room all day is kind of weird.

- The garage isn't a storage room. It's to park vehicles. If you can't park vehicles because of stuff being in there, find somewhere else to put the stuff or throw it out.

- Storage rooms / attics are to store things. You shouldn't have boxes and storage containers piled up in closets, bedrooms, bathrooms, the kitchen, in the garage, or underneath beds. If you're not using it right now, get it out of the way. Hoarding is terrible and unhealthy.

EVERYTHING HAS ITS PLACE

100% of the things in your home need a place so you never lose and misplace anything. You know what you have, where it goes, and its location at all times. It's smart and makes everything easier.

All items, keys, wallet, money, etc. should all have a place. Clothes and shoes go in closets. Dirty clothes go in hampers. Towels go in bathrooms. Trash goes in the trash cans, not the floor. Dishes, pots, and pans go in kitchen cabinets. Everything should be in place and accounted for.

As an Aircraft Mechanic working on secret and experimental aircraft, the rules were strict and clear: every tool, screw, nut, bolt, rivet, hi-lok, etc. has a place and no one goes home until every tool and piece of hardware is back in place and accounted for. The person in charge didn't suffer from Obsessive Compulsive Disorder and want to make our lives miserable, it was because tools and hardware left in an engine or somewhere else on the aircraft could lead to it crashing and killing people onboard and on the ground. It was 100% necessary that every single tool and piece of hardware was accounted for. We did this by "shadowing" tool boxes and putting as many accountability procedures in place as necessary. Every drawer of every toolbox had the shape of the tool cut out into foam and at the end of the day, the tools went back in their place. If it wasn't there, it was missing and all operations on the aircraft stopped. We separated into search teams to find it. The tools not stored in toolboxes were traced onto walls so they were quickly and easily seen if they were being used or missing. When we checked out hardware, it was counted out and we documented EXACTLY how many screws, rivets, nuts, bolts, etc. we used. If it got thrown away, we documented that too. We left no room for mistakes. These intense and strict accountability procedures kept everyone on the aircraft safe, it kept us sharp, and it saved time and effort when doing our job.

A CLEAN HOME IS A CLEAR MIND

Again, your home reflects your mind. If it's cluttered and disorganized, your mind is cluttered and disorganized. If it's clean, clear, and intelligently organized, your mind is clean, clear, and more organized.

If you're not developing emotional attachments to everything you own and regularly throwing out and giving away the things you don't need, you're mentally and emotionally retaining only what's necessary and useful and throwing out the thoughts, emotions, and habits not serving you.

When your mind is cluttered and unorganized, look at your home – it's probably the same or getting there. When you're an emotional wreck and your mind is all over the place, your home becomes a wreck.

Cleaning is good for your mental health. When you clean and organize your home, it does the same for your mind. It's therapeutic.

From 200+ years of reports and studies, militaries understand this concept better than anyone.

When a unit loses a battle, there's usually an investigation conducted as to what happened, what they did differently, and what variables contributed to it. One Russian commander reported that when the soldiers stopped shaving, they stopped caring, they became sloppy and complacent, and more of them were killed. Superiors don't make soldiers shave, iron their uniforms, make their beds right, and keep their rooms spotless because it's fun. It's because they need soldiers to remain sharp, disciplined, and detail-oriented. If they look sloppy, they act sloppy. If their uniforms are wrinkled and dirty, their behavior and attitudes suffer. If they don't keep their bed sharp and perfect, they become lazy and careless in other areas. If their room becomes a mess, their mind becomes a mess.

A CLEAN HOME IS HEALTHY

The chronically sick are usually very dirty, disorganized, and unsanitary. They don't keep things clean, wiped down, sanitized, there's a lot of dark and wet places around the home, and they don't clean on a regular basis. They get used to the smell, mask it with air fresheners, or completely ignore it. They don't give their home the attention it needs. The bathrooms have urine and fecal matter everywhere. Mold is growing in the shower. Rotting food is in the fridge, behind the stove and refrigerator, and splattered all over the microwave. Dust is everywhere. Dishes aren't getting washed, floors aren't getting swept and mopped, vacuumed, and shampooed, and old and bacteria-filled furniture isn't getting cleaned or replaced.

Over time, mold, germs, and bacteria grow and release particles into the air and those who live in the house breathe it in, get sick, and develop problems. Old food particles and residue left behind from lazy and pathetic kitchen habits rot, decay, and attract bugs, insects, and other things you don't want in your home. The bugs and insects mate, vomit, and defecate all over the place and their feces and vomit rot and release, even more, bacteria and germ particles into the air.

Wash bed sheets. When you cook and eat, wipe down counters and stovetops with disinfectant. Keep the dining room table wiped down. Every month, wipe off the top of the refrigerator, take everything out of it, wipe it down, and throw out all of the old and rotting food. Keep the inside of the microwave clean and disinfected. Pull the stove out, most stoves usually roll, and sweep, mop, and disinfect underneath it. Keep your toilet clean and disinfected – inside and outside. Keep showers clean and disinfected. Wipe down sinks and bathroom counters. Keep floors swept, mopped, vacuumed, and shampooed. Keep your home clean, healthy, and disinfected. It's important to your health.

PRACTICE MINIMALISM

Some facts about our excessive consumption and "owning" habits:

- Shopping malls out number high schools and we consume twice as many material goods as we did 50 years ago

- The average American home has tripled in size over the past 50 years and has over 300,000 items

- There are more television sets in America than there are people

- Americans spend $100 billion a year on shoes, jewelry, and watches and $1.2 trillion a year on non-essential goods, the average woman owns 30 outfits and spends 8 years of her life shopping, and the average American throws 65 pounds of clothes away per year

- 3.1% of the world's children live in America but they own 40% of the world's toys

- Storage is the fastest growing real estate industry in the past 4 decades and there is 7.3 square feet of storage space for every single person in the U.S.

- 25% of people with two-car garages park in the driveway because the garage is full of stuff and 32% can only fit one car in it

Every single thing you own is one more source of spent money instead of saved money. One more source of worry. One more source of stress. One more thing to keep track of. One more thing to pack and move. One more distraction.

Since we're emotionally out-of-control and we shop for therapeutic purposes, we end up owning more non-essential items than we will ever need, we don't know what to do with all of it, and they end up owning us. Society says the more "things" you have, the more freedom you have but it's, actually, the more you spend, buy, and own, the more of a slave you are to your "stuff".

Only buy what you absolutely need and one or two "toys" here and there.

Minimalism is keeping the things you don't need to a minimum so you don't live in a cluttered home and aren't overwhelmed by belongings.

If you're not a minimalist, get rid of or sell 80% of the things you own and it improves your quality of life, happiness, and peace of mind. It gives you more freedom.

Realistically, you only need 40 – 50 articles of clothing. You don't need the DVD's and Blu-rays you never watch. You don't need the clothes you never wear. You don't need the shoes you never wear. You don't need the toys your kids have outgrown. Every room in your home can be minimized to the basics.

In the movie Fight Club, Edward Norton is a very timid, tense, and anxious man. In one scene, he's acting like a victim because his fancy apartment blew up with all of his belongings in it. He says, "I had it all. A stereo that was decent. A wardrobe that was getting very respectable. I was close to being complete. And now it's all gone." Brad Pitt, who is very laid back, doesn't own many things, and, in essence, is a minimalist, gives his take on it, "Do you know what a duvet is? Why do guys like you and I know what a duvet is? Is this essential to our survival in the hunter-gatherer sense of the word? No. What are we then? We're consumers. We are the byproducts of a lifestyle obsession. Murder, crime, poverty. It doesn't concern me. What concerns me are celebrity magazines. Television with 500 channels. Some guys name on my underwear. Rogaine, Viagra, Olestra. Martha Stewart. Martha's polishing the brass on the Titanic. It's all going down, man. The things you own end up owning you."

QUARTERLY DETAILED CLEANING

Besides cleaning on a daily and nightly basis, it's important to clean, organize, simplify, and minimize your home top to bottom every three months.

- Vacuum/clean dust, spider webs, etc. from tops of doors, pictures, corners of walls, floors, ceiling, ceiling fans, vents, light fixtures, shelves, etc. You're breathing in that dust if you don't clean it.

- Clean all baseboards so they look new – I make my kid do this when she doesn't listen, misbehaves, or brings home bad grades

- Move all furniture and clean underneath and behind it

- Clean, simplify, and organize all drawers, cabinets, and pantries and get rid of everything that isn't used

- Wipe scuff marks and dirt off of walls, doors, and especially around light switches, plugs, and places where people put their hands a lot.

- Remove all furniture cushions and pillows and clean inside of couches, chairs, etc.

- Vacuum your mattress to remove dust mites eating dead skin and hire a steam cleaning service to clean your mattresses once a year. You are inhaling dirt, dead skin, and dust mites if you have an old mattress.

- Unplug, organize, and simplify all wires in places where you have a lot of electronics

- Pull everything from closets and underneath beds and get rid of non-essential items that aren't being used

- Most importantly, regularly give away and throw out what you don't need

PART 12: GETTING YOUR WORK ACT TOGETHER

WORK COMES BEFORE FUN

Working to reach goals, continually moving forward, and becoming better is more important than working only to relax and have fun.

Most of us have it backwards – we want to play as much as possible and work as little as possible. We only work when we run out of play money and, as a result, we're constantly behind the curve, broke, and miserable.

If you stay focused on reaching goals, becoming debt-free, and putting goals and work before fun, life is more rewarding. You'll have more fun and "play money" than most and the comfortable life you want will take care of itself.

Those who are successful through putting work first live by the motto, "Life is easy when you live it the hard way and hard when you live it the easy way." Life is hard for most of us because we focus on what's easy instead of what gets us the best results.

The time we're spending playing and doing "fun" things because we're bored could be, wisely, invested in learning, growing, and working toward bigger goals. When done over and over and over again, this small sacrifice few are willing to make adds up to life being dramatically different. It adds up to life becoming better and easier than everyone else's. All because you chose to take the more complicated and difficult route early on rather than the simple and easy one.

Force yourself to do the hard things or someone or something else will force you to do them later. Do you want to control the situation or be controlled by it? Do you want to willingly go through a little pain and work towards a life of your choice or be put in the situation where you're forced to work just to keep your head above water? Unfortunately, most of us are choosing the easy and comfortable route and when it catches up to us, we're controlled by the situation rather than controlling it.

"PARENT" YOURSELF

Across all industries and jobs, even in the SEAL teams and other military Special Forces units where everyone is expected to be fully responsible for their decisions, behavior, and habits, there are always a handful of individuals who can't keep themselves on track and have to constantly be parented. Instead of keeping themselves in line, their co-workers and superiors have to, continually, go out of their way and spend time doing it for them. They have to parent another grown adult. They keep getting in trouble for the same things, have to be continually reprimanded, and someone has to continually repeat themselves to them. It's like having a child in the workplace.

I used to be this guy. I was constantly being parented instead of parenting myself and I was too blind to see how selfish and counterproductive it was. Regardless of how many times I was reprimanded and asked to correct my behavior, I kept getting off track, acting like a child, and breaking the rules. Needless to say, I'm probably not welcome back at 99% of the places I worked.

Lacking the maturity to parent yourself is selfish, counterproductive, and unfair to your co-workers who are there to do the same job as you but keep getting sidetracked and distracted by having to keep you on track – something you should be doing yourself. It doesn't make you a lot of friends.

Parent YOURSELF. Be 100% responsible. Get YOURSELF to work on time. Another adult correcting you and telling you to show up on time is insulting and ridiculous. Keep YOURSELF focused, on track, and following the rules. Again, another adult, who's no smarter or better than you are, shouldn't have to be reprimanding you and teaching you right from wrong like you're a child. You should know better.

BE THE EXAMPLE

Not only should you be setting the example for yourself, family, and friends with how you live your life and how much you have your act together, but you should also be setting the example in the workplace for your co-workers, and even, superiors. Instead of letting them parent you, do the opposite - be the example. Be the standard. Give everyone something to look up to. Parent them if necessary.

Whatever it is you're supposed to be doing, make an effort to do it better, faster, and more efficiently. It's not a competition, but it doesn't hurt to do the best you can and raise the bar for everyone else. If you know everyone is slacking, don't do what they're doing. Do what you know they're capable of as well if they have their head on straight.

If it's obvious you're trying to compete with and outdo others, it makes you look insecure and like you have something to prove. That's not the goal. The goal is outdoing yourself and doing your job better and better every single day. Once this becomes a natural habit, co-workers will notice how good you are and they, unconsciously, will step their game up too.

Just because someone is your superior doesn't mean they're perfect and have it all figured out. You can set the example for them as well.

Just because the company is lenient about what time everyone shows up doesn't mean you have to do what everyone else is doing. Be there 15 minutes early every single day. Be predictable. Be reliable. When everyone else is standing around, being lazy, and talking during the time they're supposed to be working, it doesn't mean you have to do it too. Set the example. Stay focused, move forward, get things done, and be more productive than everyone else and they will start doing the same because you're setting the example.

START ON TIME

Time management is incredibly crucial to having your act together and it says so much about you. If you have trouble starting anything on time, it means you have some work to do and adjustments to make in your thoughts, emotions, actions, decisions, lifestyle, and schedule. Tweaks need to be made across the board so you're automatically doing what needs to be done and when it needs to be done. It doesn't matter if you're self-employed, you work from home, or you go to a job every day, the most important thing you can do is start on time. The worst thing you can do is create a time in your mind that you want to start but you slack off and make something else more important. Once it becomes a habit, it's hard to break and you never get back the time you wasted standing still instead of moving forward.

You make the most progress when you start working the very minute and second you planned to. That focus, decision making, and execution sets the tone and mood for the rest of the day and if you don't start on time, you're stressed and more likely to be feeling guilty, uncomfortable, and anxious. Negative thoughts and emotions are likely to get in the way of your focus. But if you start on time, negative thoughts and feelings won't exist and, in fact, feelings of accomplishment, pride, and confidence take their place. When you develop the habit starting when you feel like it instead of when you're supposed to, you, unconsciously, lose respect for yourself, your job, your projects, your goals, and your life. You lose respect for the process and it happens so slowly you don't notice it until it's become a deep-rooted habit and problem.

Those who are successful and have their act together start on time with everything. They wake up on time, get dressed on time, leave for work on time, show up on time, and get started on time. It's automatic. Starting late is completely unacceptable for them.

YOU'RE NOT AT WORK TO MAKE FRIENDS

We're distracted at work because we're getting socially involved in unnecessary ways like gossip, rumors, and the personal lives and business of others. Some workplaces resemble being in high school.

You're not at work to talk and hang out. You're not at work to catch up with your friends on how their weekends were. Realistically, your job is to be an asset to the company. To partner with the company in being productive, taking care of tasks, reaching goals, and helping the company make money. To do the job you applied and got hired for. Nowhere in any job description or any application does it say "come to work, hang out, socialize, and make friends". You're there to do the job you were hired for to the best of your ability in exchange for monetary compensation for your time and effort. So many of us lose focus of this reality and it gets in the way of our focus, productivity, and effectiveness.

Not being at work to make friends doesn't mean being rude, unsociable, and making enemies – it's socially intelligent to be polite, courteous, a team player, and to communicate as much as necessary in order to do your job helping the team reach goals. But you're not there to "hang out", watch YouTube videos, play on social media with your co-workers, and to share personal details of your life that have nothing to do with your job. If you want to hang out with co-workers and make friends, do it outside of work and leave your "friendship" details out of the workplace.

There's way too much time, focus, and productivity lost from grown adults having "friendship" drama and issues and being part of fighting, gossip, and rumors in the workplace. If you're really going to have your act together, separate yourself from the individuals who think making friends at work is more important than staying focused and doing what they were hired for.

DETERMINE GOALS BEFORE YOU START

No one goes to war without a plan – especially if they're invading. In your case, you're invading your job, projects, and goals, conquering them, and taking everything you can get. To win, it's smart to have your targets written out - starting with the highest-priority ones.

Besides starting on time, a clear game plan makes you more productive, focused, moving in the right direction, and hitting one target after another without having to stop and figure out what's happening next. Have a clear picture and layout in your mind and on paper of everything that has to happen so nothing gets left to chance. Once you have that clear picture and plan, get everything else out of the way and move forward.

Having your goals laid out before you start makes your job easier and eliminates unsureness and mental chatter. You're not wasting time figuring out what needs to be done. Going into your workday without goals and a plan is sloppy, complacent, and incompetent.

As an aircraft mechanic, I created my game plan in my mind as I drove to work. Then, in my morning meeting, I'd look up at the aircraft, remember exactly what I did the day before, created a list of what needed to be done, and organized my paperwork in the order the work needed to be done. In my mind, the entire day's work was planned out and I'd usually complete it faster than I anticipated. When done day after day, it added up to a lot of time and effort saved for the entire team, project, and company.

Write down your top 10 goals and targets every night and cross them out as you accomplish them. When you rewrite your goals that night, replace the ones you crossed out with new ones. Before you know it, your goals will be accomplished and done faster than you anticipated.

USE FOCUS BOXES

Comedian Mark Unger says, "Men's brains and women's brains are different! Men's brains are made up of little boxes and we have a box for everything. We have a box for the car. We have a box for the money. We have a box for the job, a box for the kids, a box for you, a box for your mother... somewhere in the basement. And the rule is the boxes do not touch. All right? When a man discusses a particular subject, he goes to the appropriate box, slides it out, opens it up, will discuss only the content of that particular box and then when he is done, he puts it away hoping not to touch or disturb any of the other boxes. Now a woman's brain is made up of a big ball of wire and everything is connected to everything. It's like the Internet super highway."

Although he is explaining the differences in how men and women think, you can use this concept when you work.

To preserve energy, structure your mind, and start having better focus, train your mind to use "focus boxes". Separate every single part of your job into a different mental box. When you're in meetings, you're in your "meeting box". You're completely disconnected from everything else. When you're on break, you're in your break box. You're completely disconnected from everything else. When you're working on a particular project or towards a particular goal, you're in that box and nothing else. Put the other boxes away. Nothing else matters but getting everything in that particular box done. If you have more than one box open at a time, you're wasting time and energy going back and forth and multitasking.

Cut off all thoughts and only focus on one thing at a time. Stop multitasking. Stop juggling tasks. Studies prove multitasking lowers IQ, kills performance, and limits brain power. You're more productive, efficient, and effective when you only focus on one thing at a time.

LOSE THE SHORTCUT MENTALITY

Zig Ziglar says, "There is no elevator to success, you have to take the stairs." How many of us see a set of stairs and decide to take the elevator instead?

Most of us don't want to take the stairs because it's easier to take the elevator. Taking the stairs requires more effort, takes longer, and is a little more painful, but it makes you stronger. On top of that, stairs aren't suspended from cables that could break and lead to you plummeting to your death. Think about it.

The habit of taking shortcuts is not only physical, it's mental – with everything! We're constantly finding shortcuts and easier ways to accomplish what takes a lot of hard work, dedication, and sacrifice. When you get to the bottom of it, it's just plain laziness and weakness. We're too weak to face the hard things and do them.

When I was having a lot of trouble getting ahead and making things happen in my life, I was, unconsciously, trying to take shortcuts, skip steps, cheat, trick the system, and avoid hard work. I was lazy and weak.

Lazy bodybuilders who use steroids to get faster results instead of spending the adequate amount of time in the gym to get the same results experience a lot of unnatural and negative side-effects that would be avoided if they didn't try to shortcut the system. The results don't last as long, it affects their health and mind, and long-term use has very destructive consequences.

When we skip steps and cheat, it comes back to bite us in the ass. Every step you skip shows up as a negative in your life. Every time you cheat, you reinforce weakness and laziness instead of becoming stronger. Lose the desire to cheat and take shortcuts. Get it completely out of your system. It doesn't work.

STOP THINKING AND JUST DO IT

When something needs to be done, stop thinking about it, analyzing it, and trying to find the right time to do it. Just get the ball rolling. Get started. Start making it happen. You will figure it out as you go. The more you think about it, the more you hesitate, stall, think yourself out of it, and the longer it takes. What you're actually doing is more powerful than what you're planning on doing. What you're planning on doing holds no weight.

Get out of your head, lose the mental chatter, lose the emotional chatter, and just get to it.

Brian Tracy says, "When you decide you're going to do something, do it. They've done dozens and dozens of studies over the years and they find that there's one major difference between successful people and unsuccessful people is successful people launch. They start. They get on with it. They just do it. Unsuccessful people get the same ideas and the same information but they've always got an excuse for not starting."

If a particular operation or procedure is complicated and requires time to think about and figure out, by all means, do so. Failing to plan is dumb. But for repetitive and mundane tasks, just get on with them. If you have a physical job, stop thinking about how your knees and back hurt, how it's hot, and how that task sucks. It doesn't matter. Those thoughts and emotions don't get the job done. They don't contribute in any way. The easiest thing to do is to turn your brain off, suck it up, move forward, ignore the weak and useless thoughts, and get it done.

The more you stop thinking about what has to be done and you just do it, the more it becomes second nature.

The most productive people are the ones who get to it and make progress before everyone else is done thinking about it.

PUSH THROUGH BORING MOMENTS

Eric Thomas says, "Everybody wants to be a beast until it's time to do what beasts do. When it gets hard, they quit. When it gets boring, they quit. When it's no longer fun, they quit. Being a beast isn't just killing the gazelle, it's the hunt. It's remaining calm and strong during the process."

Understandably, you will have boring moments in everything you do. EVERYONE has boring moments. What sets you apart from the rest who don't have their act together is how you handle boring moments. Do they get the best of you and cause you to whine and complain like a little girl or do you hunker down and push through them? Do you handle them like a winner or a loser?

Rock stars have hours and hours of boring moments in the studio, on tour, during interviews, etc. and sometimes it's so boring that it doesn't seem worth the money. Professional athletes have boring moments when they have to constantly train, practice, and travel. We think Navy SEALs and Special Forces teams are always doing cool things like shooting guns and blowing things up but we don't realize they only do that 10% of the time. The rest of the time they're sitting in classrooms, training, and doing what most of us would consider extremely boring. Internet marketers who make millions sit behind a computer for hours and hours a day doing a bunch of boring things. Aircraft mechanics don't only fix aircraft, they have to spend hours and hours cleaning thousands of tiny spaces where metal and trash could be. It's boring as hell and it sucks.

It doesn't matter what job you have or how successful you are, there will, undoubtedly, be boring moments. You just have to suck it up, stop crying about it, and power through them. Boring moments are a part of life. The more you handle the boring things, the easier it gets and, eventually, doing the boring things no longer bothers you as much.

BREAK IT DOWN INTO SMALLER GOALS

If your biggest and most time-consuming goals are too intimidating, break them down into manageable sizes. This process doesn't make you lazy, incompetent, or weak - it makes you smarter, more efficient, and more effective.

It's easy to get intimidated writing a 80,000+ word book, like this one, but it's easier to do if you take it one page at a time, like I am.

I hate to keep going back to the subject but when I was an aircraft mechanic and had to load my 1,000-pound toolbox onto a truck and drop it off at a new facility, I did it myself by removing each drawer, lifting one side of the box at a time onto the truck, loading the drawers onto the truck, and then re-installing them back into the box. If the facility didn't have a forklift and no one around to help unload it, I repeated the process in reverse. It took a little longer, but I was able to break a large goal down into more manageable sizes.

Also, when I had very large repairs to accomplish that required hundreds of hours, thousands of rivets, hi-loks, screws, nuts, and bolts, and dozens of steps, I did the same thing. Instead of looking at the thousands of fasteners and hundreds of hours, and dozens of steps as one giant and intimidating goal, I broke it down into smaller times, sizes, and steps by analyzing what needed to happen, making a to-do list, shutting my mind off, and just getting to it. If I was removing the damage, I determined how many hours it would take and broke it down into smaller and more specific steps. Then, I'd pull out my "remove damage" focus box and work from there. I did each step one at a time until the damage was removed and simplified and repeated this process over and over for each step until the entire repair was finished.

Anything that takes a lot of time and effort, break it into smaller pieces.

USE TIME CHUNKS

The process of writing this particular book is extremely time-consuming and instead of focusing on how much time it will take, I take it one day at a time and break each day into manageable time chunks.

If I know I have to work 10 – 12 hours each day to complete this book, then instead of focusing on the whole day, I break it down into smaller time chunks and focus on reaching my next break. If I start writing at 4 AM, I focus on writing until 6 AM, taking a 15-minute break, and focusing on reaching the next break time, 8 AM, and I repeat it until the workday is over. This process makes it extremely easy to make a lot of progress and to stay focused in the moment instead of focusing on the entire day. It also makes the day go by faster. I'm not focused on 8 hours from now. I'm only focused on the 2 hours in front of me.

Time chunks work for long and grueling days. Don't focus on making it to the end of the day because it'll make your day seem longer. Focus on making it to your next break time. Once you reach your break time, forget about the last few hours you just endured and move onto focusing only on the next few hours. It's less stressful and less overwhelming. Once your mind adjusts, making it through a 12-hour day is no big deal.

One Navy SEAL, when asked his mental process for making it through BUD/S, Basic Underwater Demolition/SEAL Training, a 24-week training course that pushes you to your physical and mental limits, said that the only way he made it was focusing on making it through the current evolution (training exercise). He didn't worry about making it to the end of the day, week, month, and course. He knew that if he focused on the current evolution and nothing else, he'll make it through it and he can keep repeating the process over and over until he reached the ultimate goal of graduating BUD/S and becoming a Navy SEAL.

SELF-EVALUATION

Evaluations aren't bad. They help you determine which path you're on, how you're doing, and the direction you should be headed. Most of us hate evaluations because we're subjecting ourselves to criticism – and criticism never feels good. So, to limit the negative, take ammo away from those looking to find fault, and to make it easier, regularly evaluate yourself and your own performance. You don't need another person, who is no smarter than you, telling you how you're doing and how you can improve. You should be able to determine that yourself.

Evaluating yourself instead of letting others evaluate you helps you become more open to learning, finding your weaknesses, and getting better. You're less likely to get your feelings hurt and feel insulted.

Before you start a project, analyze everything that has to happen, determine the objective and big goal, figure out all the steps involved, break it down into manageable sizes, and set a performance standard for the project. Visualizing yourself doing each step of the project and making a detailed list makes it easier. Once it's broken down and documented, figure out about how long each step will take, give yourself a time limit to do it, and then get to work hitting each target and completing each step. This helps you go into it with a clear mind.

As you're completing the project, evaluate your performance at the end of each day and see where you can improve, save time, and push yourself harder to do better the next day.

Once the project is completed, look back at the entire process and evaluate your performance throughout the entire process. Be honest. Document it in detail as if you're the boss evaluating an employee. Take detailed notes on what you believe you did well, what you could have done better, and then focus on improving for the next project.

SIMPLIFY, SIMPLIFY, SIMPLIFY

"Life is really simple, but we insist on making it complicated." – Confucius

"Simplicity is the ultimate sophistication." – Leonardo Da Vinci

"Simple can be harder than complex. You have to work hard to get your thinking clean to make it simple. But it's worth it in the end because once you get there, you can move mountains." – Steve Jobs

"Everything should be made as simple as possible, but not simpler." – Albert Einstein.

The most successful businesses and people operate from the mindset of keeping everything simple. It takes more time, energy, and work to simplify than to create complexity. It's a natural truth that seems to defy logic but makes perfect sense once you consider how often we unnecessarily complicate everything beyond what is necessary.

Simplifying is stripping away any and all unnecessary elements and only leaving behind what's needed. Simplifying seems so "simple", but most of us don't get it. We don't take the extra time and effort to simplify tasks so we can get them done faster, better, and with less effort. Simplifying before you start working and in the middle of working makes you more productive, more effective, and more efficient.

Simplify every single step of every single project and goal as much as you can – even if it means more planning and evaluation.

While everyone is complicating their goals, targets, and job and stressing out over the complexity, you're breezing through it because you were proactive enough to simplify as much as possible before starting. If something seems more complex and harder than it needs to be, figure out how to simplify the process and make it easier for yourself and everyone else.

DOCUMENT ALL TASKS AND TO DO'S

It may seem unnecessary and overboard to document every single thing that needs to be done, but it's not. It's better and smarter to document every to-do rather than attempting to commit it to memory and fail.

The length of the list doesn't matter - as long as your top 10 goals are at the top. Every single day, go through the list and cross off what you're getting done.

I use an app, available for windows, mac, apple, and android, called Wunderlist and it's 100% free. Once you download it and create an account, you can put it on all of your devices, log in to your account from each one, and all of your to-dos will be in one place.

When I need to add to my to-do list while I'm away from home, I open Wunderlist on my phone, add it, and when I get home, I can open Wunderlist on my computer and my new note will be there. Very useful and easy to use.

Don't let the length of your list intimidate you. If you get up on time and get things done, your list will shrink very fast and you will make things happen faster than everyone else around you.

The most successful people, even billionaires, carry notebooks around all day to keep track of everything they're doing and that needs to happen. They know trying to remember everything instead of writing it down is dumb and they'll forget a lot of very important information.

Use note taking apps on your smart devices, keep notebooks in the car, and keep notebooks lying around the house.

Once a week, or every day if you'd like, take your notes, copy them to one place, preferably an app with cloud backup, and cross off or delete your other notes from other notepads, notebooks, and places.

USE CALENDARS

Use calendars to track when things need to happen. This is a big "duh" but, once again, we use up too much time and energy trying to remember everything.

If you're old school, use a physical calendar. It doesn't hurt anything.

If you're technologically savvy, use an app.

Google Calendar or similar, to be exact. You can do the same with Google Calendars that can with Wunderlist – keep track of all events in one place. And Wunderlist lets you incorporate Google Calendar as an add-on.

When I need to add to my calendar, I can add it using any device, it's backed up in case I lose my phone or computer, and I can access it from anywhere.

Again, don't exert yourself trying to commit events and to dos to memory. This is where it's ok to be lazy and take a shortcut.

SCHEDULE EVERYTHING

Strict schedules keep you sharp, precise, and on top of everything.

Eric Thomas says, "The difference between those who are successful and those who are broke is how they spend their 24 hours. It doesn't matter if you're Bill Gates, Oprah Winfrey, Ted Turner, etc., you only get 24 hours a day and how you use your 24 hours makes the difference. The difference between you and Oprah is Oprah uses her time wisely. I went from being broke to selling 6,000 copies of my book in 6 months. What happened? I changed how I use my 24 hours."

Live by the clock. Respect your 24 hours. Every minute wasted is gone forever. Account for every minute. Assign times and time limits for your activities and then stick to a schedule as closely as you can. It creates clearer, more focused, and more aggressive action. You know what needs to happen, when it'll get done, and how long it'll take.

Kevin Kruse asked over 200 billionaires what their best time management tips and secrets were and, across the board, they said very specific schedules work better than anything else. They schedule EVERYTHING and if it's not worth scheduling, it's a waste of time. Specific schedules keep them in line and on track. Specific meaning, literally, minute by minute. They account for every single minute of the day and get more done than everyone else. From the time they wake up to the time they go to sleep, they know exactly where they'll be, what they'll be doing, when they'll be doing it, and how long it will take. No time is wasted. They manage time wisely and use their 24 hours as much as they can.

Starting today, schedule every single thing you do and force yourself to stick to the schedule. Fill up your calendar. Schedule your sleep, breaks, lunch, leisure time, etc. Schedule each step of each task, project, and goal. Track every single minute of your day and don't deviate from it.

PART 13: GETTING YOUR SOCIAL ACT TOGETHER

HAVING IT TOGETHER MAKES YOU LIKEABLE

When you have your act together, you're setting the example. You're raising the bar. You're giving others something to admire and look up to. You're a symbol of strength, doing what others wish they could, and controlling yourself in a way they can't. They admire your discipline, strength, focus, and motivation. You're causing them to look at themselves and realize you're doing something beyond what they are.

Body builders, CEO's, athletes, and everyone doing something great in life have thousands, and even millions, of social media followers, but how many of those followers are actually operating on their level or using them as an example and blueprint to get there? Not many. They're followers because they like them and look up to them. They possess behavioral traits and characteristics that make them more likable and that we wish we possessed.

Your personality and social skills reflect how much you have your act together. It's automatically and unconsciously detectable. It's hard to be likable when you're physically, mentally, emotionally, habitually, and socially sloppy. It's hard to be likable when your life is a wreck and you're not focused, making an effort, and taking action to improve it. It doesn't make you someone others, naturally, gravitate to. When you open your mouth and start speaking, it's immediately noticeable something is "off" and you have some work to do on your mind.

Everyone likes you better when your personality, behavior, and habits communicate you're working every day to improve yourself and become better than you were yesterday. That you're straightforward, focused, driven, and a no-nonsense person. That you're not someone just consuming, taking up space, and floating aimlessly like a kite.

Your life and habits communicate more about you than your words do.

SOCIAL RESPONSIBILITY

Social sloppiness and getting the life you want do not go hand in hand. Instead of being seen as socially-reckless, you want to be seen as socially-responsible and intelligent, in control of yourself, and aware of your personal conduct. Social irresponsibility hurts YOU more than anyone else and the more socially-irresponsible you are, the deeper you dig yourself into a hole.

Having your act together is knowing the very real positive and negative consequences your communication has on your reputation, standing, and positioning and how much you're liked and respected by those who can make your life a lot easier and better.

When you have your act together, you attract the right people into your life who help you move in the right direction and stay on the right path but it takes social responsibility to maintain those relationships. It requires social intelligence, discretion, and discernment. You don't want to unintentionally tear anyone down, needlessly destroy important relationships, and burn important bridges.

As society is becoming less and less classy and more and more socially irresponsible, judgmental, ignorant, and sensitive, it's important, now more than ever, to develop a full sense of social responsibility – even if you don't agree with or like the direction society is headed in.

Social responsibility is being careful who you associate with because, not only do they influence your mind and thinking, but the social ties paint a picture of who you really are – regardless of accuracy.

It's making sure you protect your image and reputation. Not your ego's image and reputation, but your image and reputation of being a person who's intelligent, aware, and has their act together. That reputation is what makes people like you and want to help you in any way they can.

Social responsibility is making sure you don't rub anyone the wrong way and come off as an ignorant and offensive moron on social media. It's being aware of the position it puts you in and the picture it paints of the type of person you really are. Do you absolutely have to share crude and tasteless humor and jokes on your newsfeed? Do you absolutely have to rant, rave, complain, and vent to your social media "friends"? Do you absolutely have put others down because of their political affiliations? Do you absolutely have to share your negative feelings, perspective, and opinions on different topics? What are you getting out of it besides a temporary sense of approval from people who don't really like you or care about you? Are YOU posting, sharing, and "liking" on your social media or are your ego and emotions doing it for you? Pay attention to these things. Your posts, pictures, comments, and "likes" all tell a story about the type of person you really are and how much you have your act together. It tells a story of how your mind works.

Employers, now more than ever, are looking up and reviewing social media accounts before calling potential employees because it gives them a more accurate picture of who that person really is and what kind of employee they'll be rather than listening to them put on an act during the interview process. They don't want to hire the person whose profile picture is of them doing drugs. They don't want to hire the person who is constantly posting how much they hate work. They don't want to hire anyone who's extremely negative, appears to have a horrible attitude, and doesn't uphold the same values as the company.

Because of social irresponsibility, people are losing jobs, destroying careers, and severely limiting themselves. Celebrities, athletes, CEO's, and others are losing opportunities, money, and customers. They're posting public apologies for something irresponsible they said, posted, tweeted, shared, or commented on. It's ALL completely avoidable if you take the time to think about what you say, do, post, tweet, etc.

MAKE YOUR BOUNDARIES CLEAR

It's important to have social boundaries and be 100% clear on them or anyone and everyone with a tyrannical, abusive, or bully nature will see the opening, treat you however they feel, and be pretty sure you won't say or do anything about it. Humans are extremely observant, both on a conscious and unconscious level, and it's blatantly obvious when you don't tolerate any sort of disrespectful words or behavior and your boundaries on how everyone should conduct themselves in your presence are easy to detect. You're not hanging a sign around your neck or verbally communicating, "My boundaries are this, this, and this." Your boundaries are communicated, nonverbally, by the way you conduct yourself at all times and in all situations.

When you're physically, mentally, emotionally, and socially sharp and you have it together in all areas, others are likely to come to the natural conclusion, "This person probably doesn't tolerate any bullshit from anyone so I'm going to watch myself around them." This is what you want. This keeps the peace. This protects you from abusive people. This keeps the respect. This helps you keep your power. You don't want anyone concluding, "This person looks like a doormat and I'm going to be a complete asshole to them and dominate them to stroke my ego and feel better about myself."

Socially, what are you not willing to accept from others? What type of attitude, tone, words, and language is unacceptable and unreasonable to you? What are you not willing to accept from yourself in social situations?

Think about it, make a list, and enforce it when one of those things comes up. You don't have to be a dick about it. Just be calm, cool, and collect and let the person, or yourself, know you're not cool with it.

ALWAYS REMAIN CALM AND CLASSY

No situation can ever force you to conduct yourself in an ignorant, trashy, belligerent, and childish way - even if your emotions tell you different. You are in 100% control of your behavior 100% of the time. Even if a situation or person is pushing you to conduct yourself in a way unbecoming of someone who has their act together, never give them the satisfaction of seeing you lose your poise, composure, and class.

A few years ago, my ex-girlfriend who lived with me was going out with her best friend, a girl, pretty often and since I'm a secure and confident guy, I didn't have a problem with it. But when I found out her best friend was dropping her off at some dude's house and then picking her up and bringing her back to me, it hurt my feelings, as you would guess. What do you think I did? Went crazy and destroyed her stuff? Threw it in the driveway and put on a show for the neighbors? Of course not. I wasn't about to look weak and give my power away to anyone, especially her. While she was gone, I calmly packed her stuff, set it nicely by the front door, and when she got home, in confusion, she asked, "What the f*ck is this?" to which I, nonchalantly, replied, "Oh, that's your stuff." "No shit! What is it doing here, Marc?" to which I said, "I'm helping you leave so you can go move in with the guy you've been seeing 3 nights a week. Figured it might save your friend some gas money." Mad that I was being so nonchalant about it, she went completely berserk. Screaming, yelling, calling me names, etc. Again, what do you think I did? Got angry and defensive? Yelled back? I remained calm, cool, and collected and didn't call her names back. After she left and harassed me with angry and abusive texts and calls, I continued to conduct myself in a classy manner.

When others are acting trashy and ignorant, let them behave the way they're going to. You only have the power to control how you conduct yourself in that moment and stooping down to their level won't help.

RESPECT OTHERS

When you have your act together, you, naturally, respect everyone, from the man begging on the street corner to the man signing your paychecks, because you're secure and don't have anything to prove to anyone. You respect everyone the same. You have no need to look down at others and feel "better" than them. You have no need to think certain people don't deserve to be treated the way you'd like to be treated. You have no need to EVER disrespect anyone – even if they're disrespecting you. It's the same as, "Never argue with an idiot because anyone watching won't be able to tell the difference." Be the bigger and smarter person. Never stoop down to anyone's level and become socially-irresponsible and immature. Disrespect communicates ignorance, weakness, selfishness, arrogance, and lack of tact and self-control.

You don't get respect if you're not giving it. In the show Game of Thrones, Joffrey Baratheon, the tyrannical and psychotic boy king, is in a council meeting with his mother Cerci, his uncle Tyrion, and his grandfather Tywin and he's not getting his way. So, as a desperate reach for respect, he angrily shouts, "I am the king!" His grandfather, Tywin, just remains completely calm, stares at him in a disappointed fashion, and says, "Any man who says, 'I am the king' is no true king." in an attempt to teach his ignorant and bratty grandson that if he wants respect, he has to earn it by, first, giving it to others. That respect isn't taken by force.

Respecting others is recognizing importance, value, differences, perspectives, boundaries, decisions, and privacy and not stepping over any invisible, yet real, lines. Treating others with respect shows good character and is just as important as respecting yourself. If you don't respect yourself, you're less likely to respect others. Work on having the utmost respect for yourself and you'll notice that you'll, naturally, be more respectful to everyone around you.

KEEP YOUR WORD

Keeping your word is a huge part of social responsibility. It's meaning what you say and only saying what you mean. It's keeping your promises. It's selfless. It's being honorable. It's being respectful. It's being trustworthy. It's being dependable. It's investing value in yourself and your relationships.

Not keeping your word does a lot of damage to your reputation and communicates your lack of self-discipline, self-control, and personal power. It communicates how much you value relationships and other's time. You can't expect anyone to keep their word to you if you don't keep your word to them.

Every time you go back on your word or fail to keep it, you hurt your reputation, devalue yourself, and lose trust and dependability. You damage valuable relationships. You burn bridges. It's like the boy who cried wolf. He cried wolf, everyone came running, and he laughed at all of them because he played a joke on them. He did it again, they came running, and he laughed at them again. When an actual wolf came around, he cried wolf, no one came, and the wolf killed him. Break your word once, it's accepted as coincidence. Break it twice, you awaken skepticism. Break it again and you've lost all credibility. No one will ever take you seriously. They don't actually believe you respect them, their time, or your relationship with them. They believe you're selfish and don't care about anyone but yourself - and they're right. Not keeping your word is downright selfish, immature, and arrogant.

Keeping your word is the greatest self-service possible. Do what you say you're going to do. Get things done when you say you're going to get them done. Call when you say you're going to call. Show up when you say you're going to show up - even if it means inconveniencing yourself.

SHOW UP ON TIME

Speaking of showing up, punctuality communicates just as much as keeping your word. Punctuality IS keeping your word, but only with time management. It's a verbal contract and agreement with another person that you will be somewhere at a given time and not a second late.

It communicates you're an admirable and highly-respectful person, how much you respect relationship, and it paints a picture of how you live your life. It communicates your level of humility. It takes humility to put everything back burner, prioritize the agreement, and keep your word on what time you will show up. It involves making sacrifices and putting other's needs before your own.

Sloppiness with time communicates, you're, more than likely, sloppy with everything else in your life. Punctuality, once again, is one of those things that provides clues and insight into what kind of person you really are. If you regularly manage your time and show up when you're supposed to, it's admirable and respectable. If you're always late, you're looked down upon and your credibility is ruined.

Showing up late is disrespecting and wasting everyone's time. It communicates you're lazy, irresponsible, sloppy, unorganized, unprofessional, and you only care about yourself. It communicates horrible time management skills. It communicates arrogance and tells everyone waiting on you that your time is more important than theirs. It communicates you're selfish and undependable. Most of all, it communicates you don't fully understand or care what it means to be a responsible adult instead of an immature child.

If you need something from someone and you show up late, they're less likely to give it to you. You disrespected them by not being on time.

LISTEN MORE THAN YOU SPEAK

"Wise men, when in doubt whether to speak or to keep quiet, give themselves the benefit of the doubt, and remain silent." – Napoleon Hill

It's often said, "Those who talk the most know the least and those who talk the least usually know more than they let on." This is hundreds of years of wisdom packed into one sentence. Wisdom that gets you very far in life. Wise men listen and fools never stop talking.

Anything of low-value is of lower quality, cheaper, and more abundant than anything of high-value. It's limestone compared to diamonds. Talk is cheap and worthless if it's too abundant and extremely valuable when used sparingly. Those who use words sparingly are more likely to be listened to and those who never stop talking are often ignored.

It's far better to hang back, be observant, and collect the information you're looking for than to be talking so much you can't hear the answers over the sound of your own voice.

In any social interaction, those who talk the most are losing, giving away their power, and not learning. Those who are quiet and listening are winning, gaining social power, and collecting information. They're revealing less about themselves and keeping their personal power.

Not only does listening display self-control, but it makes you more likable. People enjoy being around you more because, sometimes, they just want to hear themselves talk and enjoy you listening without judgment. It communicates you value their words and perspective more than your desire to hear yourself talk. When you make anyone feel this special and important, they like you, want to be around you, and are more willing to help you in any way you want.

CULTIVATE THE PAUSE

A period of silence before you speak or reply is extremely powerful, communicates wisdom, and does more than words ever will. Wise people take their time responding because they know not thinking about what they're saying communicates ignorance. They know it's wise, in any situation, to pause and think about the effect their next words will have. It's experienced, strategic, sharp, and targeted communication.

In the HBO show Game of Thrones, Tywin Lannister is wise, ruthless, doesn't tolerate nonsense, and keeps everyone in line. After telling King Joffrey, the boy king who speaks without thinking, "Any man who must say, 'I am the king' is no true king. I'll make sure you understand that after I've won your war for you.", Joffrey loses his temper and replies with, "My father won the real war! He killed Prince Rhaegar! He took the crown while you hid under Casterly Rock!" Tywin knows this isn't true and King Joffrey is accusing his own grandfather of being a coward. But being wise, experienced with conflict, and knowing how to think before replying, Tywin keeps his cool when most of us would explode and defend ourselves. He simply pauses, looks at Joffrey in a threatening "You just f*cked up" fashion, and very calmly replies, "The king is tired. See him to his chambers." The pause allowed Tywin to calm himself down before saying something that could make him look weak and unstable.

In tense, negative, or extremely exciting situations where emotions tell you to say the first thing that comes to your mind, it's wise to pause and think about what you're going to say. Speaking on impulse, in most cases, makes you look weak, unstable, and out-of-control. You lose your upper hand and positioning. If your first instinct is to reply with something negative, hurtful, childish, or ignorant, something most of us do during bouts of excitement, simply pause, think about how it will reflect on you, and choose to reply with something more stable and intelligent.

REACTING VS RESPONDING

As you're learning, logic beats emotion 99% of the time. Failing to pause and think about what you're going to say or do next is a product of emotion. Stopping yourself, calming yourself down, and thinking of an intelligent and appropriate thing to say or do is a product of pure logic.

Most of us react. We don't take the time to think about what we're doing and the position it's putting us in, we're just doing it. Reacting is letting your ego, emotions, and your inner-child have control and you're saying, "I don't care what position this puts me in, how it makes me look, or the repercussions of it. Saying or doing this particular thing right now will make me feel better." Sounds like a child, doesn't it? Reacting gets poor results, ruins relationships, burns bridges, and makes you look weak, sketchy, and out-of-control. We think reacting by getting angry solves problems, makes things better, and gives us control of situations. We think reacting by raising our voice, yelling, and throwing a temper tantrum gets us the results we want and makes us more effective. We think reacting by freaking out helps release the scared, anxious, nervous, and frightful energy and makes us feel better about the situation we're facing. But all of it only makes us look very weak and immature.

Responding, on the other hand, is the wiser and more logical choice because you're taking everything into consideration before making a move. When you want to get angry, you ask yourself, "Will getting angry make this better, undo what happened, or give me more control of the situation?" When you want to yell, you ask yourself, "Will yelling give me appearance of self-control or weakness and immaturity?" When you want to freak out and get scared, you ask yourself, "Will freaking out increase everyone's confidence in my ability to keep it together and lead them in the right direction or will it make me look scared, weak, and lame?" Responding communicates wisdom, strength, and self-control.

LISTEN TO ACTIONS, NOT WORDS

When I work with coaching clients to figure out the problems they're having with women and dating, there's always a common issue leading up to their problems – listening to words more than listening to actions. They're basing their thoughts, emotions, and actions off of everything she's saying instead of paying attention to what she's doing and it's causing severe conflict and confusion. They're saying, "She said this, this, and this, but she's doing this, this, and this and it doesn't make sense. I don't know what to say or do to fix this." My reply is always, "Stop listening to what she's saying and pay more attention to what she's doing. Her actions tell the truth. She can lie, exaggerate, or paint any picture she wants you to have in your mind with her words, but she can't do the same with her actions because they're so concrete and harder to manipulate. Her actions will ALWAYS tell you every single thing you need to know about her and your relationship with her."

Only suckers listen to words and ignore actions. Stop getting fooled. Develop an "I'll believe it when I see it" attitude and prevent yourself from being easily manipulated. Become very observant and stop believing everything you hear. Even if they're trying to justify actions with words, actions are, still, more truthful.

This doesn't make everyone a liar, it simply means most of us don't understand the power of behavior in comparison to words. It's harder to manipulate behavior because it's where thoughts, emotions, and motivations manifest themselves and we use words to cover up the things we don't like, not knowing, the behavior will still shine through.

Words have less power than you think and actions tell everyone the pure and unadulterated truth about thoughts, emotions, habits, and how much anyone has their act together. Listen to actions, not words.

ATTENTION, APPROVAL, AND VALIDATION SHOULDN'T MATTER

Needing validation, approval, and attention communicates, "I'm weak, unhappy, and I need other people's opinions to make me feel better about myself." It sends out negative energy that makes everyone who encounters it feel uneasy and uncomfortable. People aren't bending over backwards to be your friend and they're, more than likely, avoiding you because you're difficult to be around.

Those who get the most attention, approval, and validation are the ones who don't need it, don't really care for it, and don't look for it. They're happy with themselves. They're giving themselves attention. They're giving themselves approval. They're validating their own thoughts, emotions, behavior, and habits. They're letting their own opinion validate who they are.

Logically, it doesn't really make sense to not care about the attention, approval, and validation of others but once you think about the negative energy communicated when seeking validation, approval, and attention, you can easily see how its presence far outweighs its absence.

You're more likely to get validation, approval, and attention when you're not looking for it because you're only sending out positive energy and everyone responds positively to your positive energy by liking you more and, voluntarily, giving you validation, approval, and attention. When it's obvious you're desperate for everyone to like and approve of you, they feel the desperate, needy, and clingy energy and, as a natural reaction, associate it with YOU. It's not that they don't like YOU, it's that they don't like the negative vibes and energy you're constantly putting out.

Only seek attention, approval, and validation from yourself and constantly improve yourself so you remain happy and content.

NEVER BE TOO IMPRESSED OR DISAPPOINTED

Instead of seeking approval, giving too much of it communicates the same negative energy of, "I want you to like me so I'm going to over communicate how much I like you." It has the same negative effect and causes people to think something's off with you. Not being too impressed isn't a negative trait. It doesn't mean you're being a cocky asshole. It doesn't mean you don't like them. It doesn't mean you think you're better than them. It means you're not giving away your positioning. You're not being too easy to read. You're not being too transparent. You're not letting anyone know exactly what you think.

When someone has you completely figured out, they hold all of the power and you're powerless. You gave it away when gave all of your approval. It comes back to respect and boundaries. When someone knows exactly how much you like them, they, unconsciously, stick you in their back pocket and think, "I own this person. I can have whatever I want from this person. I can have my way with this person." This leads to less respect for you and your boundaries. It leads to cockiness and thinking they can do whatever and whenever they want. This puts you in a powerless position. With great leaders, if one of their favorite people blows them away by doing an amazing job, they don't give away power and authority by getting their panties wet and worshipping them. They give them the appropriate amount of praise and move on.

The same goes with being disappointed. When you're too disappointed - angry, upset, crying, yelling, and acting tyrannical – you're communicating weakness. You're communicating, "You have power over me. You own me. You have the power to steal my happiness and make me lose control of myself." Keep your power by always remaining calm.

KEEP COMPLAINTS TO YOURSELF

Speaking of losing power, there's no better way to give all of your power away and communicate, "I am weak and not strong, smart, or mature enough to deal with a little hardship" than whining, complaining, and bitching about what you don't like or what makes you uncomfortable.

Celebrities, CEO's, athletes, news networks, and millions and millions of people in the U.S. sobbing, crying, whining, bitching, complaining, and acting personally-victimized didn't change the outcome of the Clinton/Trump election, did it? It only did the opposite. So, in essence, complaining was, and still is, a waste of time.

As an aircraft mechanic, I often had to work in holes that were dark, hot (104 degrees Fahrenheit), the size of a coffin or smaller, with spiders 6 inches away from my face, at a 45 - 65 degree decline with my head at the lower end, sweat pouring into my eyes, laying on metal ribs that felt amazing jamming into my ribcage and leaving bruises and, sometimes, fracturing ribs, with no fans, ventilation, or air-conditioning. Freaking out, whining, bitching, crying and complaining couldn't get the repair done. I couldn't let micro-emotions and mental chatter distract me. I often listened to music on my phone, sang, or just turned my brain completely off until the job was done. The key was to remain completely calm, cool, collect, and confident because if I got negative, started complaining, and freaked out, my body would swell and I would get stuck in there and die.

No matter what uncomfortable situation you deal with, talking and complaining about it doesn't do anything to make it better. In fact, it only reinforces the imagined pain in your mind. The more you complain about what you don't like and what makes you uncomfortable, the more you're rewiring and programming your brain to be negative, anxious, and weak instead of positive, motivated, and strong.

BE OPEN TO FEEDBACK

Not listening to criticism or, at least, being open to it is the worst social move you can make. It causes you to lose respect, admiration, friends, jobs, and opportunities. While you're thinking you're smarter than everyone else, they're thinking you're too dumb and insecure to handle a little advice, correction, and direction. It means your ego is too delicate and you're an extremely weak-minded person.

No one likes the person who isn't open to feedback, can't be told anything, thinks they're perfect, and knows everything because that person is dangerous and will wind up making catastrophic mistakes.

The aircraft mechanics who never accepted feedback and never admitted they needed some help ALWAYS lost their jobs, made costly mistakes, and put people's lives in danger. Just because they failed to stop and say, "I need some help in this area" or "I can make some improvements", they caused MILLIONS of dollars in damage and even, in a few cases, ruined entire airplanes that now sit in aircraft boneyards in deserts. One time, I was 2 inches from getting crushed to death by a horizontal stabilizer because a mechanic failed to stop and ask what a certain tag meant – a tag that meant another person was in the tail and the lever with the tag should not be touched or moved.

You will NEVER know everything. EVER. Even if you consume more knowledge per day than anyone else in the world, you will still be extremely ignorant in most areas and others will always have more experience and wisdom when it comes to new things. You should be completely open to consuming whatever feedback and knowledge they provide. If you don't like feedback, at least think long and hard about what they're saying to see if they have a valid point and they're hitting a blind spot in your thinking, behavior, and habits.

PART 14: GETTING YOUR MONEY ACT TOGETHER

MIXED FEELINGS ABOUT MONEY

Our main system of trade is money. If you don't like it and can't change it, then learn how to better understand it and get better at it.

Jim Rohn said, "I used to say, 'Things cost too much.' Then my teacher straightened me out on that by saying, 'The problem isn't that things cost too much. The problem is that you can't afford it.' That's when I finally understood that the problem wasn't 'it' - the problem was 'me.'"

We wrap negative and emotional energy around the idea of money because we're upset we can't keep what we have and get more of what we want. We're angry we spend it on what we don't need and we're not responsible and mature enough to save it for when we really need it.

Our negative thoughts about money directly reflect our financial habits and discipline. We're not mad at money - we're mad at ourselves. We secretly resent those who are better at making, managing, and keeping it because we're mad at our own poor financial choices. We have a scarcity mindset around money and automatically associate people with a lot of money with greed and corruption. We take our self-anger out on everyone with money because we see it as unfair and we think they're, somehow, cheating in life. Our own bad financial habits and decisions paint a false picture of what money really is and how it works.

Those who are broke and say, "Money isn't as important as everyone makes it", are secretly holding a grudge against it because others have more than them, they can't hold onto it, and they don't have the motivation and focus to reach their goals so they can be more financially independent, debt-free, and have a comfortable life. If it's coming from a person WITH money, it's because they're taking it for granted and devaluing its importance. Ask them how important money is when they're dead broke. They'll automatically move it up to the top of the list.

"BROKE" ISN'T AN AMOUNT MONEY

It's true 1% of the world's population owns 99% of the money, but have you ever really thought about why? It's not an economic conspiracy to keep money out of the hands of the poor. That's crazy. It's because 1% of people behave differently than the other 99% of us – not only with money, but across the board. They're not part of the herd. They're not following trends and doing what they see everyone else doing so they can remain part of the pack.

"Broke" and "Rich" are mindsets, not amounts of money. Your personal behavior is your financial behavior. If you're physically, mentally, and emotionally sloppy, you're financially sloppy. If you're undisciplined and unstructured, you're financially undisciplined and unstructured. If you're impulsive and impatient, you're financially impulsive and impatient. The only way to change your financial behavior is to change your personal behavior. Your broke mindset is keeping you broke.

How is it possible more than half of us, including millionaires, are living paycheck to paycheck? How is it possible 99% of broke people who win the lottery are guaranteed to lose it all and be, even more, broke within 5 years? How is it possible half of all Americans have $0 in savings? How is it possible we're taking out loans against our homes and vehicles for emergencies and Christmas Shopping?

More money doesn't solve "broke" when your emotions, ego, and inner-child make all of your buying decisions for you. Money doesn't solve "broke" when you can't develop more mature spending habits. More money means eliminating the "broke" mindset by controlling your ego, emotions, and inner-child.

A proper and respectful relationship with money requires maturity and a clear-headed, organized, and disciplined mindset.

BROKE MINDSET

- "It's not my fault I'm broke. This person, product, or company ripped me off and took my money."

- "I'm broke because I don't get paid enough. It has nothing to do with my spending habits. I NEED my expensive car and bills."

- "I hang around broke people because they're 'victims' just like me. They understand me and I don't feel so bad about being broke."

- "My thoughts, emotions, habits, and buying decisions aren't the reason I'm broke."

- "There's no way I can make over this amount of money. No one will hire me and I'm not good enough to make more."

- "The only way I can make money is by trading my labor and time."

- "Bills are bad, unfair, and I'm getting ripped off by this greedy company."

- "Work sucks and I'm only going to do it enough to make some spending money."

- "I'd rather relax, have fun, and spend money than to do anything that feels like working."

- "Monday sucks because I have to work and I can't be lazy for the next 5 days."

- "Friday is the best because I can be lazy for the next few days."

- "Rich people are rich because they know people, are from a good family, have rich parents, or have the right skin color."

- "Money is a toy and it's only used to have fun."

- "I would rather borrow and spend someone else's money through loans and credit than to only spend what I have in the bank."

- "Shopping, social media, gambling, food, drinking, smoking, drugs, television, games, and other addictions make life fun and less boring."

- "I'm going to spend money right now to get this thing I want rather than waiting to buy only what I need."

- "I would rather spend most of my money on minor conveniences than to wait a little longer for what I want."

- "I get paid again next week so it's ok to blow this paycheck."

- "The more material things I own, the more successful I feel."

- "I'm going to buy this expensive thing so I can attach my identity to it, impress people, and make myself look better."

- "I'm buying the latest car, smart phone, shoes, headphones, gaming devices, etc. so I can keep up with everyone else."

- "Buying this will help me feel better and happier with myself."

- "Buying this will show everyone how much money I have, how 'good' I have it, and how successful I am."

RICH MINDSET

- "Money is not a toy. It's a tool to help me gain resources that lead to a better life."

- "I don't take or request handouts. I prefer to earn every dime I have."

- "I only see the ways I can make money instead of the ways I can't."

- "I can make as much money as I want – as long as I'm willing to put in the time, effort, and energy to work for it."

- "If I'm broke, it's my fault. My financial situation is the product of my maturity, spending habits, and decision making."

- "Rich people are rich because they have their priorities and goals laid out and they're only focused on what moves them forward."

- "Rich people are not bad. They know things I don't and it's an opportunity for me to learn some financial skills from them."

- "If you're not moving forward, you're dead. Working, reaching goals, and hitting targets is more important than constantly hanging out and having fun."

- "Trading my time for money is only worth it if I can demand my own price. Other than that, I would rather create, produce, sell, and repeat."

- "I have a job because it's providing me the financial means to reach goals and I'm gaining experience in a certain trade."

- "Monday is a good day because I can finally start being productive, making more progress, and contributing again."

- "Friday sucks because it means I'm losing several days of schedule and productivity."

- "The masses are losing money doing _____ so I'm going to be smart enough to avoid doing it too."

- "Loans, credit, and debt put me in a losing position and I have to pay back more than I borrowed."

- "I save my money first, then make sure my bills are paid, and then I might buy one or two things I would like to have."

- "Saving money doesn't hurt as much as being broke."

- "I pay my bills because I keep my word. I got myself into this financial agreement and I'm mature enough to keep up my end."

- "Spending money does not fix social and psychological problems."

- "Those who spend to impress are always broke."

- "Those who spend for minor conveniences are always broke."

- "I spend logically, not emotionally."

- "I don't need the newest phone, headphones, and gadgets. If it's not completely broken or outdated, it does the job."

- "I don't spend my money on addictions and anything that doesn't make my life better."

- "I am mature and respect myself enough not to spend money if it's going to put me in a bind."

- "If I can't afford what I want, I only get what I need."

- "I don't own a lot of material possessions and knick knacks because the more I own, the more trouble it is."

- "It doesn't matter if I get paid next week, this money can be used towards saving or something productive."

THE ILLUSION OF MONEY

When you see a nice home with new cars in the driveway, remember there's a 97% chance it's an illusion. The next time you see someone shopping at the mall and buying, what looks like, a bunch of nonessential items, remember it's probably an illusion. There's no need to get upset that they have more money than you because, most of the time, it's just an illusion of money. An illusion of success. An illusion of stability. An illusion of security. An illusion of happiness. They're probably worth less than you and it's not their money at all! They borrowed it! 97% of us are borrowing money to create the illusion of having money and only 3% of us actually have money and own what it looks like we own.

We think of "debt-free" as some kind of wonderful accomplishment when it's actually what normal is supposed to look like!

The average household and family create the illusion of being worth $136,643.00 – but that's actually how much debt they're in. Debt meaning, they OWE that much money! They don't own the house, the cars, and, probably, even the furniture. It's all owned by the lenders until they get paid back. When you drive a brand-new Cadillac, other people see the illusion of your success and that you "paid" $50,000 out of your own pocket for it. But the truth is you only paid $3,000 out-of-pocket and you still owe the lender over $50,000 because of fees and interest. Instead of being a "successful" person driving a Cadillac, you're a "f*cked" person driving a Cadillac because you're now worth a negative amount. A poor person may have very little money but they don't owe any money to anyone either. When your home, cars, and furniture is borrowed, the poor people who can't get loans are richer than you.

It's better to be debt-free and poor than to borrow money to make life easier and create the illusion of having money.

EMOTIONALLY DETACH FROM MONEY

It's ok to think money is important and can make life more comfortable but separate yourself, emotionally, from it. There's no need to make yourself miserable and commit suicide over it. Don't feel one way or the other about it. It's not worth as much as you think it is. It's just paper that comes and goes based on your logical decision-making process.

Emotions and money are like fire and gasoline – together, they're completely destructive. Emotional sloppiness plus emotional attachment to money equals financial sloppiness. We spend during emotional highs because we feel good and then spend during emotional lows to make ourselves feel better. We blow the little we actually have left to counteract the feeling of not having money!

Spending isn't the problem – the emotions are. Emotional attachment to money plays no part in helping you get more. Has freaking out, crying, and getting extremely angry and worried ever caused money to multiply itself in your bank account? No. It only caused it disappear faster. Emotions take the idea of "money" and blow it completely out of proportion. The less we have, the more important emotions say it is.

Getting more money is easier when you separate your "self" and emotion from it. Remove emotion from the idea of "making money" and instead, focus and invest emotional energy into the activities that help you reach the goals and get the results that automatically bring more money. The time you're spending looking at your bank account and watching the money grow can be spent doubling-down on the habits and activities that make you more money.

Danielle LaPorte says, "Think of money in the same way you regard time. It's a form of energy. It comes and goes according to your intentions. The clearer your intentions, the more the money flows."

YOUR FINANCES ARE NO ONE'S BUSINESS

When I first became an aircraft mechanic, I made a big mistake that put me a very bad and compromising position. I was 18, making $20 an hour, and wrongfully assumed everyone else was getting paid the same. I didn't realize I had less experience and was getting paid more than the guys around me because I was a contractor and they were direct employees. So, while working, I, carelessly, made a loud comment like, "I can't believe I'm getting paid $20 an hour to do this!" The guys around me heard, instantly didn't like me, and eventually convinced the boss to get rid of me. Announcing my financial situation put me in a very bad position and ended up costing me my job.

Never tell anyone how much money you have and make. Your finances are 100% your business. You're not required to tell anyone how broke or rich you are. Since we handle everything like children and get our feelings hurt pretty easily, the last thing you want is the people you thought were your friends hating your guts because they're, ignorantly, associating your identity with your income. You don't want them being jealous and envious of your financial status.

Keeping your financial status private puts you in a much better position. If you tell everyone you're completely broke, they won't take you seriously and think you're only calling them for money. If you tell them you're rich, you will have a lot of haters and people pretending to be your friend so they can get something from you. Let everyone assume what you have but never confirm or deny it.

Don't reveal how much your house, apartment, condo, etc. costs. Don't reveal how much your car costs. Don't reveal how much your bills are. If it involves money, it's 100% your business. Besides religion and politics, add personal finances to the list of things you don't discuss.

MONEY IS A TOOL, NOT A TOY

Money is a tool to make sure you don't wind up in a position of being screwed. When you don't have enough money for a deductible or co-pay in a medical emergency situation, you're screwed. When you develop unexpected car problems that you can't afford to fix and missing work means losing your job, you're screwed. When your electricity and water get cut off because you played with your money instead of using it as a tool, you and anyone else living with you is screwed. When you have that million-dollar business idea requiring a little overhead to get started but investors don't want to help, you're screwed.

All of these situations are easily avoided if we simply cram it into our brains that money is a tool and not a toy.

The problem with most of us who can't get our financial act together is we, thoughtlessly, buy, buy, and buy instead of saving, paying, and then buying. We use money to play. When we get paid, instead of putting money in savings, paying bills, and THEN looking at what we want, we immediately spend most of our money on non-essential items and experiences and then complain about having bills that we agreed to have. Much of the time, we're paying bills late and paying reconnection fees because we choose to buy instead of pay bills on time.

Every single time you get paid, experts recommend putting 20% in savings. Then, pay your necessary bills so you and your family can have water, lights, air conditioning, heat, food, and everything necessary for comfort and survival. Last, if you're dying to buy something, buy one or two things you can actually afford – things that don't require loans and still leave spending money for unforeseen occurrences. The more you follow the save, pay, and buy process, the more financially secure you'll become.

HANDLE YOUR MONEY PROBLEMS ASAP

Handling money problems requires making more money, putting it in savings and investments, getting out of debt, and hanging onto it.

If you're not making any money, get a job or start a business. Create an income. If your job income doesn't provide a comfortable living, do something about it. Get raises, find a higher paying job and quit, or make more money on the side through a business or another job. If you make money in your business through selling products, create more products and services until you're satisfied with the cash flow. Separate emotions to do what's necessary to increase your income ASAP. Without more money, you can't save, get out of debt, and invest in the future.

Pay yourself 20% and put it in savings or invest it. Hire expert investment strategists and follow their advice. For example, if you invest an average of $110 a week into a 9% interest Mutual Fund over the course of 7 years, after 7 years, you can stop putting money into it and it will keep growing on its own. Eventually, it'll be worth millions and the interest, alone, will be enough to replace your income from a job. Let your savings and investments build and build and don't touch them unless it's a REAL emergency.

Pay your bills, balances, and eliminate unnecessary bills. If you owe on credit cards, pay them off. If you have a car payment, sell the car and buy another car cash or start throwing money at the balance after you've paid yourself 20%. The same with your home. If you can't afford to go out to eat and buy the things and experiences you want while you pay off your debt, suck it up and deal with it. Be as uncomfortable as necessary to get yourself out of the financial situation you put yourself in when you decided to borrow money to create the illusion of having money.

After this is done, DO NOT SPEND YOURSELF BROKE.

STOP ACCEPTING A MEDIOCRE INCOME

The job I lost because I was running my mouth about how much money I was making, I got it because I wanted it and applied for it. That's it. I wasn't scared of hearing "no". I wasn't scared I wasn't good enough. Even though I didn't have the skill level required for it, I figured I'd learn after I got hired. Even my dad saying it took him 20 years to get to that amount didn't stop me. Before that job, I made a measly $10/hr. and I, literally, doubled my income overnight when I became unhappy with my mediocre income. I knew I was worth more than $10/hr, I knew I wanted $20/hr. or more, and nothing was going to stand in my way.

If you're unhappy with how much money you're making, why are you still there? Why are you not asking what you need to do to get a raise and then doing it better than what they expect? Why are you not proving you're better at your job than everyone else? Why are you not on hiring websites and in the newspaper classifieds every single day looking for higher paying jobs? Why are you not updating your resume and sending it out? Why are you not filling out applications? Why are you not starting a side business? What are your excuses for your mediocre income? Why are you choosing to complain about your income instead of doing something about it? Why are you accepting it?

Stop thinking you don't have the job skills to get hired. A lot of the time, they'll hire and train you on the job! Stop thinking you aren't good enough. There are people a lot dumber than you making a lot more money simply because they went after it. Stop being afraid of the job "change". The change of pace and environment is completely worth it.

Increasing your income is easy when you stop doubting yourself. Decide you're going to do whatever it takes and just do it. It's possible to make as much money as you want – you just have to believe you can have it.

GET RID OF UNNECESSARY BILLS AND EXPENSES

Saving money is painful but necessary. We're spending money in so many ways that our ego, emotions, and inner-child say is necessary, but in reality, they're not. We're wasting money on things that help us avoid discomfort, but are also non-essential to our health and survival. To get your finances together, trim the financial fat. Get rid of every single expense you don't need. Stop spending money at places you don't need to spend it. Find every single hole money is leaking out of and plug it.

Do you really NEED a cable or satellite subscription with 250 channels? No. Do you NEED cable? No. Do you even NEED a TV? Not really. Do you NEED a timeshare in the Bahamas? Of course not. Do you NEED a PlayStation subscription for online gaming? No. Do you NEED porn site subscriptions? No. Do you NEED a $600/mo. car payment? No. Do you NEED an $1,800/mo. apartment or house payment? No.

Until you get your financial act together, you can't afford non-essential, entertainment, and luxurious items. You can't afford the illusion of success and money. You can't afford the luxurious car. You can't afford the expensive home. You can't afford valet parking. You can't afford the casino. You can't afford going out and partying. You can't afford the cigarettes, alcohol, and drugs. You can't afford vacations. You can't afford restaurants. You can't afford pizza and delivery. You can't afford shopping at the mall. You can't afford cable television. You can't afford Netflix, Hulu, and Amazon Prime. You can't afford the latest smartphones. You can't afford the latest headphones. You can't afford the newest pair of Jordan's. You can't afford the latest clothes and fashion. You can't afford online video games. You can't afford internet subscriptions for your sexual addictions.

DEBT IS NOT ALWAYS YOUR FRIEND

Debt, credit, and loans should only be considered if you can afford to back up 100% of the loan using your own money and/or property and assets or you own a project or business already generating enough money to pay the loan back very fast. It's only smart when you'd like to use someone else's money, don't absolutely need it, and you can pay it all back whenever you want without screwing yourself over. It's like jumping into a hole but also being smart enough to tie a rope at the top so you can get back out whenever you want.

When we're not lucky enough to have this good positioning and take on debt, loans, and credit without it being risky, borrowing money is a terrible financial position to be in. It's like jumping into a hole without a rope and then offering to give whoever has a rope whatever they want to save you. It's not very smart.

When you're in that financial hole, or think you're in one, credit card companies, banks, and institutions drop a rope down just far enough to dangle it barely out of reach and before lowering it the rest of the way, ask you to sign an unfair contract saying if they help you get out of the hole you put yourself in, they own you until you do a lot more for them than they just did for you. 99% of the time, the rope isn't even necessary! With time and effort, we can climb out of any hole and not fall back in it.

Instead of saying, "F*ck your rope and your contract, I'll climb out by myself.", we're saying, "This hole is very uncomfortable and I don't feel like getting myself out of it. Throw down the rope down I'll sign any contract you stick in my face. Just save me from having to work and be bored and uncomfortable."

Be the person with the rope and avoid being in the hole. If you're already in the hole, learn how to climb or make enough rope to get yourself out.

F*CK YOUR STANDARD OF LIVING

It's sad. A lot of us think our standard of living and financial appearance is more important than saving money and getting rid of debt and it's putting us in a hole so deep that it's almost impossible to get out of. When you notice you're in a hole, stop digging! Stop spending! Stop trying to keep up with the lifestyle that feeds your ego, emotions, and everything else except you.

If your standard of living hurts your financial situation, adjust it and forget what your ego, emotions, and inner-child want. They're don't get a say in how you live your life because they're only interested in spending.

The house your ego wants but you can't really afford is creating more debt and preventing you from saving. How is other people being impressed by your nice house helping you? Is the temporary feeling of success you get when people say you have a beautiful home worth the financial hell you're living in? The expensive car your ego wants you to drive but you can't afford isn't eliminating your debt and saving you money either. How is being the person with the cool car helping you improve your financial positioning? Are the emotional highs you get from people saying "cool car" worth the financial bind you're putting yourself in just to own it?

The financial hell of being broke and being in debt isn't worth the fake emotional highs you get from creating the illusion of success and money.

Stop keeping up with the Joneses. Stop looking at your neighbor and wondering why they have more instead of wondering if they have enough. Stop showing off and feeding your emotions and ego. Many musicians who boast about living large invest in jewelry, cars, and clothes before saving or paying off debt. They wear $250,000 worth of jewelry but their car is getting repossessed because they don't pay the bill.

WANT VS NEED

Musicians Pitbull and Ne-Yo have a song called "Time of Our Lives" and the first time I heard it, I couldn't believe what I was hearing because the chorus paints a perfect picture of the mindset of someone who's seriously financially-irresponsible and sloppy and why they're in the financial bind they're in. The lyrics say, "I knew my rent was gon' be late about a week ago, I work my ass off, but I still can't pay it though. But I got just enough, to get off in this club, have me a good time, before my time is up."

Lyrics are subliminally powerful and, basically, the song is saying it's ok to be irresponsible with money and place want over need. It's basically saying, "My lifestyle is beyond my means and as a result, I don't have enough money to pay my rent. So, instead of paying what I have at the moment and saving until I have the rest of it so I can be as responsible as possible, I'm going to completely blow off my responsibility to pay bills and put a roof over my head, be irresponsible, and go out and spend my money partying, drinking, and dancing because life is short and having a good time is more important than being a responsible adult. Forget the consequences of not paying my bills. Forget the agreement I gave to the landlord. Forget keeping my word about paying what I owe."

Even if you have the money for it, if there's something you really want but it's going to take a chunk out of your bank account or it's a non-essential item, use the 24-hour rule. Instead of buying it right when your emotions want you to buy it, sit on the decision for 24 hours and see how you feel about it then. Usually, once 24 hours have passed and your emotional high goes away, you don't feel like you "need" it anymore.

Develop the habit of asking yourself, "Do I absolutely need this thing or can I use my money towards savings and getting out of debt?"

PAYING BILLS ON TIME

Not only is it extremely important to track every single bill and every person and company wanting you to pay them, but it's also extremely important to, consistently, pay those bills on time. Signing a financial agreement and not paying it is financially-irresponsible and your credit suffers for it. A credit score isn't only to buy things. It's also used to tell what kind of person you are. For example, you can't have a low-level secret clearance if you have a low credit score. A low-credit score makes you look financially-irresponsible and if you're not in control of your finances, it means you're not in control of yourself.

Mint.com is a useful and helpful tool for tracking bills and expenses. It's free and both iPhone and Android apps are available. Since most companies now offer a safe and secure way to pay your bills online, you can connect those online accounts to Mint.com and track when bills are due, how much is due, etc. Having all of your bills in one place makes it less of a headache.

An alternative bill-tracking solution is to create a Microsoft Excel Sheet or a Google Sheet, label it, "bills" and create a "tab" or "sheet" for each bill. Along the top of each sheet, enter the company name, the bill's due date, date paid, amount paid, payment method (cash, bank card, check, etc.), the balance left over, and whether you paid it on time or late. This can be done by filling in the last cell red or green. If it's green, it was paid on time. If it's red, it was late. Very simple system. Each month the bill is due, create a new line and fill in the information.

Every time you get paid, after paying yourself 20%, develop the habit of opening Mint.com, your spreadsheet, or your other method of tracking bills and pay what you owe. This habit reinforces the "bills come first" thought and you're less likely to blow money on things you don't need.

TRACK WHERE YOUR MONEY IS GOING

As crazy, meticulous, and overboard as it sounds, never spend any money without tracking it and categorizing the expense. It's important to create a clear picture of your spending habits so you can adjust and budget when necessary. Not having a clear picture of where your money is going is what makes and keeps you broke.

When I started this habit, I went to the bank, printed out the last 5 years of bank statements, and was disgusted by what I found after going through and categorizing each and every transaction. As much as I thought I was in control of my spending habits, the numbers told a much different story. After adding up and categorizing all non-essential expenses over the last 5 years, I discovered that if I would have taken 75% of non-essential purchases and, instead, transferred that money to a savings account, I would have saved tens of thousands of dollars and it would be collecting interest! But instead, there was NOTHING. I spent all of it and saved none of it – like half of all American households. "Fun" and spending emotionally made me completely broke. Instead of blowing my money, I could have saved and bought a high-end car with no payments. I could have moved into a big and beautiful home and paid half of it completely off before I even moved in. I could have done anything I wanted if I would have saved better. It was a very hard lesson and I'm sure if you take the time to see where your money is going, you'll come to the same conclusion.

Mint.com connects to your bank accounts to help you track each and every transaction. If you're using cash, pull out your phone, quickly add the transaction, and categorize it. Once you have enough transactions, you can generate reports to show where your money is going and how much you can save if you create a budget.

PART 15: REACHING GOALS

WINNING IS A PROCESS

Les Brown said, "There are losers and there are people who haven't learned how to win." Angelo Ajayi says, "You're still learning how to win so when the losses start piling up, the natural inclination is to say 'It's too hard. I can't do this. I quit.' Nobody wants to be committed to something they're losing at and to the area that's defeating them. But the strange thing about winning is that it looks like losing. It looks like frustration. It looks like anger and feels like betrayal. If this sounds strange to you, it's because you're still learning how to win. You're still learning that winning is a process. Winning is not the suspense and the magic of game 7. It's not even the highs and lows of the season. It's the sweat, the tears, and the mixed pains of each play on that court from the moment all those years ago they decided they wanted to be a ball player. It's the pain but it's also the joy. Winning is about the lows and the highs. Winning is a process."

Reaching goals, getting your act together, and getting the life you want is a process and if you can't handle the process and learn to love it from beginning to end, you won't make it. You have to become incredibly comfortable with the discomfort of the process.

Those who are in great shape love the pain of exercise and working out and that's why they make so much progress with it. Those who are living life on their terms and getting what they want love the pain of the daily grind. They love the pain of the struggle to reach the next level. They love the pain of pushing and pushing and pushing to gain that one inch in the right direction. They love the pain of coming up short because they didn't focus or try hard enough. They love the pain of knowing they'll still fall down, get scraped and bruised, and have to get back up and keep moving forward. They love the lessons they learn every single time they make a mistake. Get comfortable with the discomfort of the winning process.

TIME IS THE MOST IMPORTANT

When you're getting a lot more done than everyone else, you say things like, "My time is extremely important", "I have to use my time wisely", "I don't want to waste my time", and "That's a waste of my time". When time is the thing that's most important to you, you're more focused, clear, efficient, and living with a constant sense of urgency. You know time is running out, you don't understand why everyone else is screwing around, and you know you won't be dying with any regrets. You know you're going to get every single thing done that you want to get done.

You can never get time back. The sand never stops falling in your hourglass and you can never take the sand from the bottom and put it back into the top. Once it falls, it's there forever. What are you doing with that time? Are you making sure it's not a waste or are you just sitting there and watching it?

As long as the sand is falling in your hourglass, you have no time to waste on low-value thoughts, activities, habits, and people. You can't afford not to be on the ball, focused, and getting as much done as you can.

Be as meticulous with your time as you are with keeping track of your money. If you don't purposely waste money, don't purposely waste time.

Find where you can use your time more wisely and plug the holes where time is leaking out and being wasted. Time spent listening to music in the bathroom, car, at the gym, walking, etc., could be spent listening to people who teach you, help you, and make you better. Spend that time listening to lectures, motivational speeches, podcasts, or audiobooks that provide value, help you learn and grow, or solve problems for you.

Squeeze every second out of your day and don't let a minute slip by. When you sleep in for an extra 2 hours, instead of ignoring it, remember that you just lost 120 minutes you can never get back. It's important.

SCHEDULE AND ROUTINE IS EVERYTHING

Whenever you're trying to reach goals and accomplish anything, create a strict schedule to weed out potential wastes of time and stick to it until you've reached your goal and hit your target. If you're like me and consistently creating and hitting goals, then create a permanent schedule and routine to help you quickly move forward, hit targets, and reach goals.

Your schedule is how your time will be used and your routine is the collections of behavior and habits that help you stick to your schedule. It's hard to stick to a schedule without a routine and the good part is if you focus on sticking to a schedule, your routine handles itself.

There's no time for guessing when the job will get done. There's no time for guessing how much time you'll put towards getting it done. When you have a lot to do, there's no time to waste. If you can use an empty block of time in a productive way, merge it into your schedule. From the time you wake up until the time you go to sleep, jam up your schedule with as much as you can so you're forced to stay busy, focused, and making progress. Make reaching goals faster and easier. Make it inevitable.

"A schedule defends from chaos and whim. A net for catching days." – Annie Dillard

"The key is not to prioritize what's on your schedule, but to schedule your priorities." – Stephen Covey

"So many people are insanely busy nowadays, and it's easy to say, 'Ah, I'll work out tomorrow.' But you have to set aside a time and stick to that schedule." – Derek Jeter

"Plan your work for today and every day, then work your plan." – Margaret Thatcher

YOUR AUTONOMIC NERVOUS SYSTEM

The goal in getting your act together is making effective and useful thoughts, behaviors, and habits completely automatic so you don't have to constantly think about what you're doing. It's programming your Autonomic Nervous System with the effective and useful thoughts, behaviors, and habits you want to occur automatically and deprogramming your Autonomic Nervous System of the inefficient and useless thoughts, behaviors, and habits you don't want.

The Autonomic Nervous System takes care of breathing, blinking, and walking for you. If we had to think about these things as we did them, we'd be miserable! Fortunately, it's automatic for a reason and you can program your mind and Autonomic Nervous System to do the same with any thought, behavior, and habit.

Clear, focused, and purposeful thoughts, behaviors, and habits, when purposely repeated, program your Autonomic Nervous System and conscious thought, behavior, and habit restriction deprograms it. If you're a smoker, you programmed your Autonomic Nervous System to smoke because you purposely and repeatedly picked up and lit one cigarette after another. When you quit smoking, you're deprogramming your Autonomic Nervous System because you're purposely not picking up cigarettes and lighting them. You're reprogramming yourself not to smoke.

Programming your Autonomic Nervous System allows you to engineer your ideal self and life. It allows you to be the architect of your results. It allows you to design what happens automatically in your life and what doesn't. The result is a calculated and well-designed mind that directs purposeful second-nature thoughts and behaviors and pushes you towards the life and habits you actually want.

THROW YOUR HAT OVER THE FENCE

Put yourself in situations and create situations that force you to do what you're supposed to be doing and don't give you any other way out. Eben Pagan calls this the "inevitability factor". It's to make it inevitable that the things that have to happen, will happen. That's there's no possible way they won't happen. That there's no possibility of you wiggling your way out of it. It's "throwing your hat over the fence". If you have to climb and jump over a fence but you're not feeling motivated enough to do it, throw your hat over so you have to go get it.

For me, "throwing my hat over the fence" was knowing if I wanted to be self-employed and take my business and life in the direction I wanted, I was going to have to suffer. I was going to have to put myself through a lot of pain so that my only options were to stand on a street corner with a sign or do what needed to be done in my business to keep a roof over my head and put food on the table. I took drastic measures to wake myself up, get out of my comfort zone, and get going. This meant making the deliberate decision not to get another job after I got fired from my last one. If I accepted another position or got another job, I would have been so comfortable that I would have used it as an excuse not to work hard to grow my business and get it to where it is now. But, I made it inevitable and struggled, starved, and went into debt. And you know what? Everyone hated me for it! They took my pain and made it their pain! They asked, "Why are you doing this to yourself?" and "Being self-employed isn't worth going through this much trouble and completely ruining your life and credit."

When you make your goals and getting your act and life together inevitable, don't listen to anyone not doing the same. They don't understand. To them, you've lost your mind. To you, you're making it 100% likely to happen because you're eliminating all other possibilities.

BECOME FRIGHTENED BY LAZINESS

Anne Frank said, "Laziness may appear attractive, but work gives satisfaction." Sitting around doing nothing IS attractive. It feels fantastic to not have to move, exert ourselves, and answer to anyone or anything. We can just have a smooth, easy, and lazy day. While that sounds incredibly attractive and I could do that all day, every day, for the rest of my life, there's major problems with it - nothing happens. Nothing gets done. Nothing gets produced. Nothing gets created. Progress isn't made.

You should place as much importance on things getting done as you do your time. You should be terrified of not getting things done and making progress. You should be terrified of waking up tomorrow and you're exactly where you were this morning. Denzel Washington says, "I'd be more frightened by not using whatever abilities I'd been given. I'd be more frightened by procrastination and laziness."

Personally, I am so terrified of laziness that I can finish a major project that will dramatically improve my life and while I'm out having dinner, a beer, and watching the game to celebrate my little victory, I'm thinking, "This is great but I'm being lazy. I'm not making progress or getting things done. I can be making progress on my next goal RIGHT NOW. I could be eating this in my office." I picture myself being the shirtless and overweight guy laying down on the couch with greasy potato chips all over his chest while he's watching TV and his mom is picking up his mess and I say, "Not in a million years will that ever be me."

Battling laziness is more than just telling yourself to get up and do it because there are too many problems and mindsets piled on top of each other and contributing to the laziness. Battling laziness requires digging into your mind, untangling everything, finding each contributor, and fixing one a time until they're all taken care of.

USE YOUR SUFFER BANK

Former Navy Seal David Goggins had a rough childhood and in one of his interviews, he says he uses his pain and suffering to push him forward. He uses his pain and suffering to accomplish his goals. That he doesn't want to let his suffering be for nothing. He doesn't want it to be a waste. It's the fuel that drives him. It's what made him who he is today.

Everything that's ever happened in your life, everything that's made you feel like a failure, everything that's made you feel real pain, put it in your "suffer bank". Put it in one place and when you need the strength to push forward and keep going, pull it out and look at it. Look at the pain you went through and remember how you felt. Remember that you never want to go back there and experience that pain and suffering again. As Eric Thomas says, use your pain to push yourself to greatness. Use your pain to keep you from regressing and moving backwards. Use your pain to push you as far as possible in the right direction.

Remember when they said you couldn't do it. Remember when they said you weren't good enough. Remember when no one believed in you and supported you. Remember when everyone laughed at you and doubted you. Remember when you were all alone and no one came to your side. Remember your lowest points and how it felt like you would never have the strength to get up. Use it as strength and motivation to get to where you want to be. Use your pain and suffering as fuel to drive you.

Chase your suffering. Chase your misery. Chase your pain and store it away. Don't forget where you came from. Don't forget what you had to go through to get to where you are now.

I'm not telling you get all emotional and cry about it. I'm just telling you to be realistic and use it to remind yourself that if you made it past that pain and made it out of those situations, you can make it anywhere.

SET TOO MANY GOALS

Set more goals than you think you can handle. Have more targets than you think you can hit. Be a little more ambitious than you usually are. Seek to accomplish more than you think you can. Les Brown says, "Most people fail in life not because they aim too high and miss, but because they aim too low and hit." If you usually have 10 goals, set 20. It's better to aim for 20 and accomplish 14 than to set 10 and reach 10.

It's about outdoing what THINK AND BELIEVE you can do. It's proving you are mentally tougher than you think. It's forcing yourself to develop an, even deeper, sense of urgency to push yourself to accomplish. It's about knowing you can go beyond what you think is possible.

It's said you have to be crazy to be wildly successful and those with mediocre minds stop and give up. They place limits on themselves because they're afraid others will think they're crazy. You have to believe and do things that defy logic. You have to aim to accomplish more than what anyone believes is possible. Steve Jobs said, "Here's to the crazy ones, the misfits, the rebels, the troublemakers, the round pegs in the square holes... the ones who see things differently. They're not fond of rules. You can quote them, disagree with them, glorify or vilify them, but the only thing you can't do is ignore them because they change things... they push the human race forward, and while some may see them as the crazy ones, we see genius. Because the ones who are crazy enough to think that they can change the world, are the ones who do."

In one of his dating programs, Eben Pagan talks about a guy who was very successful with women actually believing every woman he met wanted him. Did every woman he met actually want him? Probably not. But believing it gave him the confidence to carry himself in a way that made him more attractive.

STAY OVERLY-SPECIFIC ABOUT GOALS

It's easier to accomplish goals when you're extremely specific about any and everything relating to each individual goal. Not only do you want to be specific, you want to be overly-specific, clear, and obsessed - like cutting a lawn with a pair of scissors and making sure not to miss a single blade of grass.

Cover, analyze, and familiarize yourself with every single little detail involved in the goal-reaching process and every single detail about the actual goal itself – the two can involve very different details. Each detail you overlook and fail to catch increases the difficulty and decreases the likelihood of reaching that goal.

Again, when Conor McGregor beat Eddie Alvarez and became the first and only UFC fighter to hold 2 championship belts simultaneously, he repeated over and over that he wasn't surprised he was the champion because he was so certain about what he wanted. That it's all he concerned himself with. That he saw it clearly in his mind over and over. That he obsessed over every single detail. That he was extremely specific and backed it up with extremely specific hard work and training.

You can't just say, I'd like to be successful. You need to be as specific as possible about what's involved in getting there. Each goal involves hundreds and thousands of tiny details and being "successful" can involve accomplishing hundreds of goals before you get there. If you can familiarize yourself with each detail and the details that surround each detail, reaching your goal is 100% certain to, eventually, happen. If you overlook and ignore the details and don't see them as important, you diminish your chances of ever reaching that goal. While everyone else is just looking at the goal and missing the details, you're handling the details first so you're more likely to reach the goal.

STAY OVERLY-FOCUSED

We live in a more distracted society than ever before and with a new distraction popping up around every corner, it's important, now more than ever, to be and stay overly-focused on goals and targets. Average focus tolerates distraction but overly-focused tolerates no distraction. It's deliberately, purposely, and energetically keeping your attention on what you're accomplishing and immediately destroying each and every distraction as it pops up. It's forcing yourself, regardless of how you feel about it, to see it through to the end. It's a level of focus so intense that others say it's unhealthy, to take it easy, to take a break, and to quit being so hard on yourself. If others aren't saying you're a little too involved in what you're doing, you're not focused enough.

When I was talking about not being lazy and said that even if I reach a big goal and go out to celebrate for a few hours, I still fail to detach my mind from my job. I'm still overly-focused, obsessed, and unable to take a break from thinking about the next goals, the details surrounding those goals, and how they relate to the bigger picture. I'm consistently focused on moving forward and there is never a second throughout the day that I'm not thinking about what needs to happen, how it's going to happen, and when it's going to happen.

With a high-end camera, if you focus on everything at once, the thing you want to focus on isn't as clear as you'd like it to be. But if you zoom in and focus on that one specific thing, everything else becomes blurry. That's what being overly-focused looks like. When you're focused on one goal at a time and want to make it easier to reach, nothing else should matter. Everything else should be blurred out. There should never be a second throughout the day that you're not thinking about and obsessing over the details and figuring out as much as you can. It's full-immersion focus. It's so focused that it's hard to be concerned with anything else.

STAY OVERLY-AGGRESSIVE

You should be taking constant and aggressive action as often as you breathe. More action than you think is physically possible. So much action you forget to eat, take breaks, and sleep. So much action the whole day goes by and you don't even notice.

Squeeze everything you can out of your days and life. Become aggressive about getting everything done. If you normally get up at 7 AM, get up at 4, 5, 6 AM and start earlier. If you take 30-minute showers, cut them down to 7 minutes to give yourself an extra 23 minutes to get things done. Clean up your timing, sharpen the sword, and improve your precision and execution.

Do more than you're normally willing to do and be the aggressive person who, not only, gets more done than everyone else, but does it better. Be the person who's always asked, "How do you do it? How do you make so much happen? How are you always on the ball?"

To portray just how much he has his act together and how aggressive, precise, and efficient Andy Garcia is in the movie Ocean's 11, Matt Damon is briefing Brad Pitt on what he's learned about the guy. "He arrives at the Bellagio every day at 2 p.m. Same town car, same driver. Remembers every valet's name on the way in. He works hard, hits the lobby floor at seven on the nose. Spends 3 minutes on the floor with his casino manager. There's rarely an incident he doesn't know about or handle personally. He spends a few minutes glad-handing the high rollers. He's fluent in Spanish, German, and Italian, and he's taking Japanese lessons. As I said, a machine. He is as smart and ruthless as they come." The casino owner, Andy Garcia, takes so much action and is so precise in everything he does, it's extremely impressive and intimidating to the guys who are studying him as their target.

STAY PERSISTENT AND CONSISTENT

My dad once said I would have hard time in life because I was way too stubborn - and I didn't completely disagree. He was both right and wrong. Right in the sense that I did have a hard time when it came to doing things I didn't like or want to do – like working for people I didn't respect and didn't believe should have authority over me. In that situation, I'm like a scared cat getting dipped in ice water – I'm not having it. But wrong in the sense that he failed to recognize my stubbornness would take me extremely far if I pointed it in the right direction and stayed consistently persistent.

Calvin Coolidge said, "Nothing in this world can take the place of persistence. Talent will not; nothing is more common than unsuccessful men with talent. Genius will not; unrewarded genius is almost a proverb. Education will not; the world is full of educated derelicts. Persistence and determination alone are omnipotent."

When it comes to reaching goals, remain consistently and persistently stubborn. Never quit. Never give in. Never collapse. If you know you're headed in the right direction, aggressive and consistent persistence gets you there. Persistence turns your mind into an unstoppable tank and aggressiveness turns goals into cardboard boxes. Your goals are no match for a persistent mindset. If a tank encounters a wall, it doesn't turn around go back – it blows a hole in the wall and drives through it!

Once you're persistent, make it consistent. Do things consistently well. Not just sometimes - ALL OF THE TIME and without fail. Each and every time you work towards a goal, do it well. Do it great. Do it to the best of your ability. Anyone can consistently do an OK job but not everyone can consistently do a great job. Consistently OK beats inconsistently great but nothing beats consistently great. Only persistence gets you there.

KEEP MOVING FORWARD

Getting your act together, reaching your goals, and getting to where you want to be is like being on an old train – it's dirty, ugly, loud, uncomfortable, rough, and the fastest way to reach your destination is to just toughen up, tighten your grip, and deal with the rough ride. If you just hang on, don't complain, and don't try to slow the train down, it'll get there faster than you expect. Those who have their act together, reach goals, and reach their destinations in life are the ones who just hang on, deal with the ride, and don't complain about anything. Those who don't have their act together, don't reach goals, and aren't where they want to be are the ones who complain about the ride. It's ugly. It's dirty. It's uncomfortable. They don't have a window seat. The ride is too rough. It's moving too fast. There's no air conditioning. It's too loud. It smells bad. They find any and every excuse to either slow the train down, stop it, or get off completely and that's why they don't reach their destination. That's why they don't get their act together. That's why they don't accomplish anything. When anything gets the least bit painful, scary, or uncomfortable, they want to slow down and take a break or stop completely. What should take a year to accomplish ends up taking 10 - or it never gets accomplished at all.

When things get painful, deal with it. When things get uncomfortable, get used to it. When things are moving too fast and the ride is rough, instead of trying to slow down, learn how to hold on tighter. You don't have time to slow down and complain. You don't have time to be afraid. You have to make it there on time and that means dealing with whatever happens on the ride.

Keep moving forward. Stay aggressive. Stay persistent. Keep pushing. Keep striving. In a lot of cases, the ride to the life you want sucks and it's ugly, but if you don't worry about it and just hold on, you'll make it there.

TRACK DAILY GOALS, BEHAVIORS, AND HABITS

It makes perfect sense that schools use behavior and habit tracking sheets as a learning tool for kids. If the kids listen, follow directions, are polite, and don't get in trouble, they get a cool little sticker or happy face on their chart that gives them a sense of pride and accomplishment. The sticker, smiley face, and the teacher's "good job! ;)" comment reinforce good behavior and make it more likely that they'll keep it up. It also makes a lot of sense that if the child isn't up to par on their behavior and habits that day, the teacher provides feedback and educates the child on what they can work on and why it's important.

What doesn't make sense, however, is why this behavior and habit tracking system, instead of getting more sophisticated as the child moves up through grade levels and gets older, fades out and becomes rendered useless. Getting older doesn't make the system obsolete. We still feel pride and accomplishment when we know we're on the right track.

As adults, it's still useful to track the consistency of our good habits and behaviors. It's useful to see the patterns and where we can improve.

When I found this practice to be extremely helpful and useful in getting my act together, I created a "Personal Behavior and Habit Tracking Sheet". Along the side, I listed each good behavior and habit I wanted to work on and improve and along the top, I listed each day of the week. Next to each behavior, each day either had a green or a red dot.

I started off with mostly red and each week after that, each sheet became more and more green until, eventually, it was 99% green all of the time. Seeing so much red woke me up to the reality that I had a lot of work to do and as the sheets got greener and greener each week, I felt a deeper and deeper sense of accomplishment and being on track.

PART 16: GET EACH DAY RIGHT

GETTING UP LATE IS NOT AN OPTION

Ben Franklin said, "Early to bed and early to rise makes a man healthy, wealthy, and wise." Eric Thomas says, "I studied the top millionaires in the world and I discovered that they all wake up at 3-3:30 in the morning." Dozens and dozens of studies continue to show early risers perform better. They're happier, clearer, sharper, more relaxed, mentally tougher, more optimistic, more productive, more consistent, less distracted, better prepared, make better decisions, get better grades, outperform everyone around them, and they sleep better.

The good decision of getting out of bed when you're supposed to sets the tone for the rest of the day because when you start off with a good decision, you're likely to make good decisions for the rest of the day. When you start your day off with the lazy, poor, and sloppy decision of hitting the snooze button and going back to sleep, you're likely to make the same kind of decisions for the rest of the day. Again, your decisions, inevitably, add up to you having your act together and having a great life or not having your act together and having a life riddled with problems.

Jocko Willink says, "While you are resting, you are getting no closer to your target." When you get to the bottom of it, getting up late is, simply, a waste of time. If we're sleeping an extra 2 hours each day of the week, that's 14 hours of productivity lost. Each month, 56 hours. Each year, 672 hours. In 5 years, 3,360 hours. If we're sleeping an extra 2 hours per day, each year, we're losing 16.8 weeks' worth of productivity! And we say, "I don't have the time" to get things done. We do have the time! But we're deciding to waste it. If you're too tired when your alarm goes off, reschedule your bed time so you can get more rest.

What are your excuses for not getting up? Get rid of them. ALL OF THEM. Nothing is stopping you from you getting up. You're stopping yourself. "I'm not a morning person" and "I'm grumpy in the morning" are excuses used to dodge blame and responsibility. They're used to avoid having to suck it up and get it together.

If you can't master something as easy as getting out of bed when you're supposed to, how will you master anything else? Seriously. How are you going to consistently do anything harder than getting out of bed early if you can't even get out of bed early? You won't. You can't master the big things if you can't master the smaller things first.

Getting up early, when you think about it, really isn't that hard and if, at the moment, it actually is hard, you can still program your Autonomic Nervous System to make it happen automatically. When the alarm goes off, it only involves throwing the covers off, sitting up, turning, standing up, walking to the bathroom, and doing whatever it is you do when you start your day. Yes, it's hard when you're not used to it. But the more you do it, the more it becomes an automatic behavior. Eventually, you don't even have to think about it or put any energy into it. It just happens.

It also helps if you have a powerful reason for getting up early each and every day instead of being lazy and staying in bed. Eric Thomas says, "My WHY wakes me up every single morning!" What is your reason for waking up early? If you don't have one, get one because it will motivate you more than anything else. Personally, I get up early because it's tough and I'm not looking for life to cut me slack. I get up early because it's uncomfortable and I aim to get comfortable being uncomfortable. I get up early because I'm tired of sleeping when I could be improving my life. I get up early because the more I get done, the more income I generate, and the more comfortable I am. I get up early because my competition is still sleeping and when they get started, I've already been at it for hours.

Squeeze every minute out of your day and make things happen. Sleeping past the time you're supposed to be up is unacceptable.

MORNING RITUAL

Not only do 90% of all very successful people get up before 6 AM, but they also have strict, precise, and purposeful morning rituals and routines. If you look as far back as you can into the history and stories behind the world's most successful people, ALL OF THEM had some form of ritual and routine that contributed to their success. Gary Vaynerchuk has a 3-hour morning routine that gets and keeps him on track. Patrón Founder John Paul DeJoria has 5 minutes of quiet reflection. Disney's CEO Bob Iger is up at 4:30 a.m. to read and the CEO of Twitter, Jack Dorsey, is jogging at 5:30 a.m.

A morning ritual helps you start your day right and puts you in the right mindset and mood for the day. It clears the mind and gets you focused on what's important. It's a series of actions, behaviors, and habits that, when done in the morning, lead to a better and more productive day. It's the morning routine before your morning routine. It's what gets you physically, mentally, and emotionally ready to handle whatever comes your way. It's your first goal for the day, your first target, and if you're able to accomplish that first goal, you'll have the confidence to continue moving forward and executing.

Your morning routine doesn't have to be like anyone else's. It can be whatever you want as long as it helps get your mind in the right place. Some drink an entire bottle of water as soon as they wake up to hydrate their body. Others hit the gym. Others get out of bed, make it exactly how they think it should be, sit on the floor next to it, do breathing exercises, and meditate for 30 minutes. Others, like me, stretch for 15 minutes to de-stress their muscles and mind. On top of stretching, part of my morning ritual is going through my house and double-checking that everything is squared away and in place. Knowing everything is clean and in order allows me place 100% of my focus on what I'm doing.

MAKE YOUR BED

Making your bed goes beyond what the bed looks like and how it adds to the presentation of the room. It goes beyond the fact that you're going to mess it up when you go back to bed. It goes beyond looking sharp and organized.

Making your bed is mental and the first step in a day full of accomplishment. It sets the tone for the rest of the day and kicks off your organized mindset. Making your bed is a principle. According to Navy Seal Adm. William McRaven, it's the best way to start the day. "If you make your bed every morning you will have accomplished the first task of the day. It will give you a small sense of pride and it will encourage you to do another task and another and another. By the end of the day, that one task completed will have turned into many tasks completed. Making your bed will also reinforce the fact that little things in life matter."

If you're feeling too lazy to make your bed, something requiring very little effort, what else will you feel too lazy to do during the day? What other easy and simple things will you fail to accomplish and how will those failures add up day after day, week after week, month after month, and year after year? But, if you just make your bed and don't worry about how you feel about it, how many other things will get done during the day because you tackle them with the same mindset? How will that benefit your life day after day, week after week, month after month, and year after year?

If you see a sloppy person who doesn't seem to have it together, you can guess, with 95% accuracy, that they probably don't make their bed. On the other side of the coin, if you see someone who seems to have it together physically, mentally, and emotionally, you can guess that they probably make their bed every single morning and you'd be right.

RELAX YOUR BODY AND CLEAR YOUR MIND

The tone you set for the day matters. The value and importance of ensuring clear-mindedness and a relaxed body at the beginning of each day cannot be overstated because the mindset you mold and develop in the morning automatically follows you throughout the day.

Waking up late, panicking, and getting in a rush makes you edgy, freaked out, and sketchy, your body automatically switches from a state of rest to a state of panic and alarm, and for the rest of the day, you're edgy, freaked out, sketchy, and in a state of panic and alarm. It ruins your whole day. It ruins your mood. It ruins how you react to and handle important situations throughout the day. Being proactive, waking up early, and taking the time to clear your mind and relax your body before doing anything else helps you avoid this situation and ensures a more predictable day. It ensures you're not physically, mentally, and emotionally on edge and freaking out. It ensures you're mentally and physically relaxed, calm, and composed. It ensures you're more likely to stop, think, and respond to situations rather than just blindly and thoughtlessly reacting to them.

As part of your morning ritual, completely wipe and settle your mind before starting the day. Get rid of the worries and anxiety. Get rid of the tension and frustration. Get rid of the useless thoughts and emotions. Use your drama book to "take a mental dump" and get the negative nonsense out of your system that can, and will, get in the way of more important things. You don't need that junk floating around in your mind and robbing you of brain power. At the same time, get rid of the stress and tension in your muscles by stretching every single muscle in your body, doing yoga and breathing exercises, and anything that helps your body to relax. The state of your body directly affects your mind and the calmer your body is, the calmer your mind is.

DECIDE WHO YOU'RE GOING TO BE

Successful people start their road to success with a moment of truth and a decision. A decision to change. A decision to improve. A decision to become more mature. A decision to no longer put up with their own bad behavior and habits. A decision to stop making their own life a complete mess. They wake up and decide, "Enough is enough and if I want better results and a better life, I have to do better."

After getting up early, making your bed, and going through your stretches and morning ritual, look yourself in the mirror and decide who you're going to be on that day and every day after. Mentally plan and rehearse being that person. Mentally plan and rehearse the good decisions that person makes and avoids. Mentally plan and rehearse that person staying cool, calm, and composed if they encounter tense and unsettling situations.

Decide to be better than you were yesterday and tomorrow you'll be better than you are today. Decide any kind of weak and second-rate thoughts and behavior from yourself are unacceptable. Decide second-rate planning, execution and results are unacceptable. Decide to raise the bar and do only what pushes you forward and improves your life rather than sets you back.

Every morning, after making my bed and doing my morning routine, I have a meeting in my mind and I start asking questions. "What will I do today that'll make a positive and permanent difference in my future? Is who I'm choosing to be today contributing to that positive future?" Then I start making decisions. "I'm going to make wise decisions today. I'm going to make the right decisions. I am going to take action and not be lazy. I'm going to do better than I did yesterday. I'm going to BE better than I was yesterday. Results are what matter – not my weak feelings."

STRAIGHTEN UP AND CLEAN FIRST

It only takes 5 - 10 mins a day to keep your home clean and presentable. Scrambling to pick up and clean when you're expecting company isn't normal if you have you act together because "normal" is keeping the house so clean that when someone comes over, you just have to push in a chair or two and you're done. You should never be in the incompetent position of having to tell someone they can't come in because your home isn't presentable. If it does get to that point, you should be really hard on yourself and pressure yourself to tighten it up and get it together. You should make yourself feel terrible for letting your home reflect the condition of a lazy kid's bedroom.

It doesn't matter how busy you are, you can make 5 – 10 minutes each morning and night to straighten up, organize, and wipe things down to ensure you don't have a "dirty house" problem. If you have kids and a girlfriend/boyfriend/husband/wife, then it really shouldn't take more than 5 minutes a day because you should be strict on everyone about picking up after themselves and not being lazy. If everyone is physically capable of cleaning up, there are no exceptions or excuses.

5-10 minutes each morning of cleaning and straightening up not only helps you avoid crazy, chaotic, and tiring "spring cleaning" and "summer cleaning" days, but it also has the same effect as waking up early and making your bed – it puts your mind on the right track, narrows your focus, and leads to a day full of accomplishment. You're already getting up early and making your bed – adding a few minutes of straightening up and cleaning means you're accomplishing more before you leave the house than many accomplish in a whole day! If you don't spend a few minutes cleaning and straightening up each morning and putting everything where it goes, you're more likely to be sloppy and complacent in everything you do for the rest of the day.

REVIEW YOUR GOALS

When you write a goal down, you're making it a seed in your mind and reviewing it helps you water it, grow it, and make it stronger until you accomplish it and make it a reality. Memorized goals are better than no goals, written goals are more powerful than memorized goals, but written goals reviewed morning and night are 100 times more powerful. Les Brown says, "Review your goals twice every day in order to be focused on achieving them."

In pay-per-click marketing, studies reveal average prospective customers must see an ad 5 – 10 times before they click it because you have to prime their brain with your ad. Reviewing goals over and over primes your mind to accomplish them. The first few times you review them, you understand they're important, but you don't feel that intense urgency and burning desire to accomplish them. But once you've reviewed them over and over and over, they're etched into your brain and go from being things you'd like to do to things you absolutely have to do.

Your list of goals is your roadmap. It's your blueprint. It's your guide. Your goals tell you what direction you're headed in and that's why it's so important to look at them first thing in the morning before you turn on your TV or you start looking through your news feeds on your phone. It's crucial to prime your mind with your goals. It's important to water the seeds you're planting every time you write down a goal.

The Reticular Activating System seeks out familiar. When we get a new car, we suddenly see it everywhere. When we own a certain hat or shirt, we see someone wearing it from a mile away. When you constantly review goals and water those seeds, your Reticular Activating System helps you notice everything and everyone related to making that goal a reality. Without priming your mind with your goals, this wouldn't happen.

DO THE HARD THINGS FIRST

When I was a kid, my parents made me eat everything on my plate or I'd be in trouble. I wasn't given a choice in what I ate, but they didn't care how I ate it. All that mattered was the plate got cleared I didn't get caught giving food to our little Chihuahuas. Most kids in that situation eat all of the food they like first and then spend 2 hours eating the food they don't like. But I did the opposite – I ate the nasty stuff first and then the delicious stuff last. If I ate the nasty stuff first, it was over with and I could enjoy the rest of my dinner and also, I didn't have to finish with the taste of the food I hated still in my mouth.

When it comes to accomplishing our goals, you can finish in pain or you can finish feeling good. It's up to you. Many of us are like the kids who want to eat the tasty food first and the nasty food last. Instead of handling the difficult things first and getting them over with, we put them in the very back and do the easiest things first. Bad idea. When we do the easy things first, it's an uphill battle and it will only get harder and harder and harder. By the time we get to the hard things, we're worn out and we don't have any fight left. But when we do the hard things first and when we have the most energy, we come out of the gate swinging with everything we've got and we do major damage to the hard things. Once the hard things are done, it's all downhill and we coast our way through the rest of the list.

Most people allow the hard things to intimidate them so they choose to do what's easy until they're backed into a corner and they have no other choice but to do the hard things. But by the time they're backed into a corner, they're so used to everything being easy that they completely give up. It's like a spoiled kid who's never dealt with hardship – they want everything easy and they're very likely to quit at the first sign of difficulty. Do the hard things first so the rest of your day is a breeze.

CONSTANTLY BE ON THE MOVE

I mean this both physically and metaphorically.

Those who are successful, make things happen, and have the life they want are constantly on the move and getting things done. They're not standing still and waiting for opportunities to come to them. They're out finding them, capitalizing on them, and monetizing them. If they have a new idea, they don't sit on it until they feel ready, they start accomplishing whatever steps they can in the moment – even if it's just preparation for bigger steps.

There's always something that has to and can be done.

Plan your life around being fully-functional at all times. Constantly be on the move. Get things done. Make things happen. Be finishing and closing things out. Be crossing goals off of your list and adding new ones. Fill your days up with making progress.

Stop sitting down, taking breaks, and taking it easy. Being still doesn't make anything happen. It doesn't get anything done. Your goals don't accomplish themselves. Your bank doesn't fill itself up. Your bills don't pay themselves. The life you want doesn't seek you out.

It's good to have plans and ideas, but being on the move and taking action is what will take it from thought on paper to being real.

Forget anyone telling you to slow down and take a break. Forget anyone telling you you're too busy. Forget anyone telling you you're going to burn yourself out. Tell them to find something to do and they won't have time to notice how busy you are.

Don't mistake this for staying busy doing nothing. Tons of us are incredibly busy doing things that don't produce any results. Constantly being on move means always taking action towards beneficial goals.

FEED YOUR MIND

Feeding your mind is as important as feeding your body. A starving mind eats anything and believes it tastes good like a person, if driven to extreme thirst, will drink salt water or motor oil in an attempt to stay alive. If you don't feed your mind what makes it stronger and healthier, it will feed on anything and you will suffer. Just like eating a healthy breakfast to give your body energy and make it stronger and healthier, it's crucial, as early as you can in the day, to feed your mind something healthy. I'm not talking about social media, television, death metal, rap, negative radio shows, etc.

A healthy mental breakfast is listening to, watching, or reading what moves you closer towards your goals. That makes you think. That makes you mentally tougher. That makes you smarter. That helps you make wiser decisions. That helps you learn and grow. That wakes you up from your dumb mindsets and habits. That helps you recognize your faults and weaknesses. It's listening to intelligent and successful people talk about what they know and what they've learned. People who have something to offer and are genuinely interested in helping you. People who want you to become greater than they are and to achieve more than they have. It's learning something you've been wanting and needing to learn. It's listening to podcasts designed around helping you become better, wiser, and stronger. It's feeding your mind anything that causes you to have higher-value and higher-quality thoughts, emotions, and habits.

You won't learn anything or become better from looking at social media news feeds. You won't learn anything or become better from listening to the newest # 1 song on the radio over and over as loud as you can. You won't learn anything or become better by watching the latest Instagram and Snapchat models show off their asses and titties. You're only teasing yourself. You have to feed your mind stuff that makes you better.

HIT YOUR TARGETS

Targets are your goals for the day, week, month, year, etc. They're what you're focused on. The things that have to be done as part of your schedule They're the things that come back and make your life harder in the future if you don't destroy them now. You don't want to only hit each target, you want to destroy them. There should be nothing left of the target by the time you get done. Each target should look like you drove over it with a tank or shot it with a missile.

There are no excuses for not hitting your targets but it does happen from time to time – especially if you're on a strict and tight schedule. Time flies, you're moving fast, and the target is approaching so fast that you don't have enough time to aim or get a shot off and you miss it. That's ok. Once again, it happens. You can get it tomorrow. What you never do is back up to go get it. It'll be there tomorrow. You let it go and keep moving forward at the same pace because if you back up, it means you're stopping and backtracking. Stopping means losing time, killing momentum, and slowing down progress. When you move backwards, you multiply the amount of time and progress you're losing. It's just extremely counterproductive. Simply add the missed target to your list of goals when you go to bed and be sure to circle it and not miss it again.

You know why people don't make progress, seem to be standing still, and nothing is happening in their life? Because they don't have targets and if they do, they don't have enough. They don't have goals. They don't have anything to stay focused on, move towards, and to destroy. They're not getting up and moving through their targets with aggression and precision. They don't have the blinders on. They're walking, checking out the birds, stopping for water, talking on the phone, complaining about the weather, and finding excuses for why they're not completely focused on getting things done. Every day, hit your targets. No excuses.

KEEP YOUR HEAD ON STRAIGHT

While you're moving quickly and swiftly through each one of your targets, it's vital you keep your head on straight. If you were a Special Forces team member in the military and started freaking out in the middle of an operation, it would be bad news for everyone. The worst time to lose your head is during the day and in the middle of moving forward and hitting targets because it has detrimental effects on your focus, clarity, and progress.

When you get your day going and it's time to get things done, emotions, micro emotions, and weak thoughts stay out of the picture. There's no place for them while you're trying to work and move forward.

That's why it's important to calm your mind and body at the beginning of the day because it plays a big part in helping you keep your head on straight while you're trying to get things done.

SCHEDULE DISTRACTIONS AND INTERRUPTIONS

You can play on your phone, take calls, text, check email, take a break, play games, take a nap, and anything else you want to do – on your own time. Don't do it on your schedule. Do it before work, after work, or during breaks.

When you allow distractions and interruptions to happen during your schedule, the time requiring you to be overly-focused, you get slowed down. You get moved in the wrong direction. They get in the way of what you're supposed to be doing.

Allowing interruptions and distractions is making them just as, or even more, important than the goals on your schedule. It's making them more important than what they should be.

Your schedule is king. The things on your schedule are there because you're saying they're important. You put them there because they push you forward and make life better. They move you in the right direction. Allowing distractions and interruptions is disrespecting your schedule.

Studies show it takes 25 to 40 minutes to get back on track after you get distracted and lose focus. That's 25 to 40 minutes of productivity lost. If you get distracted once an hour in an 8-hour workday, you're only getting 3 to 4 hours of work done. The rest of the time is used in getting yourself refocused. If you work full-time, that's 15 to 20 hours of productivity lost each week. Each month, 80 hours. In a year, 720 hours!

When your mind is in the zone and you're focused and making things happen, keep your blinders on. It's tiring having to get back to where you were over and over. Turn off or silence your phone, silence computer sounds, wear earplugs, tell people you're busy, and get it done.

TAKE NAPS

If it's not absolutely necessary, don't try to force yourself to stay away awake so you don't lose 30 minutes to an hour of productivity. If you don't give yourself a break and allow your mind and body to rest, you're going to lose that time anyways through poor performance. It's hard to be productive, stay motivated, and get things done if you run out of energy and don't take time to recharge. A full night's rest is great but if your schedule and work demand a lot out of you, it's easy to become drained and worthless without a nap.

According to Sleep.org, a lack of sleep costs the U.S. $63 billion a year in lost productivity and a lot of smart companies are now developing a stronger commitment to employee wellness and realizing if they don't help employees manage energy by allowing naps, it costs more in the long run than just money. These companies are realizing the benefits of naps far outweigh the negatives. Japan is now encouraging workers to take afternoon power naps on the job because it improves alertness and performance, boosts productivity, and minimizes fatigue-related mistakes and injuries. It's called a siesta. It's also common in Portugal, Spain, Philippines, Malta, and in Latin America. In the 1990's, NASA experimented and allowed employees to nap and, unsurprisingly, their performances "skyrocketed".

Extremely busy men and women get more done by taking naps. Eleanor Roosevelt napped before speaking engagements. Thomas Edison's productivity was boosted by napping. Napoleon Bonaparte would nap anywhere he could because he was so busy he didn't know when the next opportunity to rest would present itself. Leonardo Da Vinci took 15-minute naps every 4 hours and slept less at night. On top of 10 hours of sleep a night, Albert Einstein claimed small naps boosted his brain power. Aristotle believed napping was necessary for genius.

CONSTANT LEARNING IS KEY

The heightened awareness you experience while learning something new, never turn it off. Ever. Keep it on. Keep the antennas up. Keep the radar on. Keep it scanning. Keep it collecting data. Never stop learning. Instead of asking, "Why do I need to know that?", just absorb it and say, "That will be useful one day." Constant learning is important because you never know when you'll need that information. It's better for it to be there than to reach for it and it's not there. When you don't have time to think and the situation demands an automatic reaction, you'll need to pull from what you already have – not what you can think of, find, or create.

Learning shouldn't be scheduled. It shouldn't only happen during school. It shouldn't only happen when reading a book or watching a video. It should be constant. You should be learning from your thoughts, actions, behavior, habits, and results. You should be teaching yourself as you reflect on your actions and experiences and analyze how those situations helped or did damage. You should constantly ask yourself, "What can I learn from that?" and "What did I learn today?" Spend time figuring out every little thing happening within and around you so you can turn it into knowledge, wisdom, and experience. If you don't learn from it, it's not wisdom and experience – it's just wasted time. Most of the stuff you're learning in this book is stuff I've figured out and taught myself!

Constantly learn throughout the day. Be observant, ask questions, study results, and watch people. You can never learn and know everything. Devour knowledge and information. Stop wasting time reading books and watching shows that were made up. There's so much to learn about the world, stop wasting time in fantasy. Learn about people. Listen to their lessons. Take notes and review them. Always be the student. Use their mistakes and wisdom as a shortcut to get to where you want to be.

RESEARCH EVERYTHING

Never be afraid to admit when you don't know something. Don't be afraid to go to a library and research it. Don't be afraid to get on Google and find the answers. Don't be afraid to ask others.

Before the internet, I was always at the library because there was always something my mother wanted to learn and know. She'd have a legal pad and we'd be there for hours while she read books and took notes. If it was too much to learn in one sitting, she'd check the books out, bring them home, and learn all she could. I am truly blessed to have been able to witness such a beautiful thing because most kids aren't fortunate enough to learn such a powerful lesson at an early age. If they don't know it, they don't have the awareness to seek it out.

It's better to say, "I'm dumb and I don't know this thing" than to say, "I'm smart and there's not much I don't already know." Saying you're dumb isn't putting yourself down – it's communicating self-awareness and wisdom. Saying you're smart and know a lot is putting yourself down because it communicates ignorance. Who do you think gets hired more often? The person who says, "I'm willing to learn." or the person who says, "I don't need training."? No one wants a "know it all" working for them because they're dangerous and less effective.

Find mentors. Find coaches. Find consultants. Find guides. Find people who have been there, done that, they're still doing it, and they're willing to teach you everything they know. Absorb everything they're willing to share and give. Follow those who are doing what you want to do. Learn their thinking, emotional, and behavior habits. Learn how they operate. Learn why they do what they do. Learn their secrets.

There are models and templates everywhere around you, all you have to do is be wise enough to recognize and use them.

WAS TODAY A WIN OR A LOSS?

As your day is winding down and coming to a close, besides asking yourself what you learned and reflecting on the lessons of the day, determine whether the day was a win or a loss. Determine whether you let the day knock you around and take advantage of you or you knocked the day around and took advantage of it. Which side of it were you on? Were you the victim or the victor? Were you the aggressor or the retreater? Were you the hunter or the prey?

Ask yourself, "Was today a win or a loss?" and then determine why. Take your day and dissect it, break it down, deconstruct it, analyze it, and learn from it. Look at every little detail. Find where you did a great job. Find where you could have done better. Find you can improve. Find the things you weren't even aware of. Learn from all of it.

Break your day down into as many parts as necessary and document what you learn. "Was the first part of today a win? Why? What did I learn? What can I work on for tomorrow? Was the second part of today a win? Why? What did I learn? What can I work on for tomorrow?"

If you want rapid learning and progression, this is the way to do it. Go into your mind and relive the day. Relive the thoughts, emotions, and experiences. Draw from them. Learn from them. Document them. Study everything about them. Learn about yourself so you can develop a deeper understanding of how you work and why you work that way. Figure yourself out so you get along and work with yourself better.

A life well lived is, simply, the product of focusing on one single day at a time. If you can win today, you can win tomorrow. If you can win tomorrow, you can the rest of the week. If you can win the rest of the week, you can win the month. If you can win the month, you can win the year. If you can win the year, you can win the rest of your life.

EVENING RITUALS

Successful people also have evening rituals and processes they go through before they go to bed because it helps them to relax, get quality sleep, and wake up ready for the next day.

1. **Read, learn, and prime your mind** – don't finish your day with junk in your brain. Just like brushing your teeth, clean your mind and feed it something useful and healthy.

2. **Completely unplug and disconnect** – do something completely different than what you've been doing all day long. Disconnect and unplug from work, projects, school, your cell phone, etc. Give your mind and body a break. Spend time watching your favorite show, listening to music, etc. Allow your mind and body to de-stress.

3. **Spend time alone or in silence** – Meditate, go walking, jogging, or do something that allows you to hear yourself think. Something that allows you to process the day and sort it all out.

4. **Stretch** – morning stretching gets you loose and relaxed for the day ahead and stretching at night gets you loose and relaxed for bed. If your body is relaxed, you sleep better. If you've never stretched before bed, try it on a night you can afford to sleep through your alarm. One of my former co-workers didn't come to work the next day because he said he slept better than he had in 30 years.

5. **Journal/drama book** – if you've had a long day, talk about it in your journal or drama book. Get the negativity, stress, anxiety, and anything else that isn't good for you out of your system.

6. **Review and update your goals** - go through your list of goals and cross off what you accomplished, add anything new, and review what needs to happen for tomorrow.

FEED YOUR MIND AGAIN

Ever fell asleep watching TV and then had a dream related to what you were watching or woke up thinking about what you saw the night before? It's because, again, your mind is constantly consuming and programming itself with whatever you're feeding it.

What you feed your mind before you go to sleep is what you're telling it to process and program itself with all night long. It doesn't care if it's negative or positive, smart or stupid, or quality or garbage. It can't tell the difference or decipher it. That's your job. Your brain's only job is to find a place to put the stuff you're feeding it. It doesn't say, "This is garbage" or "I can't use this." It only says, "I can't tell and don't care what this is. You put it in here so I'll put it away."

Be smart and give your mind something good to process and program itself with while you sleep. Give it something that'll make you wiser, faster, more competent, and more knowledgeable. Something that will make you a better person. Something that will make reaching your goals and becoming the person you want to be easier.

The last thing you feed your mind is extremely likely to influence the next morning's thoughts and mood. If you want to motivate yourself to go running when you wake up, devour some content on running and when you wake up, you'll, naturally, be more motivated to put on your shoes and go running. Your brain spent all night processing and programming itself with the last thing you put in it – running.

Feed your mind something healthy and beneficial before you go to bed so it's not processing and programming the junk music you had on in the car or the fear, worry, and anxiety you got from watching the news.

Control what you put into your brain because it will, with 100% certainty, manifest itself in your thoughts, emotions, behavior, and habits.

ADVANCED MENTAL PLANNING

My problem in the morning isn't waking up – the problem is the physical act of getting out of bed. I wake up and the lights come on, but nobody's home and I say "f*ck it" and go back to sleep. Sleepy Marc doesn't care about anything but sleeping. It's like another person altogether. To fix this problem, I started something I call "Advanced Mental Planning". I visualize, with extreme clarity and detail, the entire process of waking up, getting out of bed, and starting my day. If I just say, "I'll get up", it won't happen. But if the night before, I clearly plan and envision the entire process of getting and staying out of bed, I do it 100% of the time. I prime and program my mind with the specific and detailed plans I want it to carry out.

I clearly plan, visualize, and execute what will happen when I wake up: "When alarm goes off, sit up, turn my entire body to the left, put both feet on the ground, stand up, pick up my phone with my right hand, unlock it, turn off the alarm by tapping the screen with my right thumb, take 5 steps to the bathroom, open the door with my right hand, turn on the light with my left hand, take 3 steps to the sink, turn left, turn on the cold water with my right hand, use both hands to scoop the water and splash it on my face, use the tips of my fingers on both hands to clean my eyes, turn the water off with my right hand, turn 180 degrees towards the towel, grab it with both hands, dry my face, turn 180 degrees back towards the sink, turn cold water back on with my right hand, open my left drawer, grab my toothbrush with my left hand, grab the toothpaste with my right hand, unscrew the cap with my pointer finger and thumb, set the cap down, put toothpaste on my toothbrush, and start brushing my teeth."

Try it with anything you struggle with. It works. When you visualize your plan with extreme clarity, you make it more likely to happen.

CONCLUSION: KEEPING YOUR ACT TOGETHER

STAY FOCUSED AND HUNGRY AT THE TOP

Keeping your act together is harder than getting it together because it's easy to think you can relax, stop working, stop trying, stop setting goals, and stop making an effort at the top. It's the mindset of those who reach the top, get too cocky, lose their footing, and fall!

The top isn't flat. You can't lay down, rest, and nap. It's pointy and steep. Staying at the top requires constant awareness and hanging on and watching your footing. It requires never getting cocky. It requires watching your back because there's always someone working 24 hours a day to knock you off of the top. The minute you relax and become complacent is when someone grabs your leg and starts pulling. If you pay attention and stay aware, they'll never have that opportunity.

Conor McGregor says to remain the champion, work like you're in 2nd place and trying to reach 1st. To train harder than everyone else. He says most champions relax, get cocky, stop training as hard, get knocked out the next fight, and lose the belt.

Learn from those who relaxed at the top and paid dearly for it. There's countless documentaries and stories on the web. In UFC 168, Chris Weidman knocked out Anderson Silva, the champion, because Anderson got too cocky. He started putting his hands down, getting cute, talking trash, taunting him, and he caught a left to the jaw. JaMarcus Russell, considered the biggest NFL bust of all time, was named MVP in the 2007 Sugar Bowl, picked 1st in the NFL draft, and got too cocky, partied, gained 35 pounds, and his career when down the drain. It's the reason 80% of NFL Players go broke and bankrupt after leaving the league. They think they no longer have to work.

Don't get cocky, comfortable, or complacent. It takes more work to stay at the top. Get comfortable being uncomfortable. Thanks for reading.

PLEASE REVIEW THIS BOOK:

Hey it's Marc. Thanks for reading and if you found valuable answers to your questions, please go to amazon and leave me a review. It only takes a few seconds and it helps me out more than you can ever imagine!

Thanks again...

-Marc Summers

Leaving a review for this book is simple:
1. Go to Amazon.com
2. Type "Declare War on Yourself" in seach bar
3. Click on "Customer Reviews" under the title
4. Click "Write a customer review" button

Customer Reviews

⭐⭐⭐⭐⭐ 71
4.9 out of 5 stars ▾

5 star		92%
4 star		7%
3 star		1%
2 star		0%
1 star		0%

Share your thoughts with oth... ...omers

Write a customer review

See all 71 customer reviews ›